Marketing Wireless Products

Marketing Wireless Products

Sarah-Jayne Gratton and Dean A. Gratton

ELSEVIER
BUTTERWORTH
HEINEMANN

AMSTERDAM   BOSTON   HEIDELBERG   LONDON   NEW YORK   OXFORD
PARIS   SAN DIEGO   SAN FRANCISCO   SINGAPORE   SYDNEY   TOKYO

Elsevier Butterworth-Heinemann
Linacre House, Jordan Hill, Oxford OX2 8DP
200 Wheeler Road, Burlington, MA 01803

First published 2004

British Library Cataloguing in Publication Data
Gratton, Sarah-Jayne
  Marketing wireless products
  1. Cellular telephone systems – Marketing   2. Cellular telephones   3. Wireless
  communication systems   I. Title   II. Gratton, Dean
621.3'8456

Library of Congress Cataloguing in Publication Data
A catalogue record for this book is available from the Library of Congress

ISBN 0 7506 5936 X

For information on all Elsevier Butterworth-Heinemann
publications visit our website at http://books.elsevier.com

Typeset by Newgen Imaging Systems (P) Ltd., Chennai, India
Printed and bound in Great Britain

To D, for finding me and making me yours forever.

To Charlotte, for being my miracle, my inspiration and my immortality.

To my mother, Mona, for loving me no matter what.

To Mam, Dad, GranJoyce and all my extended family in Wales, for your love and support and for showing me how to use a tea-towel!

And to my father, Henry John Camden, who never stopped believing in me.

Contents

About the authors

Sarah-Jayne Gratton

Sarah-Jayne Gratton is a leading voice in technology marketing, with her articles being regularly featured in a number of national magazines and newspapers. She became President of the Women in Business Society in 2000, and is the co-founder and Director of both GA Technology and Camden Publica-tions (a UK publications house specializing in consumer-related magazines and journals). Sarah-Jayne holds an upper-second class honours degree in Education and Psychology, along with a Masters Degree in Psychology. She is a prominent member of the CIMTech and her company, GA Technology, is an adopter member of the Bluetooth SIG. In 2000, Sarah-Jayne launched eWomensWeb.com, an e-magazine for UK executive women that has been described by the national press as 'the best of all the sites' aimed at women today.

You can contact Sarah-Jayne at sarah@ga-technology.com.

Dean Anthony Gratton

Dean Anthony Gratton is the co-founder of both Camden Publications and GA Technology, of which he is the Managing Director. GA Tech-nology is a wireless-focused consultancy spe-cializing in software development, training, marketing and visionary engineering. The com-pany has provided consultancy services to a number of leading organizations, including TDK Systems Europe,

Alcatel Microelectronics, Plantronics, Sony and 3Com Europe, where Dean became editor of the Bluetooth LAN Access Profile and was an active member of the Bluetooth PAN Working Group. His work on defining new aspects of wireless technology has been patented. Dean has also studied for a B.Sc. (Hons) Psychology and a Diploma in Counselling. Dean is the author of *Bluetooth Profiles: The Definitive Guide* (Prentice-Hall PTR, 2002) and has already started work on his third book, *Developing Practical Wireless Applications* (Digital Press, an imprint of Elsevier, 2004).

You can contact Dean at dean@ga-technology.com.

About the contributors

Johan Åkesson, Ericsson Technology Licensing

Johan Åkesson is the Director of Marketing at Ericsson Technology Licensing, the 'Bluetooth' company within Ericsson. Johan has been in the core of the Bluetooth community since the beginning and is one of the pioneers in this field. He joined Ericsson in 1998 to work within the unit that was developing and forming Bluetooth. In 2000, Ericsson Technology Licensing was spun off as a separate entity, fully owned by Ericsson, to focus on providing Bluetooth design solutions for the semiconductor industry and OEMs. Johan has contributed to establishing Bluetooth as a well-recognized brand, and heading out a new successful Bluetooth marketing strategy for Ericsson. Combining very technical products like intellectual property for the semiconductor industry with an additional offer for OEMs in one single product is one of his unorthodox marketing ideas. Prior to joining Ericsson, Johan worked for more than 10 years at ABB Automation (formerly Alfa Laval Automation) with Process Control systems. Johan worked in the development team that pioneered *SattLine*, a process control system way ahead of its time, and nowadays a highly recognized and modern object-oriented process control system. During his years at ABB, Johan held various positions and also spent some time on international assignments. He holds a degree in Computer Science from Lund University in Sweden.

Ronald Sperano, IBM Personal Computer Division

Dr Sperano is the Program Director for Mobile Market Development at IBM Personal Computer Division (PCD). He is responsible for worldwide marketing initiatives and strategy development for PCD's wireless initiatives for the IEEE 802.11 Wireless Local Area Network (WLAN) specifications along with Bluetooth wireless technology for Personal Area Networks (PAN) and cellular technologies for Wide Area Networking (WAN). Prior to his current position, Dr Sperano was the worldwide Marketing Manager for the Ultraportable segment of the notebook computer market responsible for the conception, development, introduction and launch of many of the IBM ThinkPad products. During Dr Sperano's 29-year career with IBM, he has been associated with Mainframes, Mini-computers and more recently Personal Computers. Dr Sperano was one of the original members of the IBM ThinkPad development team, where he remains today. He holds a BBA in Accounting, an MBA in Marketing and a Ph.D. in Computer Technology in Education.

Gary Evans, Toshiba Information Systems, UK

Gary Evans is Head of Business Development at Toshiba Information Systems, UK. A 10-year veteran of the mobile computing industry, Gary Evans is responsible for developing The Computer Systems Division's value-add proposition in the UK. After graduating in Mechanical Engineering from University College Cardiff in 1984, Gary pursued a career as an avionic and optical design engineer before a change in direction led to varied sales and business development roles within the Computer Aided Design and most recently the Mobile Computing industries. This diverse background gives Gary a wide perspective of both the technical and commercial applications of mobile and wireless computing technology.

Nick Hunn, TDK Systems Europe

Nick Hunn is the Managing Director for TDK Systems Europe Limited, leading TDK's European design team for communications solutions. Nick was one of the two founders of Grey Cell Systems, which was acquired by TDK in 1997 as their European Communications Design Centre. Over the past 12 years, Nick has been responsible for the full range of products designed by Grey Cell Systems and TDK Europe. They have been at the forefront of bringing new technologies to market that enable mobile communications, from one of the first Ethernet PCMCIA cards through a gamut of GSM data solutions to today's wireless products. Prior to his involvement in the PC industry, Nick developed a diverse range of products, ranging from robot vision systems to laser gyroscopes and semiconductor processing equipment. He was also responsible for a world-leading range of sperm and embryo freezers that was awarded the Queen's Award for Technology. He is a frequent contributor to explaining technology trends, both in print and at conferences. Over the years he has appeared in print on cryobiology, plasma chemistry, surface mount manufacturing and communications. He speaks regularly throughout Europe on the future of mobile communications. He is also an executive director of the Mobile Data Association, promoting all forms of wireless data communication.

Nick can be contacted at nick.hunn@tdksys.com.

Wade Gillham, Mobilian Corporation

Wade Gillham is the Marketing Director at Mobilian Corporation. He has won many industry awards and recognitions as an advanced and accomplished marketing expert in wireless technology. He has also worked at Dell Computer Corporation, Electronic Data Systems and as a management consultant at Renaissance Worldwide (now Adventis). Wade holds a Masters of International Management (MIM) from l'Ecole Superieure de Commerce, Dijon, France, an MBA from Texas A&M University and a BA from Baylor University in Texas.

He can be reached at wade_gillham@hotmail.com.

Tom Siep, Bluetooth SIG

Tom's background is firmly planted in both the 802.11 and Bluetooth worlds. He is the former General Manager of the Bluetooth Special Interest Group (SIG) and was a seven-year member of IEEE 802.11. As a member of technical staff for Texas Instruments he was the primary architect of the development of several mobile short-distance wireless prototype products in the late 1980s and the mid 1990s. Responsibilities ranged from product definition to user interfaces to protocol design. From that experience base, he helped define and design the initial WLAN Standard for 802.11. Based on his IEEE 802.11 experience, he became the chief technical editor of IEEE 802.15, the Wireless Personal Area Networks standards family, which includes a standardization of the Bluetooth protocol. It was that work which brought him to the attention of the Bluetooth SIG, who hired him as their first employee. While working for the SIG, Tom was involved in all facets of running a not-for-profit industry trade organization, including marketing and positioning. As GM he was the liaison for the SIG with peer non-profit organizations, commercial enterprises and the press. He is a published author, holds four US patents and is also an artist. Tom has a Masters degree in Management Information Systems from the University of Texas at Dallas, and a Bachelors degree in Behavioural Sciences from the University of California at Fullerton. He is currently an independent consultant specializing in Short-Distance Wireless product strategies and industry consortia relations.

Derrick Emeka, TDK Systems Europe

Derrick studied International Relations at Keele University, where he obtained an upper-second class honours degree. Derrick also studied at the University of Sheffield, where he obtained an MBA. Since then, he has held marketing positions within several companies, such as Railtrack, Barclays, Frost & Sullivan (International Research Consultancy) and Michelin Tyre Plc. He is presently Head of Marketing at TDK Systems (part of TDK Corporation). He is also a member of the Institute of Directors and the CMO (Chief Marketing Officer) Council, as well as a member of the Chartered Institute of Marketing. He offers marketing advice and recommendations to both small and large companies who are planning marketing campaigns or looking to adopt a marketing strategy within their businesses. Derrick is presently working closely with the Bluetooth Special Interest Group in helping them to facilitate the adoption of Bluetooth technology.

Simon Garth, Symbian

Simon Garth is General Manager of Symbian's Cambridge (UK) site, which focuses on core software development and licensee consulting and heads Symbian's London-based Market Development function addressing the needs of Mobile Operators. Simon also sits on the Board of the Open Mobile Alliance industry body. In the last 20 years, Simon has worked in a number of technology-based companies in roles including CTO and Managing Director. Before joining Symbian in 2000, he created and managed several overseas activities, including a software JV in India and a sales and development office in Detroit, USA. Simon gained his Ph.D. from Cambridge University, where he was also a Research Fellow in association with Texas Instruments Inc.

Andrie de Vries, Symbian

 Andrie joined Symbian in 2001, where he is responsible for market analysis and forecasting. Prior to this, he was product manager at Psion Computers, where he was responsible for managing the range of PDAs that Psion developed for the consumer market. Andrie also has seven years experience in strategy consulting, having worked for both Accenture and Bain & Co. He enjoys the forward-looking aspects of his position and thinks that the mobile software industry is entering a phase of rapid innovation to win the repeat business of consumers of mobile telephony. Andrie is a national of South Africa, where he studied mechanical engineering at the University of South Africa. He has lived in London since 1998, where he studied towards an executive MBA at the London Business School. He enjoys going to performances by symphony orchestras, loves cooking and keeps fit by running and swimming regularly.

Foreword

It is my pleasure to write the foreword for this book and invite you to read on. Over the past seven years I have personally been involved in launching and promoting a new class of wireless technology; this class being the worldwide, two-way, unrestricted use, personal range, wireless communications designed for a broad range of applications. We named it Bluetooth wireless technology for short. My role within Intel Corporation and as Chairman of the Bluetooth Special Interest Group (SIG) marketing team has been focused on establishing the standards, communicating the vision to the user segments and working with the industry to deliver products. I have worked with most of the contributors to this book, who have each taken the vision and concept of *new wireless* to deliver products into their individual market segments. Many of the lessons learned will be of great value to you if you are involved in bringing wireless products to your market.

The key to success is achieved through finding a clear and consistent vision that understands user benefits and adheres to the right path to implement products. The Bluetooth vision is to replace cables between devices and build a radio for less than $5. The objective was to bring together companies from different market segments, agree on the usage models, and work together to develop and promote the technology. Companies benefit through ubiquity and a broad installed base of a single standard. Details of how this came together can be found in the following chapters.

The first challenge was to bring the industry together and agree on the key directions and use objectives. For this, clear business benefits for each company needed to be defined. Each company then contributed investment in resources for product and specification development. Key marketing challenges through this phase were industry facing and focused on bringing the technology to market. Now we are in the phase of delivering products to customers and growing the installed base. Each company with a product is responsible for the specific benefits and positioning to their customers. And so, the Bluetooth SIG is shifting to a user and channel focus.

Along the way there were many challenges for the technology that will also apply to specific products using the capability. The challenges include positioning the technology against other wireless standards, gaining regulatory approval to use products in target markets (for us that meant worldwide approval), competition and meeting the expectations of the market segment.

For us marketers, the great thing about wireless is that it really is magic. 'Doing it without wires' is a benefit that is easily understood. The challenge is not so much about the primary benefit but addressing: Why now? Why this technology? How easy is it to use? What does it work with? Will it still work two years from now? And so on. These are the real marketing challenges and make this a very dynamic and exciting place to be. Good luck and have fun with your programs.

Simon C. Ellis
Intel Corporation
Chairman of the Bluetooth SIG Marketing Team

Preface

When Dean and I were given the opportunity to both write and edit this book we were quite simply overjoyed. The chance to combine both of our backgrounds and knowledge in a single publication was a thrilling challenge and one that we dived straight into with enormous gusto. We both knew that there was a great need for a book like this to be written, as very little literature on the marketing of wireless was available outside of the analyst arena. It was this understanding, in combination with many hours of discussion and planning, that helped to shape the final 'look and feel' of this book. What we have achieved here we feel is something quite unique, in that this book encompasses not only our own knowledge, but also that of some of the world's greatest wireless marketers. Collecting and editing their individual chapters has been a great personal privilege and the opportunity to pass on this knowledge to you fills us with a rare combination of pride and excitement as we anticipate the value given; value that will both positively reshape your existing marketing perspective and arm you with the confidence to succeed in your future endeavors.

Marketing Wireless Products will take you on a journey filled with new discoveries that you will want to revisit again and again. We hope that you enjoy reading its pages as much as we have enjoyed filling them.

Acknowledgements

Our sincere thanks go out to all our contributing authors: Simon Ellis of Intel, Johan Åkesson of Ericsson, Ronald Sperano of IBM, Gary Evans of Toshiba, Wade Gillham of Mobilian, Tom Siep of the Bluetooth SIG, Nick Hunn and Derrick Emeka of TDK, and Simon Garth and Andrie de Vries of Symbian. Thank you all for your support and patience in putting together this valuable collection of ideas and philosophies.

A special thank you to Tom Farley of TelecomWriting.com, Telephone History Series, for the use of his illustration in Chapter 1 (Figure 1.1).

And, of course, no book can be well written without the support of those closest to us, our family and friends, and it is with this in mind that we send out a special thank you to our parents, Mona, Tony and Sheila, and to GranJoyce, who never fails to ask us about the book's progress. We would also like to send our love and thanks to Katrina and Andrew and our dear little Godsons, Kieran and Connor for their understanding and support during the months of writing; many a family dinner is owing to you all.

Introduction

This book is written with the intention of providing you with all you need to know about the marketing of *new* wireless products. Furthermore, its content should inspire you to establish your own philosophy on the best way to bring a product from creation to consumer by taking you inside the minds of some of the greatest marketers in the wireless world today. The book is separated into three main sections for ease of reference:

Part I, 'History and Theory', introduces you to wireless technology by providing a brief history of its origins and development through the last two centuries. It goes on to consider both the architectural and developmental aspects of some of the most popular forms of wireless technology today and tackles issues of coexistence and interoperability between the various wireless technologies. Most importantly perhaps, it looks at what makes a good wireless product in the light of consumer expectations.

Part II, 'Leading Perspectives', comprises a valuable collection of chapters authored by some of the world's leading authorities in wireless marketing. Their work in introducing new wireless products to the consumer has revolutionized the way we mentally view the word *wireless* today. These chapters will, we hope, inspire and motivate the way in which you plan your future marketing endeavors and will no doubt strengthen and possibly reshape your individual philosophies whilst doing so.

Finally, Part III, 'Looking to the Future', looks to the future of wireless technology by discussing the various routes and forms that wireless may take in future years. Much can be learned by studying the developmental and promotional compounds that make up our earlier chapters, and this is taken to a further level by making educated assumptions about where we next expect advances to be made. The section will undoubtedly encourage you to form your own opinions about where we are headed and to look long and hard at the various consumer-biased elements that will make our future wireless products either revolutionary or redundant.

When read as a whole, *Marketing Wireless Products* will take you on a journey through the origins of wireless technology to modern-day consumer usage and will bring into focus the psychological *links to purchasing* that every good marketer should know and understand. Some of you may wish to dip into certain sections from time to time to gain a fuller understanding of a particular marketing or historical element but, however you choose to use the book, we hope you will find it to be an invaluable addition to your marketing reference library.

Part I

History and Theory

Chapter 1

A brief history of wireless technology

However far modern science and techniques have fallen short of their inherent possibilities, they have taught mankind at least one lesson: nothing is impossible.

Lewis Mumford

The concept of a *world without wires* is one which all technology marketers will be familiar with. It is an exciting thought; the possibilities both commercially and socially are quite phenomenal. Now, more than ever, these same possibilities seem within the reach of us mere mortals through the endeavors of the highly skilled developers and researchers that surround the continuous birth of new wireless wonders. Indeed, our commercial interpretation of *wireless* encompasses so many futuristic promises that, in our excitement, it's easy to forget its true origins. This chapter aims to provide you with a real sense of where wireless came from by explaining the basic concepts behind the birth of the *original wireless* technologies that ultimately led on to the equally revolutionary *new wireless*[1] of today. It touches upon key moments in the history of wireless product development and will hopefully excite you enough to encourage further research into your own specialized area of interest. Furthermore, it will provide you with a useful primer to Chapter 2, which will explore, in greater depth, the implicit workings of wireless.

---

[1] A term depicting the new generation of wireless technologies, such as Bluetooth and 802.11.

We begin by looking back to the middle of the nineteenth century, when communications around the globe were inconceivably slow and restrictive in comparison to today's standards. It was during this period that Morse sent his first message over a telegraph line. Although not a wireless feat, it was a revolutionary achievement and one which harkened the way forward to today's email messages. Just over a decade later, telegraph cables connected people all the way from Europe to the United States of America and led the way towards further advances in remote communication, such as Alexander Graham Bell's invention of the telephone in 1876. However, it was not until the mid 1890s that the first truly wireless telegraph system was developed by Guglielmo Marconi and a further six years before the first human voice was broadcast on a wireless set. Clearly, when Marconi initially began his experiments with radio waves in 1894, he did so with the intent that wireless communications were wholly possible. Despite much criticism from his peers, he persevered with his attempts to produce and detect sound using hertzian waves over long distances, and in 1896 he achieved the initial success he had been looking for. Over time, improvements were continually made to Marconi's now patented system, and in 1901 he was triumphant in sending a radio message across the Atlantic Ocean using Morse code (radio-telegraphy). The success and critical acclaim of this radical new discovery led to radio-telegraphy quickly being adopted by the international maritime services in the early 1900s as a means to improve safety at sea. Indeed, the technology rapidly became the primary form of maritime communication, bringing with it new levels of safety management capability and opening up a whole new world of commercial possibility for other industries, all keen to learn more about its potential. With this in mind, dozens of inventors and scientists around the world worked on different parts of the radio puzzle, each wanting to improve its capabilities and, in doing so, bring about the same recognition for their findings as Marconi had accomplished. Ironically, it was largely due to the generally poor level of communications available at this time, coupled with parallel patterns of disjointed research, that many people duplicated the work of others and often misconstrued their own findings.

Shortly after the first wireless transmitters went on the air at the start of the 1900s, information was added to the signal carriers, a process known as *modulation*. This dramatic inclusion made it possible to transmit voices and music via wireless, the medium that we now know as *radio*.

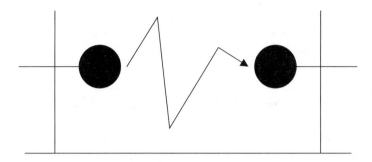

Figure 1.1 With a sufficient amount of electrical current between two points a spark will jump across them

The commercial diversification of radio waves in wireless communications was not to become fully apparent for many years, but the relationship between radio and another revolutionary form of communication, the telephone, had already been forged. It is considered by many that the first *mobile* telephone call was taken in 1879 by London-born David Hughes, a gifted inventor who, in the late 1800s, worked on a number of early wireless projects. Hughes developed a home-based telephone device and centered a number of his experiments on its workings. In particular, he was intrigued to discover a tapping noise that appeared to be present each time he used it.

Upon further investigation, Hughes realized that the tapping he heard was due to a spark caused by a loose wire in his mechanism. This finding caused Hughes to ponder over whether any information had managed to travel across the wires in the device without the presence of a fixed connection and, as a result, he accurately concluded that radio waves had been produced and then carried within the gap that the spark had moved across. Hughes quickly began developing a number of devices to test his theory. One such transmitter was operated by clockwork and tested the capabilities of circuit interruption, allowing Hughes a small degree of remote telephone usage. Initially, Hughes only transmitted signals internally, between the rooms of his London home, but he soon realized that the real test of its capabilities could be found by exploring its potential use in the outside world. And so he took to frequently walking the avenues adjoining his own, telephone in hand, as he concentrated on detecting the clicking sounds, which indicated his device was indeed transmitting wirelessly over remote distances.

Similarly, as early as 1910, it has been recorded that Lars Ericsson was experimenting with ways of using the telephone to make remote calls whilst traveling in his car. Although Lars's system was not wireless,[2] it clearly opened up his mind to the commercial possibilities and implications of being able to make calls from remote locations and without the restrictions of a fixed base telephone device. Lars's company Ericsson has continued its passion for inventing new ways to improve communications and were the very founders of Bluetooth technology, which we will discuss later on in this chapter. Indeed, you can read an excellent chapter authored by Johan [ANG]kesson, the Head of Marketing for Ericsson Licensing Technology, in Part II, 'Leading Perspectives'.

The 1920s saw radio-telephones being used for the first time in the patrol cars of US policemen. The introduction of these was revolutionary to the way in which the service was able to communicate whilst on the road. However, in these early days, the devices were far too large to be installed in the front of the vehicles and were confined to the boot or trunk, where they took up every inch of available space. This severely weighed the vehicles down and consequently limited their speed – not a positive attribute for a police car! In addition to this problem, the unevenness of the city street and the imposing city buildings caused severe disruption to the transmission of the radio-telephone signals.

However, this was all to change in 1935, when Edwin Howard Armstrong introduced *Frequency Modulation* (FM), a discovery that would revolutionize radio broadcasting, as it reduced the amount of equipment needed to carry a signal and provided greater reliability and consistency of transmission. Further advances were born when the idea of spreading or scattering the number of transmitters used in an area opened up new possibilities. The concept meant that calls could be 'handed off' from transmitter to transmitter as users traveled around in their vehicles. When brought into practice it allowed simultaneous access to the system, by reusing the frequencies across the city and, when more capacity was needed, the area served by each transmitter could be divided again.

During World War II, FM technology took the place of *Amplitude Modulated* (AM) technology. Work in radio-telephone technology

---

[2] Ericsson's system relied on the obtrusive use of long poles with hooks on the end that linked themselves over the main telephone system wires to tap into their signal-carrying capabilities.

continued, with much emphasis on its military use. Motorola was responsible for the design and development of the very first portable FM two-way radio, the *walkie-talkie*, which they named the *Handie-Talkie*. This played an impressive part in battlefield communications throughout Europe and the South Pacific during World War II. The product's much talked about success on the battlefield encouraged other companies to focus on the commercial potential of mobile communications and walkie-talkies, as we know, are still very much in use today.

We have already introduced the concept of scattering transmitters to improve access to a system. This idea worked and was a revolutionary breakthrough in mobile communications, but it actually took over 20 years to fully develop and for approval to be granted by the FCC in the United States. But, by the early 1970s, the technological stitches that made up the wireless tapestry had all been sewn and they remain the cornerstone of those in constant use today.

The preceding history has given us a flavor of original wireless technology and of the many challenges it had to overcome on its journey to the consumer of today. Indeed, it is argued that new wireless technology came into being as a result of the overwhelming popularity of the mobile communications marketplace that encompassed original wireless technology.

GSM is a success story that, like Bluetooth, we will discuss next in this chapter. It had its routes in pan-European development, albeit some 12 years before Bluetooth's initial concept had been born. A consortium of countries from the length and breadth of Europe worked alongside one another to realize a cellular-based method for wireless communications that had the potential for seamless global roaming. With the initial research having been undertaken and the theory for development being shown to be sound, the Group Spéciale Mobile, from where the abbreviation GSM first emerged, joined together in 1982 to begin developing this exciting new communications system. However, work did not progress as quickly as was first anticipated, as is often the case with new technology development, and was later taken over by the *European Telecommunications Standards Institute* (ETSI). It was not until 1991 that the first ever GSM network was finally released to a wave of public anticipation and expectation. Uptake of GSM was rapid and it was this widespread global adoption that gave way to a new definition of its letters, that of a *Global System for Mobile Communications*. It is this definition to which the letters GSM refer to today.

In contrast, the idea that resulted in the development of Bluetooth wireless technology came directly from a major telecommunications corporation, namely Ericsson Mobile Communications, in 1994. The company had decided to explore the feasibility of a low-power, low-cost radio interface between mobile phones and their accessories. They envisaged that a small radio built into both the cellular telephone and the laptop could possibly replace the cables used to connect the two devices. They decided to codename the technology after the great unifier of Denmark and Norway, Great King Harald II of Denmark, whose nickname was *Bluetooth*. It was over 12 months later that the potential of Bluetooth technology fully became clear. This new radio technology had the power to provide not only freedom from cables within the workplace, but a new way of working outside of the office. At the beginning of 1998, a consortium of telecommunications and computer manufacturing companies, including Ericsson, Intel, IBM, Nokia and Toshiba, began working jointly to extend the idea of Bluetooth into a developed and ready-to-market technology, and on 20 May 1998, the consortium created a *Special Interest Group* (SIG) to oversee the technology's evolution.

Meanwhile, another new wireless revolution had already begun to take shape. In 1990, the IEEE 802 Executive Committee formed the 802.11 Working Group to create a *Wireless Local Area Network* (WLAN) standard. This specified an operating frequency in the 2.4 GHz *Industrial, Scientific and Medical* (ISM) band and provided the foundations for a new wireless technology. Seven years later, the IEEE 802.11 was approved as the world's first WLAN standard with data rates of 1 and 2 Mbps. Fortunately, the executive committee possessed a keen marketing foresight and worked with the assumption that bandwidth would need to increase as the world grew more infatuated with power and speed. With this in mind, they began working immediately on ways of satisfying these needs through extensions to the existing technology. These extensions are discussed further in Chapter 2, and were essential components of 802.11's success and the sustainability of its market attraction.

Looking back, we can see that the concept of wireless technology has always been about freedom of communication and this is continually echoed in today's marketing of the products that encompass its capability. Throughout the history of wireless development, our main tool for the integration of its technology has indisputably been the telephone but, with the advent of computer systems, *Personal Digital Assistants* (PDAs) and other on-screen means of communication, this channel has since broadened considerably. More recently, a new generation of wireless products has exploded onto the marketplace which, in turn, have given birth to a new breed of consumer with ever-changing levels of awareness about what wireless is and about what it can do. What started as the simple concept of 'connection without wires' has reinvented itself into a philosophy of ever-increasing new possibilities, which inevitably will bring boundless new challenges for marketers everywhere.

Summary

- Wireless technology falls into two historical categories – *original wireless* and *new wireless*.
- The birth of wireless technology can be traced back to the mid nineteenth century.
- Morse code marked the way forward for today's email messages.
- The first truly wireless telegraph system was developed by Guglielmo Marconi in the mid 1890s.
- In 1901 Marconi sent the very first radio message across the Atlantic Ocean using Morse code.
- The process of modulation made it possible to transmit voices and music via radio.
- It is thought that the first mobile telephone call was made by David Hughes in 1879.
- Lars Ericsson began experimenting with remote telephone usage around 1910.
- The 1920s saw radio-telephones being used for the first time in the US in the patrol cars of policemen.
- Edwin Howard Armstrong introduced FM in 1935.
- The scattering of transmitters in an area allowed calls to be handed off from one transmitter to another during remote usage, thus accommodating increases in service use and reliability.
- New wireless technology came into being as a result of the overwhelming popularity of the mobile communications marketplace that encompassed the original wireless technology.
- The idea that resulted in the development of Bluetooth wireless technology came from Ericsson Mobile Communications and was named after King Harald II of Denmark, whose nickname was Bluetooth.
- The Bluetooth SIG was formed to oversee the technology's evolution.

Chapter 2

How wireless technology works

The creation of a wireless product is the result of a combination of design and packaging, production, hardware and software. These core stages of development occur at different phases of a product's life cycle. More often than not, a feasibility study will be conducted prior to any design stage, as a company will need to be absolutely certain that a proposed wireless product is needed and there are an ample number of consumers ready to purchase it. This philosophy seems, on the surface, to be black and white, but with *new*[3] wireless technology marketed as offering mobility, freedom and ease-of-use, it's quite easy to imagine the associated drive to lure consumers into adopting this simplicity in their everyday technology-orientated lives. Furthermore, a feasibility study may incorporate information gained through *data mining* to evaluate potential features and assist in ascertaining how a product's functionality should ultimately manifest itself to the end-user; and let's not forget the general look and feel of the product. It's incredible to note that the look and feel plays a significant part in the consumer perception of a product: is it a suitable fashion statement? Does it feel comfortable in my hand? Does it feel comfortable on my ear? (A Bluetooth headset, for example; see Figure 2.1) and so on. With such subtleties in product definition, it is evident that these factors could potentially affect both a product's initial success and its long-term market adoption.

In this chapter we present an understanding of how wireless technology works by taking a closer look inside our wireless products,

---

[3] You may recall from our discussion in Chapter 1 that we distinguished between old and new wireless technologies.

Figure 2.1 The Sony Ericsson Bluetooth™ Headset HBH-60 (courtesy of Ericsson Technology Licensing)

where we will bias our discussion towards the software and hardware architectures. Our objective will undoubtedly provide you with a valuable appreciation of most of the wireless-enabled products currently available today, coupled with an appreciation of the combined processes that bring a wireless product to life. The chapter will avoid imparting too much technical detail, but will provide sufficient knowledge to enable you to understand the basic building blocks of a wireless product which, in turn, will allow you to talk more confidently and openly about its inherent architecture.

Understanding the hardware

With such a diverse set of wireless technologies available for us to explore, it's difficult to know where to begin our initial examination of the hardware architecture. However, one common component unique to all wireless devices is the *radio*. Bluetooth wireless technology, WiFi and ZigBee all rely on this core component to facilitate communication with other similarly interested devices. Nevertheless, let's not forget that the radio is not unique to new wireless products. We can see this technology already incorporated into many existing products that we all take for granted, such as the television, satellite communications, mobile phones, cordless handsets and so on. The radio forms part of our discussion surrounding the hardware components of a wireless device and is further explored later on in this section.

For the moment, our immediate discussion focuses on the surrounding hardware components of a wireless product which, in turn, will provide some context for our radio. Figure 2.2 illustrates some of the typical components that can be found within a wireless product. In the following discussion, we break down each component to help us understand their relationship and how, together, they uniquely form a wireless product. The chosen building blocks will also impact upon many other factors, which we briefly touched upon earlier, such as end-functionality. Equally as important is product pricing, which is determined by a combination of factors and, most certainly, the hardware components chosen will affect the end-price.

The combination of hardware components, as we have illustrated, uniquely enable functionality within the device. If we refer to Figure 2.2, the radio, *power, processor, read only memory* (ROM), *random access memory* (RAM) and *input and output*, although simplified, form the basic components at the centre of any wireless product.

The processor, like any electronic-based system, is the heart of the device, which coordinates effort between all the entities shown in

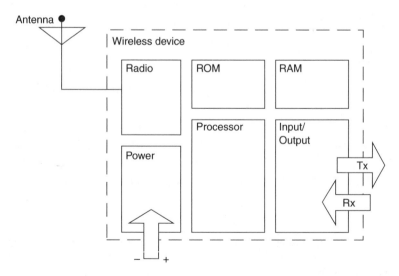

Figure 2.2 A simplified overview of the hardware components that comprise a wireless device. The illustration may represent a USB or PCMCIA device

our illustration. It relies on power to bring it to life, as well as powering the rest of the components. Power may be derived from a physical connection, such as being plugged into a wall socket, batteries or from a *host*[4] device. The processor also requires access to ROM and RAM space. The RAM space provides a dynamic working area for the processor to perform its instructions. The ROM area will contain a small *operating system* (OS) and also the *firmware*,[5] which will provide basic operation. The role of the OS is to provide intrinsic functionality of the surrounding hardware components and, additionally, it will execute the firmware. The firmware will provide the basic functionality, such as transmitting and receiving data to and from the radio and passing it to the input/output controller for use by an external device. It may also undertake instructions for retransmission and error handling when data is lost or corrupted. We can see such a relationship in operating systems such as Microsoft Windows and Linux, where effort is coordinated between the hard drive, CD-ROM, mouse and so on, and applications are executed. It is these applications that ultimately provide a fuller and broader experience for the user. With a range of wireless-enabled devices, such as a wireless access point, Bluetooth-enabled PC Card and a Bluetooth-enabled headset, more often the functionality relies on a combination of hardware and software processes. For example, when a PC Card is inserted into a notebook, not only does it utilize power resources, it exposes an interface to the rest of the wireless system. The OS residing on the host will resource applications that will understand the wireless device's interface and will then engage communication with it.

This combined architecture is fundamental to the pricing of a wireless product, as we previously highlighted. For instance, smaller ROM and RAM areas offer a cheaper end-price and so does the type of processor used. Engineers will architect the hardware solution cost-effectively which, in turn, will ultimately benefit the end-user in terms of price. Naturally, this architecture may impact upon features where not all the functionality can be offered. In some instances, if the software is too large to occupy ROM, some

---

[4] One such host device includes a notebook computer, accompanied with a wireless-enabled PC Card. When the PC Card is inserted into the notebook, it derives power from its host.

[5] Firmware refers to the software application that resides in an embedded device, such as a Bluetooth-enabled headset.

non-essential features may be removed from the product and at a later development stage (where the user has become more confident with the wireless product), the consumer may be inclined to spend a little more to have the additional features.

In the early stages of Bluetooth development, manufacturers were keen to bring down prices of their hardware to around $5 per unit.[6] With the recent introduction of ZigBee, manufacturers are more aware of the need to architect a new wireless technology effectively, as the success of the technology relies, to a large extent, on its adoption by other manufacturers. In presenting ZigBee, its associated alliance and marketing members are keen to promote a technology that will resolve some of the initial problems experienced with Bluetooth. ZigBee itself boasts: low power usage which, in turn, will extend battery life; a full protocol stack (more about this later on in the chapter), which will occupy less then 32 KB of memory, in turn keeping the manufacturing cost down; a simplified software architecture, in turn, providing rapid product development; and the ability to extend its interoperability with a larger range of devices. Nonetheless, ZigBee occupies the same unlicensed radio frequency as Bluetooth and 802.11b, which of course introduces potential coexistence issues. For Bluetooth wireless technology, the issue of resolving interoperability issues with 802.11b was introduced at a later stage of the specification's life. It was deemed to be a critical issue, as the press wallowed in the technology's perceived shortcomings, alongside their assertions that these two technologies would not cohabit harmoniously. Manufacturers such as Mobilian have benefitted from introducing technology that does indeed resolve coexistence issues. As for ZigBee, it is too early to predict (at the time of writing) if the Alliance will employ hindsight when creating the technology's future specification.

An *input/output* component within a wireless product provides an interface to the outside world. This interface serves many purposes. Some manufacturers create an interface to coexist with a host (as previously described) or to offer the user the ability to upgrade firmware. Providing this ability enables manufacturers to resolve any outstanding issues with software or to provide upgrades to the firmware, which, on some occasions, could enhance the

---

[6] This is certainly becoming more evident, as the popularity of Bluetooth wireless technology is increasing and some analysts predict that this will become the norm by 2005.

product's core features. It is important to note that the design of the hardware for a wireless product is one of the most critical parts of its development, as any later redesign is both a costly and time-consuming exercise. Manufacturers therefore invest a large part of their time ensuring that they get this stage of development absolutely right.

The radio

We touched upon the radio in our initial introduction to this chapter. This key component of a wireless product deserves its own section, as it is an exciting piece of technology that has intrinsically surrounded us for many years and, of course, is today very much taken for granted.

A radio is an electronic device that has an *antenna* attached to it; this forms one of the most essential components of a wireless system. Figure 2.3 illustrates some of the common components that make up a radio. As an independent unit the radio provides an *over-the-air* interface to other wireless devices. The radio applies a *radio frequency* (RF) current[7] to the antenna which, in turn, generates *radio waves*. Putting it simply, radio waves are transmitted and received by the radio through the antenna and converted into electrical signals, which are then communicated to and from the rest of the wireless system as data. If you again refer to Figure 2.3, you will see that a *transmit* (Tx) and *receive* (Rx) path exists to facilitate communication to and from the system. Radio waves comprise an electric and magnetic field (*electromagnetic*), which is propagated from one antenna to another. In current wireless products, radio waves are typically *omnidirectional*, although in some devices they can be *directional* (these terms refer to how radio waves are transmitted by the antenna). You may recall that we first introduced radio waves in Chapter 1.

There is a large range of radio frequencies to choose from, where each occupies a particular band and each has its own purpose and application. For example, Bluetooth wireless technology, ZigBee and

---

[7] A radio frequency current is a form of *alternating current* (AC). This type of current is used to create and propagate radio waves, as its properties generate the up and down motion of a radio wave.

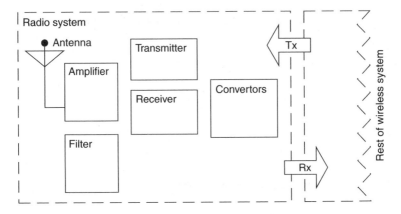

Figure 2.3 A simplified overview of the components that comprise a radio system. The ancillary components are shown in no specific order

Table 2.1 The various bands and their associated frequencies and respective wavelengths

Band	Frequency	Wavelength
Very Low Frequency (VLF)	9 kHz to 30 kHz	30 km to 10 km
Low Frequency (LF)	30 kHz to 300 kHz	10 km to 1 km
Medium Frequency (MF)	300 kHz to 3 MHz	1 km to 100 m
High Frequency (HF)	3 MHz to 30 MHz	100 m to 10 m
Very High Frequency (VHF)	30 MHz to 300 MHz	10 m to 1 m
Ultra High Frequency (UHF)	300 MHz to 3 GHz	1 m to 100 mm
Super High Frequency (SHF)	3 GHz to 30 GHz	100 mm to 10 mm
Extremely High Frequency (EHF)	30 GHz to 300 GHz	10 mm to 1 mm

802.11b all operate within the 2.4 GHz band,[8] as illustrated in Table 2.1. The choice of frequency will also affect the antenna's size (typically, an antenna on most wireless products today is very small and discreet). Essentially, as we move up through the higher frequencies, we need a smaller antenna and, conversely, lower frequencies require a much larger antenna.

Furthermore, the frequency used will have a corresponding effect on the wavelength of the radio wave, which is illustrated in Figure 2.4. A frequency refers to the number of times a radio wave moves up and down per second; this is known as its *oscillation*. A radio system will be configured to listen for a particular radio wave and, similarly,

[8] Incidentally, in Chapter 4, we discuss the problems that manufacturers are faced with when developing technologies that operate within the same radio frequencies.

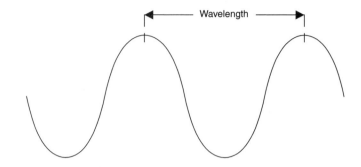

Figure 2.4 The wavelength of a radio wave

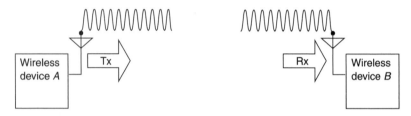

Figure 2.5 Two wireless devices are shown communicating with each other using the same frequencies

it will communicate to other devices using the same frequency, as illustrated in Figure 2.5.

One of the many key features of wireless technology is the advertised data rate or how fast data can be wirelessly transferred from one device to another. Bluetooth wireless technology has an advertised data rate of approximately 1 Mbps, whereas 802.11b has an advertised data rate capability of 11 Mbps. Primarily, 802.11b is aimed at the WLAN marketplace and data rates should be comparable to a fixed infrastructure, although, most fixed networks operate at a data rate of around 100 Mbps. Some smaller businesses may have an infrastructure that utilizes a data rate of 10 Mbps.

You may recall from Chapter 1 that the IEEE had the foresight to accommodate the increasing need for higher data rates. From their original specification, purporting rates of 1 and 2 Mbps, the current rate today of 11 Mbps demonstrates a specification that is evolving specifically to the needs of the consumer. The newer data rates are indeed extensions to the original specification, as we can still purchase access points that support the slower data rates. You may have also come across other technologies, such as 802.11a,[9] which purports a data rate of 54 Mbps, and undoubtedly we will, in time, see wireless technologies matching the data rates of our existing fixed technologies.

When we look at Bluetooth wireless technology, with an advertised data rate of 1 Mbps, and its associated type of applications, we can see that the rate is adequate. Nevertheless, the Bluetooth SIG are actively constructing a new specification, which will see Bluetooth's advertised data rate increase significantly. We can certainly anticipate the technology supporting data rates from 2 to 5 Mbps. When Bluetooth was first introduced, the technology intended to cover a large part of the application spectrum, to include WLANs. Many analysts and marketers did not anticipate that Bluetooth would succeed in this area, as the data rate was inadequate; this is quite clear when we compare it with 802.11b and, indeed, the IEEE's foresight in extending the technology. The primary problem encountered regarding a Bluetooth LAN access point was that it could only accommodate a maximum of seven concurrent users, essentially dividing the data rate between them. As such, the future of these applications is in doubt and, at the time of writing, some of the original Bluetooth Profiles[10] are being disbanded[11] and replaced with newer adopted profiles.

Finally, looking at ZigBee, which is very much in its infancy, we can glean a clear marketing message from the alliance, regarding the types of wireless applications for which the technology is intended, along with proposed implementation and functionality strategies. ZigBee has been specifically marketed as a technology that requires a lower data rate than that of Bluetooth and 802.11b. It is anticipated that the typical data rate for a ZigBee product will be between 20 and 250 Kbps. ZigBee is expected to be integrated in a larger application spectrum than that proposed by Bluetooth or WiFi.

---

[9] Wireless technologies such as 802.11b, 802.11a, 802.11g and so on all sit under the Wireless Fidelity (WiFi) umbrella.

[10] The Bluetooth Profiles are the end-functionality, which defines specific behaviour and characteristics at the application level.

[11] The profiles that may be considered disbanded and subsequently replaced are, speculatively, the LAN Access Profile, Dial-up Networking Profile, Extended Service Discovery Profile (for LAN Access) and WAP over Bluetooth. The Personal Area Networking Profiles are understood to replace the core networking profiles.

We can expect to see consumer electronics (such as DVDs, TVs and remote controls), various home applications (such as security and lighting) and healthcare equipment (such as sensors and monitors) all benefitting from ZigBee wireless technology. Naturally, applications offered by Bluetooth and ZigBee will overlap and the test of time will dictate how each technology suitably accommodates their individual application.

Moving from this hardware focus, we now turn our attention to the software components that make up a wireless product. The following section discusses the issues surrounding software architecture and its associated applications.

Understanding the software

Put in simple terms, a wireless product will allow the utilization of an application by a user. This interaction with both the software and hardware components of the product will generate data. The data comprises a series of instructions that inform the wireless product to take appropriate action. For example, a user may wish to *discover* other wireless products that are in radio range, such as a Bluetooth-enabled headset or an 802.11b access point. With this instruction, the wireless product undertakes the effort required to learn of other devices nearby. As we have earlier illustrated, data from the wireless system is communicated out through the radio system and then converted into radio waves. Other wireless devices that wish to acknowledge their existence will accordingly respond. Radio waves are then received by the radio system and converted to data to be communicated to the rest of the wireless system.

Using this simplified approach, we can begin to understand more of the underlying mechanisms that facilitate instructions between wireless products. These comprise the software building blocks that are essential in undertaking and passing on these instructions. In this section, we move on to discuss in more detail what is understood to be, and commonly known as, a *protocol stack*. Of course, the user will be unaware of this mechanism and what they will ultimately see is an application suite which, in turn, interacts with the protocol stack.

What is a protocol stack?

WiFi, Bluetooth and ZigBee wireless technology have each defined a specification that describes how a manufacturer and developer should create their respective wireless products. In these specifications, specific instructions are given that relate to the physical characteristics of a radio along with other ancillary definitions for the related hardware of that particular wireless product. A specification will also discuss particular software mechanisms that will become the essential building blocks for the software. Typically, these definitions are built upon the *Open Systems Interconnect* (OSI) model, as illustrated in Figure 2.6.

The OSI model

This model was first introduced by the *International Standards Organization* (ISO) in 1984, as a means of establishing a common framework for software within communication systems. At that time, many companies were developing numerous communications protocols but, unfortunately, none of them successfully interoperated. The ISO standard was adopted by companies wanting to develop and standardize protocol software to enable successful interoperation of communication-specific products. The result of their endeavors means that, today, if a manufacturer wishes to develop a wireless product, they can be confident that it will interoperate with another wireless product developed by a different manufacturer, as both will be referring to the same specification for development. The conceptual nature of the OSI model therefore provides an ideal foundation for creating protocol stacks. This

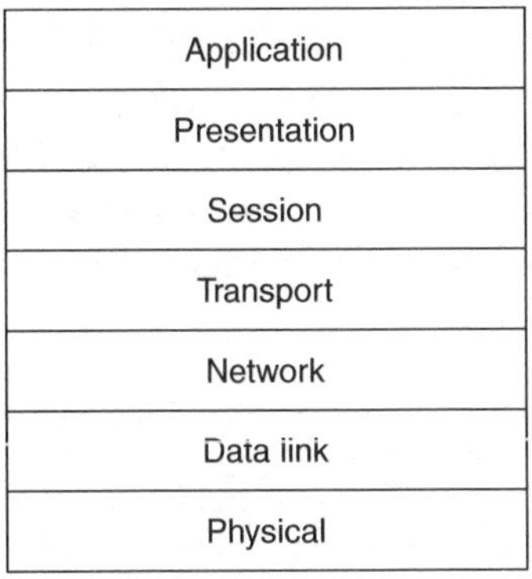

| Application |
| Presentation |
| Session |
| Transport |
| Network |
| Data link |
| Physical |

Figure 2.6 The OSI model, which is the basis for most of the wireless technologies' protocol stack architecture

underlying philosophy can be witnessed in all of the WiFi, Bluetooth and ZigBee specifications.

The interoperation of wireless-enabled products plays a significant part in the product development life cycle. You may have come across events such as the *Unplug fest*,[12] which is held annually by the Bluetooth SIG. These events allow developers to ensure that their protocol stacks interoperate successfully and, further, allow any problems to be identified early on, before the product is publicly released. Essentially, engineers will test the *peer-to-peer* interaction of each *layer* within the protocol stack (we will discuss peer-to-peer interaction later on in this chapter). Engineers will be interested in ensuring that their applications also work at the peer-to-peer level. For example, if a user utilizes Microsoft Windows Explorer to transfer a file, then the receiving device should instigate the appropriate reaction at the user interface level, as well as engaging many of the underlying stack mechanisms. These events are extremely popular with manufacturers, as they allow them to ensure that interoperation is successful between their product ranges. Marketers can then confidently proclaim that their company's products are compatible with other manufacturers to assist in achieving rapid adoption.

Each layer is an independent software block within the stack and is assigned a set of unique responsibilities and functions to perform. This has numerous benefits, effectively providing an efficient development life cycle and enabling ad hoc changes to a particular layer without affecting the rest of the protocol stack. You may recall from our earlier discussion that an interface is used to upgrade (provide additional features) or resolve issues in software.

Table 2.2 provides a broad reference for each layer's set of responsibilities and functions. This will help you understand how data is communicated up and down the protocol stack. Remember, the layered approach is used to simplify development in a structured and methodical way, and to facilitate effective changes to the software in the future. The architectures adopted within the 802.11b, Bluetooth and ZigBee specifications are based upon the original OSI model. For example, in Figure 2.7, we compare the OSI model with the

---

[12] These events are not unique to Bluetooth or any other wireless technology; many other events are organized for a whole range of technologies, for example USB. These gatherings are typically restricted to engineering personnel, allowing manufacturers to interoperate a large range of products, which utilize a communications suite.

Table 2.2 The OSI model and its respective layers

Layer	Description
Application	This layer primarily forms the top-end of our protocol stack. You may recall from our earlier discussion that a user would be unaware of the underlying software mechanisms of a protocol stack and, as such, this layer will expose an interface to the application suite, enabling it to communicate with the software building blocks.
Presentation	This layer's responsibility ensures that data received by the application layer is readable by its peer.
Session	When one device communicates with another wireless-enabled device, the two parties sustain a connection. This layer ensures that connections are created and maintained, and also disconnects the two devices when communication is no longer required.
Transport	When our session layer has created a connection, a reliable and unreliable service can be provided depending upon the type of data being communicated. For example, transmitting voice-orientated data requires a more reliable service, given the critical nature of the data. Standard data, such as transferring files, can use an unreliable service, but may employ a retransmission technique or an error recovery procedure for *data packets*[13] that were not received.
Network	Having established that we have an open connection between two devices, we need a means for identifying the end-destination of our data packet. This layer takes on the responsibility of identifying the internal references that are made to remember what is connected to what.
Data link	The data link layer is responsible for undertaking the transmitting and receiving of data packets to and from the physical layer, as well as presenting data to the network layer.
Physical	This layer is responsible for communicating data to and from the radio system. It will parcel the data to be transmitted over the air interface, in addition to collecting data from the air interface and parceling it up to the data link layer.

Bluetooth protocol stack, and in Figure 2.8 we compare the model with the 802.11 protocol stack.

It is not necessary to be able to recall individual layers within either of these examples. They have been illustrated to provide an

[13] A data packet is an encapsulated instruction set and, as it moves down the OSI model, each layer places its own additional instruction informing the next layer what to do. Conversely, when data is sent up the OSI model, the additional data packaging is removed, to provide that particular layer with its instructions.

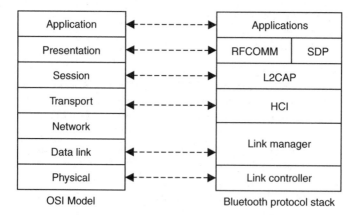

Figure 2.7 Comparing the OSI model with the Bluetooth protocol stack. The Bluetooth Specification outlines all layers of the OSI model. It can also be noticed that some of the responsibilities are shared between some layers

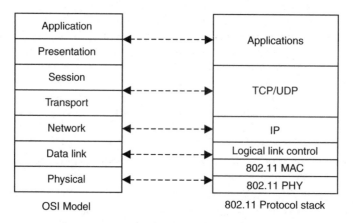

Figure 2.8 Comparing the OSI model with the 802.11 protocol stack. Primarily, the 802.11 specification outlines the lower layers of the stack (Logical Link Control, 802.11 MAC and 802.11 PHY) and typical networking implementations are placed on top, in turn, forming the network layers and above. Again, it can be noticed that some of the responsibilities are shared between some layers

understanding of the architecture and issues surrounding the development life cycle of a protocol stack. They will also allow you to understand how the specific building blocks are put together, in turn, enabling features that are inherent in wireless products.

Many protocol stack providers will offer pricing based on a one-off purchase of the stack or take advantage of a royalty-based scheme where, for each wireless device sold, a share of the product's price is passed on to the protocol stack provider. Companies tend to prefer the former scheme, as it is usually a cheaper solution, but does require that the company initially part with a substantial amount of capital. Stack providers typically offer bespoke schemes to accommodate specific functionality or for stacks that have to be built for a particular hardware platform. Some companies also provide the complete solution, i.e. the hardware and software. As such, manufacturers are only faced with the task of building their individual applications. The foundations and essential building blocks are already in place and so this 'all-in-one package' is an attractive solution for many companies, allowing them to provide rapid development of their new wireless products.

Peer-to-peer communication

Earlier in our discussion we touched upon peer-to-peer communication and this section will discuss how the OSI model achieves commonality between wireless-enabled products.

Figure 2.9 illustrates two wireless-enabled devices that share the same protocol stack architecture. When Device A communicates with Device B, Device A's layers communicate with the corresponding layers of Device B; this is referred to as peer-to-peer communication. For example, the physical layer on Device A will communicate

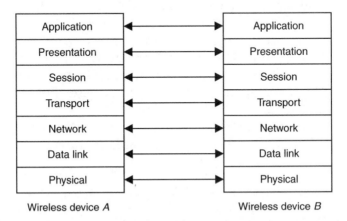

Wireless device *A* Wireless device *B*

Figure 2.9 Two wireless-enabled products share identical protocol stacks. Each layer will communicate with its peer, i.e. physical to physical, data link to data link, network to network and so on

with Device B's physical layer; the data link layer on Device A will communicate with Device B's data link layer, and so on.

This is how the OSI model establishes commonality with the development of communications-enabled products, but on occasions development effort can go astray. Many companies choose to develop protocol stacks from the same specification, as indeed they should, but if the specification itself has ambiguities, then this can lead to different development threads occurring in a particular layer, for example. It doesn't become obvious that there are differing interpretations of a specification until a company attempts to interoperate their device with another, although engineers may refer questions to the *architecture review committee*[14] in an attempt to resolve any uncertainty. This issue also highlights the benefits of such events as the unplug fests, as here a manufacturer is afforded the opportunity to test out and, if necessary, to reverse engineer software for a wireless product (usually on the fly) in an attempt to isolate any problems. However, many disagreements can then ensue. With such an ambiguity in the specification, the architecture review committee would be notified (significant board members of a committee are often present at an event). The committee will then ensure that an appropriate solution is effected by initially debating the ambiguity with both the original and other manufacturers. It is often the case that the manufacturer who has identified the ambiguity has already invested an extensive amount of development time in the product; therefore, it is in their interest to persuade the committee to take on board their recommendations, ultimately convincing them that their method is the right one. This may not be straightforward, since potentially other manufacturers might have experienced similar problems; nonetheless, it all leads to an interesting debate.

Bearing in mind our previous examination of peer-to-peer communication, this following section now discusses how each layer understands the information it receives.

Let us use our earlier example of a user interacting with an application which, in turn, generates data that is sent down the protocol

---

[14] The architecture review committee is a structured organization that would have been created from representatives of several manufacturers who have an invested interest in the evolution of the specification and its underlying technology. For example, the 802.11b working group has an organization that is typically structured with a chairman, marketing personnel, technical authorities, and software and hardware engineers.

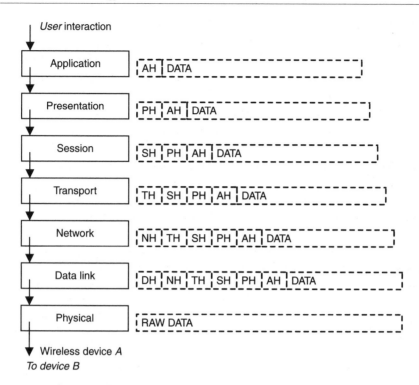

Figure 2.10 When a user interacts with an application provided by the manufacturer, it generates data unique to a given command. For example, if the user wishes to learn of other devices in radio range, data generated at the application layer will be encapsulated and passed down the protocol stack. As the data moves down the stack to each layer, the layer will append its own header as an addressing scheme for its peer

stack and over the air interface. This will help us to understand how data is distinguished by each layer. Figure 2.10 identifies the sequence of data packets that are generated when a user has interacted with an application. The application layer receives the command and begins to pass it down the stack. As the data packet moves down each layer, *header*[15] information is appended to the data packet. The header information is a form of addressing, which may also contain personal information for its peer. This form of packaging is referred to as *encapsulation*.

[15] In the illustrations we have used the first letter of the name of the layer, followed by the letter *H*, to denote header information. The data segment of our data packet is used to contain the command that is being issued by the application.

Incidentally, the physical layer is not concerned with encapsulating the data, it is only concerned with the *raw* data, i.e. the ones and zeros that make up its natural structure. This raw data can then be systematically transmitted from the wireless device to its intended party and similarly, in Figure 2.11, we can see that the raw data received by Device B is moved up the stack. As the data packet is received, the peer is aware that it should remove the header information and learn of additional instructions, if they have been attached. When a particular layer has finished with a data packet, it moves it up the stack to the new addressee.

Packets are moved between layers using an *interface*. This interface is the only means by which a layer communicates with either the layer above or below it. With the appropriate heading information identifying its destination, a layer will know where to post the rest of the data packet. This moves us on to our final section, which discusses the interface that is exposed at the application layer.

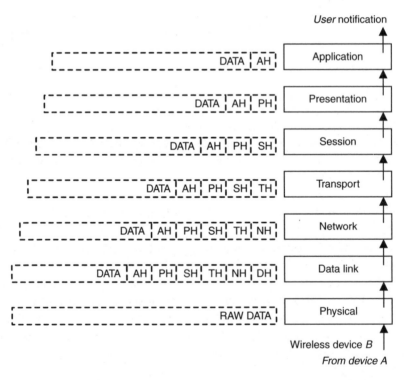

Figure 2.11 When Device B receives data from Device A, it is collected by the radio system at the physical layer and then moved up the stack. As the data packet moves up, the header information is removed to reveal the new addressee

The Application Programming Interface

The *Application Programming Interface* (API) is exposed at the application layer of our protocol stack. Software development engineers, who create applications for the end-user, will rely on this interface as a means of providing the user with as much information as possible. Specifically, this interface will comprise a series of commands that will inform the protocol stack what to do – for example, *open* or *close* a connection, *discover* wireless devices and so on. The developer will issue a command such as *open*, and will await its response. The response will contain sufficient information enabling the application to determine if the command was successful or not. If the command failed, perhaps due to the remote wireless device being busy, then the response will contain this information coupled with the reason. This information will be translated into an appropriate dialog for the user, such as: '*Unable to open the remote wireless device, as it was too busy. Please try again later.*' On the other hand, if the command was successful, then communication channels would be created between the two devices and the services that the remote device provides will be made available to the user through the interaction of the application.

Summary

- One common component unique to all wireless devices is the radio.
- Bluetooth, WiFi and ZigBee all rely on the radio to facilitate communication with other similarly interested devices.
- The radio is not unique to new wireless products; it is already incorporated into many existing products, such as the television, satellite communications, mobile phones, cordless handsets and so on.
- A radio is an electronic device that has an antenna attached to it; this forms one of the most essential components of a wireless system.
- The radio provides an over-the-air interface to other wireless devices.
- The radio applies an RF current to the antenna, which generates radio waves.
- Radio waves are transmitted and received by the radio through the antenna and converted into electrical signals, which are then communicated to and from the rest of the wireless system as data.
- Radio waves comprise an electric and magnetic field, which is propagated from one antenna to another.

- Radio waves are typically omnidirectional, although in some devices they can be directional.
- There is a large range of radio frequencies to choose from, where each occupies a particular band and each has its own purpose and application.
- Bluetooth wireless technology, ZigBee and 802.11b all operate within the 2.4 GHz band.
- The choice of frequency will also affect the antenna's size. As we move up through the higher frequencies, we need a smaller antenna and, conversely, lower frequencies require a much larger antenna.
- The frequency used will have a corresponding effect on the wavelength of the radio wave.
- A frequency refers to the number of times a radio wave moves up and down per second; this is known as its oscillation.
- A radio system will be configured to listen for a particular radio wave and, similarly, it will communicate to other devices using the same frequency.
- A key feature of wireless technology is the data rate. Bluetooth technology has a data rate of approximately 1 Mbps, whereas 802.11b has a data rate capability of 11 Mbps.
- The Bluetooth SIG is actively constructing a new specification, which will see Bluetooth's advertised data rate increase significantly; expected data rates may be between 2 and 5 Mbps.
- The radio, power, processor, ROM, RAM, and input and output form the basic components at the center of any wireless product.
- The processor is the heart of the device and requires access to ROM and RAM space.
- The RAM space provides a dynamic working area for the processor to perform its instructions.
- The ROM area will contain a small OS and also the firmware, which will provide basic operation.
- Power brings a wireless product to life, as well as powering the rest of the hardware components.
- Power may be derived from a physical connection, such as being plugged into a wall socket, batteries or from a host device.
- The role of the OS is to provide intrinsic functionality of the surrounding hardware components and, additionally, it will execute the firmware.
- The firmware will provide the basic functionality, such as transmitting and receiving data to and from the radio and passing it to the input/output controller for use by an external device.
- Smaller ROM and RAM areas offer a cheaper end-price and so does the type of processor used.

- Engineers will architect the hardware solution cost-effectively, which will ultimately benefit the end-user in terms of price.
- A cost-effective solution may impact upon features, where not all the functionality can be offered.
- An input/output component within a wireless product provides an interface to the outside world.
- An input/output interface may exist to provide some manufacturers with the ability to upgrade firmware.
- The design of hardware for a wireless product is one of the most critical parts of wireless product development, as any later redesign is both a costly and time-consuming exercise.
- When a user interacts with an application it generates data.
- The data comprises a series of instructions that inform the wireless product to take appropriate action.
- Data from the wireless system is communicated out through the radio system and then converted into radio waves.
- An application will interact with the underlying protocol stack.
- This model was first introduced by the ISO in 1984, as a means of establishing a common framework for software within communication systems.
- The conceptual nature of the OSI model therefore provides an ideal foundation for creating protocol stacks.
- Engineers will test the peer-to-peer interaction of each layer within the protocol stack.
- A device communicates with its peer layer on the corresponding device.
- Each layer is an independent software block within the stack and is assigned a set of unique responsibilities and functions to perform.
- The layered approach is used to simplify development in a structured and methodical way, and to facilitate effective changes to the software in the future.
- Many protocol stack providers will offer pricing based on a one-off purchase of the stack or take advantage of a royalty-based scheme.
- Stack providers typically offer bespoke schemes to accommodate specific functionality or for stacks that have to be built for a particular hardware platform.
- Some companies also provide the complete solution, i.e. the hardware and software. Manufactures are only faced with the task of building their individual applications.
- As the data packet moves down each layer, header information is appended to the data packet.

- The header information is a form of addressing, which may also contain personal information for its peer. This form of packaging is referred to as encapsulation.
- The physical layer is not concerned with encapsulating the data, it is only concerned with the *raw* data.
- Raw data is transmitted from the wireless device to its intended party.
- Packets are moved between layers using an interface. This interface is the only means by which a layer communicates with either the layer above or below it.
- Using the header information, a layer will know where to post the rest of the data packet.
- An API is exposed at the application layer of our protocol stack.
- Software engineers will rely on this interface as a means of providing the user with as much information as possible.
- This interface will comprise a series of commands that will inform the protocol stack what to do.

Chapter 3

What makes a wireless product sell?

'I want it and I want it now' – this is the mantra of today's society. And our cry is getting louder. The need for instant gratification in all aspects of our lives has never been better illustrated than in our growing love affair with the many gadgets and gizmos offering to give us just that. It might be considered something of a paradox that the world we live in today generates its own *need for speed* by the constant reinvention of the very products we were all perfectly content with before another faster, younger model began to 'strut its stuff'. On the flip side of the coin, the world has never been better connected. As a result of today's technological advances in all forms of communication, distances seem to melt away to nothing at the touch of a button, making the world considerably smaller and our RAMs considerably larger as a result. The barriers that have limited our communications are disappearing before our eyes. Soon our refrigerators will tell us when we need to order more milk and eggs, and will even be able to place the order for us. Our oven will know when we are on our way home and will obe-diently begin roasting our turkey in readiness for our return. Our lights will come on as we enter the driveway and our bath will begin to fill in preparation for our evening slow-down. In short, our homes will become intelligent sanctuaries, which, love or hate, we will all come to depend upon and eventually wonder how on earth we ever managed without. Wireless has become the buzzword of today, no longer causing us to think of Terry Wogan or Radio Two, but instead to focus on the freedom and convenience that wireless technology can provide. This change in concept is largely due to the skill of the marketers who have dedicated themselves to finding the best way possible to sell the wireless dream to the consumer. What they have discovered, through trial and error, is that the people who most wanted wireless solutions in their lives needed to be *told* that they wanted them. A description of what the technology could do was, to many, useless unless put into every lifestyle context. This chapter aims to illustrate what consumers are looking for in a wireless product and how marketers can effectively utilize lifestyle elements to build an effective bridge between product development and on-shelf success.

Understanding motivation to purchase

There are many aspects of the market that require analysis in order to understand consumer motivation in a way that will have a positive impact on our future marketing endeavors. Our primary objective must always be the consumers themselves, so we must be sure to center all our research and investigations around *the consumer environment*. One of the most important aspects of consumer psychology lies in the decision-making process. This comes about as an attempt to solve problems. A *problem* in this particular sense can be described as 'a need or desire that is, as yet, unfulfilled'. For example, a businesswoman may want to get to reach her office in less than 30 minutes, but is subject to constant traffic delays, which slow her down. In this instance, a service that could offer a personalized daily route planner to steer her clear of any traffic hold-ups would be of particular value, as it would fulfill a need by solving a particular problem. Problems can be major or minor. Major problems such as unemployment have an impact upon minor problems and push them into the background. This, of course, means that unforeseen changes to the economy can consequently have a huge knock-on effect upon product sales, no matter how many consumer problems they may appear to solve during times of economic growth.

Problem recognition

Consumers will often create their own problems by drawing internal comparisons based upon what their life is and what they want it to be. Discrepancies will undoubtedly be found in some areas and

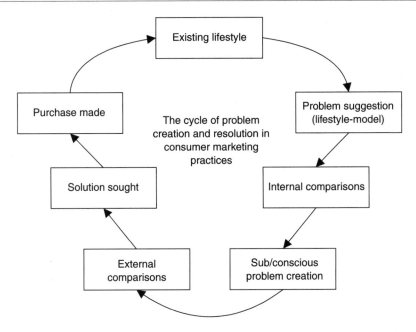

Figure 3.1 The cycle of problem creation and resolution in consumer marketing practices

once the consumer has pinpointed these, a psychological balancing act will take place to determine whether the weight or difference is great enough to justify action being taken. If justification is made, then either consciously or unconsciously the consumer will begin to search for solutions, usually in the form of a product or service. Figure 3.1 illustrates this cycle of problem creation and resolution in the consumer.

Active and inactive problems

There are two primary types of problems in consumer psychology: *active* and *inactive*. An active problem is one that requires immediate attention – for example, you have a toothache and you need to relieve the pain without delay. With an inactive problem, on the other hand, the consumer may not be aware that their situation is a problem – for example, they may not realize that they could double their modem speed by using a particular plug-in device. Maslow taught us through his *hierarchy of needs* theory that active problems

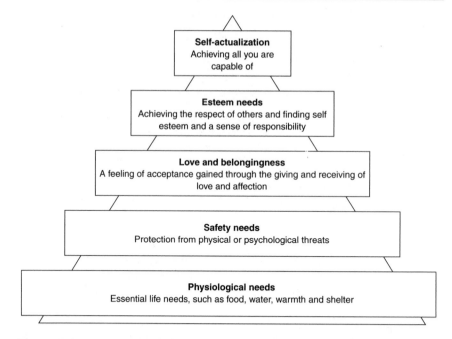

Figure 3.2 Maslow's hierarchy of needs: the original five-stage model (1954)

follow a strict order of internal significance (see Figure 3.2). In other words, once we have satisfied our primary instinctive need for food, warmth and shelter, our psyche is free to attain higher levels of satisfaction, such as those relating to self-esteem and a sense of belonging. The search for attainment of these higher-level needs initially falls into the category of inactive, as they are not primarily seen as a necessary part of our internal lifestyle model and exist for the most part on a subconscious level. Necessity is born only when our inactive needs are stimulated and enhanced by both our external and internal perceptions of the world around us. Our search for fulfillment of these needs then becomes an active problem when their characteristics become seen as necessary to our lifestyle. Furthermore, they are often effectively stimulated and reinforced by marketers in their drive to provide prospective purchasers with the perfect *lifestyle model*, which we will discuss in greater depth later on in the chapter. The power of the lifestyle model is in its subconscious link to the feelings of fulfillment and acceptance being sought by the consumer. Good technology marketers know that inactive problems are the ones most commonly used to introduce new products into the marketplace. Indeed, the marketer will often create a problem for the consumer that is initially inactive and yet gradually grows in significance to the consumer through repeated media exposure routes until it becomes an active problem that requires immediate attention.

Creating problems for the consumer

Creating problems for consumers, however unethical it may seem, will undoubtedly increase the sales of a product that does not already fulfill an obvious active problem. A tried and tested way to create new problems, and subsequent desires, is to build a *lifestyle model* – that is, a glimpse into the perfect lifestyle where the attributes of your product are seen to be the key to finding a better way of life. Images tend to play a significant part in this psychological roadmap, where consumers are taken on a journey that encompasses both the creation and the resolution of problems. A recent example of this involves a radio advertisement where a woman calls her husband on her mobile phone to describe a car she is in the process of viewing. Her inability to paint an adequate picture of the car using words alone prompts her husband to exclaim, 'If only we had the new *brand x* picture phones,' thereby creating a problem and a solution in the mind of the listener. Indeed, as well as photography, the new generation of mobile phones deliver digital video and advanced web browsing facilities. So the evolution continues until the mobile phones of today become redundant relics of a lifestyle past.

Situational influences

The successful introduction of a new wireless product to the marketplace begins and ends with understanding the consumer. This understanding should not focus purely on the behavioural psychological elements of the buying process, but needs to take into account the various situational elements of life today that will ultimately influence the buying process. The first of these situational elements that we should be aware of is the economy and its related pricing factors. A poor economy will have a subsequent impact upon consumer spending, as lower-level needs such as putting food on the table and paying the mortgage will, for the majority of the time, take precedence over any higher-level ideals of lifestyle that we seek. So it is important to look at the economic elements surrounding the proposed launch of any new product into the marketplace, particularly those products that rely to a greater extent upon increased consumer perceptions and expectations, as defined by today's new generation of wireless applications and services. Keeping track of where the economy is heading is a vital but often overlooked element of successful marketing. Knowing just when to begin promoting a product need not require psychic ability, just a keen eye on the marketplace and the economic elements surrounding it. Establishing strong networking links with financial analysts within the industry is a good way to glean insight into predicted economic change, good or bad, which may impact upon product sales within the industry. In Part II, 'Leading Perspectives', Wade Gillham of Mobilian talks about how the establishing of such networks can be of great value to wireless marketers. Knowledge is indeed power and leverage within these networks comes through the realization that the flow of information should always be a two-way process if maximum value is to be achieved by it. Through sharing your own knowledge of the wireless industry with your network links, you will provide yet another channel through which your company's message can be broadcast; this is something that we will revisit later on in the chapter.

The second situational influence is that of risk. We can define purchases as being either a *low-involvement* or a *high-involvement* process, depending on the risks surrounding them. For example, buying a tube of toothpaste is a relatively low-involvement process. We tend to find a brand that we are happy with and continue to buy it without a great deal of thought as to why we are selecting it each time we shop. The action of purchasing this brand then becomes an almost conditioned response for us, with little to no risk factor involved. By contrast, the purchase of a new wireless product comes with a perceived high-risk factor and is consequently a high-involvement process. Let's take the purchase of a mobile phone as our example. This purchase falls into the category of a high-involvement process due to its related number of perceived risk factors, such as cost, ease of use and pre-purchase information. Marketing channels may have led us towards a particular brand of mobile phone through their effective portrayal of a life model which, in turn, offers to fill our high-level needs. Alongside this, our experience of the sales team within our chosen store may have reinforced that message, but the risks remain and dictate the way in which we choose to purchase our products. Stores that offer no-deposit, monthly payment options can assist in overcoming any initial cost factors that may have an effect on the decision to purchase. Indeed, from a first purchase point of view, many of us will prefer to venture into a store where we can see a wireless product demonstrated by staff prior to buying it for the first time. This on-hand support can alleviate issues of re-education and ease of use that are again considered risks to purchase. However, as a product becomes tried and trusted by us over a period of time and the risk factors associated with our purchase become diluted, we, in turn, may be confident enough to reorder the product through other means, such as the Internet or via mail order. The difficulty in relaying this scenario to new wireless is that it is constantly evolving, and with that evolution comes change in design, features and subsequently user education. This is why many marketers believe that the only way to effectively end-market the ever-changing face of new wireless is through direct retail in stores, where demonstration and usage models are on permanent display to the consumer.

Other situational influences are more individual and relate to sociological elements, such as our home and family or work and business environment. Here, employing various methods of segmentation, including geo-demographic, socio-economic and psychographic,[16] can assist marketers in working with these variables to establish effective positioning and message value to prospective consumers on a national or even global basis. We will discuss more about the value of segmentation later on in this chapter, when we look at how wireless products are marketed within industrial, organizational and business-to-business markets.

---

[16] Geo-demographics is a mix of geographical and demographical data to provide marketers with information relating to where and how different groups of people within society choose to live. Socio-economics is the study of the economic factors that affect social groups, and psychographics in marketing relate to segmentation according to psychological aspects of lifestyle, personality and attitudes.

What consumer research tells us

Over the past decade there have been numerous studies carried out to discover what consumers really think about wireless technology. These studies range in type and size from localized group reviews to global consumer analysis. Deciding what information to use when planning a successful marketing strategy and what to discard is discussed later on in this chapter, but for now let's focus on some of the most pertinent findings related to wireless product consumerism.

Bluetooth technology is now growing in popularity, but how well is it really known by general technology consumers? According to In-Stat/MDR,[17] analysis of Technology Adoption Panel (early adopters and higher-end consumers) surveys carried out by the high-tech market research firms and the general public show that Bluetooth familiarity (i.e. usage) is considerably lower than one might expect, at just 10 percent of the general public. However, the surveys also reveal that interest in Bluetooth technology is considerably greater than its familiarity amongst consumers and additionally indicate a significant interest in residential wireless networking products. Even more interesting is the knowledge gleaned from the report that suggests that the more consumers learn about the benefits of Bluetooth technology the more interest they have in acquiring the technology and, similarly, with that increased interest comes a willingness to pay more for those perceived benefits. If we refer back to our earlier discussion on consumer psychology, we can see a natural link here between knowledge gained and subsequent needs being created in the mind of the consumer, thereby allowing for the succession of active problems to be both reinforced and solved via effective marketing of Bluetooth-enabled products.

Whilst Bluetooth is currently the leader in over-the-counter consumer purchases, the corporate marketplace tells a slightly different story. During 2001, a huge uptake of wireless networks was seen across the US, with almost $1.5 billion being spent on wireless network hardware.[18] The most common choice of technology has been 802.11, which has shifted the focus from network-based connection to peer-to-peer links and, to some extent, has

---

[17] http://www.instat.com   (http://www.wirelessdevnet.com/news/2002/274/news2.html).

[18] Giga Information Group 2001 (http://www.itweek.co.uk/Features/1127334).

taken the limelight away from Bluetooth. Having said that, Bluetooth's reign as the personal area network ruler is far from over and, now that issues of coexistence between Bluetooth and WiFi are being robustly tackled (Chapter 5 discusses this aspect in greater depth), its wireless companionship and corporate popularity is, once again, growing at a rapid pace. We will discuss more about how to reach the corporate marketplace later on this in this chapter, where we will examine the crossover between both the theoretical and the practical fundamentals in each area of marketing.

Indeed, a striking similarity between the two markets can be found within a new millennium study by the Context-Based Research Group, entitled *Wireless Opportunities: A Global Ethnographic Study*.[19] This theorizes that, despite ever-increasing levels of adoption of wireless products around the globe, manufacturers have not yet delivered the functionality and simplicity their products and services promise; a shortcoming that can be related to both the corporate and consumer markets.

The study looked specifically at how people interact with wireless products in a number of different environments. It supported the theory that social perspectives are all-important aspects of future wireless product development and marketing success. The conclusion was that a huge gap exists between consumer expectation and what is actually 'delivered' in a wireless product, suggesting that more care needs to be taken in matching the message to the model. The report also discusses the need for further 'education' of consumers in technology and dismisses much of the current marketing messages as being too technical for the average consumer to understand. It concludes by drawing upon the premise that relating products to personality and lifestyle is the way forward, and that their interactional aspects (in other words their *lifestyle benefits*, as we previously discussed) are ultimately what makes them sell.

Analysis of the European vertical retail markets paints a similar picture. A 2002 IDC report by Senior Analyst Cinzia Rinelli discusses these trends and concludes that a lack of confidence and knowledge of wireless products is a commonly noted inhibitor to wireless product sales.

The message here is knowledge, and not just knowledge of the products, but knowledge of the people to whom we are targeting them. The benefits of any wireless product must present themselves

[19] http://www.contextresearch.com/context/global_wireless.cfm.

affectively to a buyer in a way that relates explicitly to their lifestyle expectations and needs. Just saying that a product is wireless is not enough to convince a consumer that it will benefit their current way of life, yet many marketers continue to believe that the very notion of wireless is enough to excite the world into a buying frenzy – it isn't! Rapid adoption comes about through a combination of *need fulfillment* and *brand loyalty*. Loyalty or trust in a particular brand is tricky to achieve, especially for newcomers to the wireless arena. Association with a brand to a particular product crystallizes in the mind of the consumer over time and can become an automatic choice. To make a customer believe in your brand you must relate to that customer in a way that is personal to his or her needs and expectations. Empathetic messages, built into lifestyle-routed media, are key to the rapid achievement of this and, if done right, can hop, skip and jump a decade of purchasing reliance and conditioned trust fundamentals. Orange are an excellent example of this. Within two years of their messaging launch, they had achieved the kind of brand loyalty and product association that made their competitor giants stand to attention. The subject of brand loyalty through messaging is also something that Derrick Emeka of TDK Systems Europe effectively discusses in Part II, 'Leading Perspectives', and it is an area to which you should pay great attention if you need to launch a wireless product outside of your company's normal area of manufacture.

The bigger business picture

The corporate marketplace offers a different challenge to manufacturers and marketers alike; that of securing *group value*, whereby a wireless product serves a particular objective which enables radical change within a company's structure to become a positive rather than a negative occurrence. As mentioned previously, with retail customers, this is to a large extent synonymous with re-education or, where possible, the avoidance of it as a necessary part of the usage package. The business customer may well intend to unwire themselves in a variety of ways. Perhaps they intend to integrate your wireless product into their own devices or maybe they simply wish to initiate a wireless methodology into their existing communications strategy. Whatever their reasons for potential purchase, the marketing challenge will always be to latch on to these needs and to tantalize their corporate taste buds with the promise of absolute fulfillment through your product's individual offerings. On that note, as marketers, you will be aware that the individuality of a product often exists purely as a result of branding, rather than from any distinction in underlying features or physical structure. Remember that the key to success most often lies in promoting 'application rather than architecture' or, to put it in even simpler terms, 'the sizzle rather than the sausage'. With this in mind, it is easy to understand why lifestyle models, which we discussed earlier in this chapter, can play a substantial part in the formulation of a successful corporate marketing brand. After all, every corporation wants to be the biggest and the best in their particular field. Good marketers will latch on to this concept and spend time in understanding the psychology of the corporate consumer and their competitive endeavors in relation to the purchasing model, and will structure their strategies around it. There is no X-factor associated with this exercise and certainly no need for espionage or hidden agendas. The secret of building this understanding can be expressed in a single word: *communication*.

Simplifying market intelligence

To master true market intelligence is to embrace continuous change. The meandering stream of new technology distills itself with the perpetuated expectations of its waiting society, resulting in a continuous flow of product and personal evolution. This may sound rather prophetic, but it's actually a simple theory that separates the weak from the strong in the world of marketing. To a technology marketer, its adoption may be the difference between professional life or death.

Consider the current channels through which your flow of information runs. What research do you buy in and what research comes from your own networking and 'freely available' investigative routes? It's a fact that most companies spend far more than they need to on buying in overpriced market reports, when the information gleaned from them can be more beneficially acquired through personal contact routes. Here again, we emphasize the importance of building channel relationships within your stream of market intelligence. Make the time to really talk to the research analysts you buy from and find out what their reports *aren't telling you* as well as what they are. As in all good relationships, self-disclosure is key to securing these valued links. Divulge information that you *want* the analysts to use and pass on to others in the industry. Use them as a microphone through which to broadcast your company's strengths and as a vent through which to draw in the information that will set you apart from your competitors. After all, the reports you buy are probably being purchased by all competing manufacturers of wireless products. So, with this in mind, in order to gain the advantage with regards to market intelligence, you need to have an ace up your sleeve in the form of a valuable two-way link that extends far beyond the white papers flowing between you.

Developing a market information system that works

A good market information system is one that doesn't leave you drowning in a sea of data that, by the time you've finally found the time to read, has already become outdated and useless. Instead, it's a system of information acquisition and release that should, over time, become as natural to an effective marketing system as breathing in and out. There are three key words to consider when acquiring any information pertaining to your market:

Why–What–How
- Why do I need this information?
- What do I want to do with it once I've got it?
- How will it affect the grand scheme of things?

These questions are vital tools that will enable rapid prioritizing and ultimate productivity within your research activities. Far from being a drain on your time and energy, you will discover that, in answering the above questions in an objective statement format, you arrive with many additional research requirements and/or strategy incentives as a result of your accompanying knowledge acquisition. Equally, you may find that the entire exercise is unfounded and should be discounted from your research endeavors. The internal associations that evolve from the answering of these three key questions may well result in additional segmented questions being raised. This positively extended clarification will provide you with a unique *blueprint* for action, upon which your acquisition and release routes can now be based.

Consider the following example:

- Q: Why do I need this information?
- A: To assess the youth market in Bluetooth products.

The above answer warrants the further question: 'What do we need to assess within the youth market?' This can now be broken down into specific categories of potential research, such as *economic factors* and *brand trends*. We then need to return to our primary question: 'Why do I need this information?' Answers such as economic factors (to determine the right pricing level for our product) or brand trends (to look at what features we should be most promoting in our products) give us a clear objective of what our proposed research will ultimately achieve for our company.

Types of marketing information can be internal or external, qualitative or quantitative. They are all either highly valuable or a waste of time, depending on how you approach them and use them within your information system framework. Developing an effective framework for storage and use is part and parcel of the successful marketing strategy. A framework will vary from company to company and from person to person but, for ultimate flexibility in acquisition and release, it should allow for the maximum amount of flow in both directions. Figure 3.3 provides an example of how an effective market information system might be laid out.

In many respects, research for the wireless corporate market is fundamentally the same as for the consumer market, in that both utilize the same research techniques and overlapping sources and channels for both information acquisition and release.

Similarly, both approaches benefit from a willingness to get inside the psyche of the purchaser, whether that be a major corporation or a single individual. As previously discussed in this chapter, the successful wireless product marketer understands that the customer buys the benefits of the product rather than the technology surrounding those benefits – here again, we are talking about promoting the sizzle in order to sell the sausage. By coupling this understanding with up-to-date market intelligence that assesses the current wants and needs of the target consumer, a marketer can bestow him or herself with the confidence necessary to deploy their own educated approach with which to take a wireless product successfully to market.

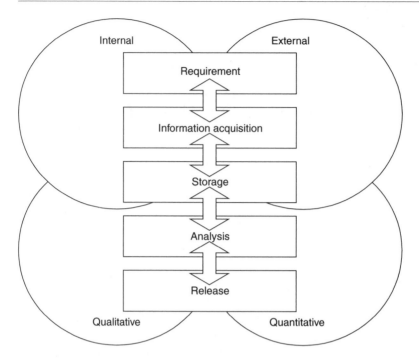

Figure 3.3   The various sources and flow of information within an effective system framework

Summary

- Today's consumers are ruled by a need for instant gratification in all aspects of their lives.
- Through effective marketing, the word wireless today has less an association with radio and more with the concepts of freedom and convenience.
- The successful introduction of a new wireless product to the marketplace begins and ends with understanding the consumer. Therefore, we must be sure to center all our research and investigations around the consumer environment.
- One of the most important areas to consider is the decision-making process, which can be stimulated through both understanding and creating problems for the consumer.
- There are two primary types of problems in consumer psychology: active and inactive. Marketers will often create these types of problem

in the mind of the consumer to stimulate the decision-making process and, subsequently, increase the sales of a product.

- Consumer understanding should not focus purely on the behavioural psychological elements of the buying process, but needs to take into account the various situational elements of life today that will ultimately influence the buying process.
- Establishing strong networking links with industry analysts is a good way to glean insight into predicted change, good or bad, which may impact upon the marketplace.
- Your network links can provide yet another channel through which your company's message can be broadcast.
- Many marketers believe that the only way to effectively end-market the ever-changing face of new wireless is through direct retail in stores, where demonstration and usage models are on permanent display to the consumer.
- Segmentation can assist marketers in establishing effective positioning and message value.
- Over the past decade there have been numerous studies carried out to discover what consumers really think about wireless technology. These show a natural link between knowledge gained and subsequent needs being created.
- Some studies have revealed that a huge gap exists between consumer expectation and what is actually delivered in a wireless product. Furthermore, it has been concluded that a lack of confidence and knowledge of wireless products is a commonly noted inhibitor to sales.
- Rapid adoption of new wireless comes about through a combination of need fulfillment and brand loyalty.
- The corporate marketplace offers a different challenge to manufacturers and marketers alike; that of securing group value.
- The individuality of a product often exists purely as a result of branding, rather than from any distinction in underlying features or physical structure.
- The key to success most often lies in promoting application rather than architecture.
- To master true market intelligence is to embrace continuous change.
- The information gleaned from expensive industry reports can be more beneficially acquired through personal contact routes.
- A good market information system is one based upon acquisition and release that should, over time, become as natural to effective marketing as breathing in and out.

- Use the Why–What–How principle to enable rapid prioritizing and ultimate productivity.
- Types of marketing information can be internal or external, qualitative
  or quantitative.
- Developing an effective framework for storage and use is part and parcel of the successful marketing strategy.
- Research for the wireless corporate market is fundamentally the same
  as for the consumer market, in that both utilize the same research techniques and overlapping sources and channels for both information acquisition and release.

Chapter 4

Comparing wireless technologies

In Chapter 2, we gained an understanding of the basic foundations of the various new wireless technologies available today, but how do we know which wireless technology is best suited to a particular product or application? This chapter answers the question by comparing the most popular new wireless technologies and assessing their individual strengths and weaknesses. It goes on to explore issues of coexistence within new product development and will enable you to gain an understanding of why manufacturers take the routes they do when developing a wireless product.

In the world of wireless technology, the 2.4 GHz band is a crowded arena, due to the appeal of its unlicensed status. ZigBee, 802.11b and Bluetooth all share the frequency, which can cause problems for consumers who have given a home to these technologies. For example, if WiFi provides the framework for a home wireless network, then trying to use Bluetooth technology to send information from one enabled device to another within its domain could result in problems, such as the inability to discover devices or to connect to a device once discovered. Indeed, in tests carried out by the Mobilian Corporation, they 'provided a demonstration of noticeable degradation ... the demonstration showed interference effects under a Bluetooth/ 802.11b colocated scenario ...'.[20]

Whilst significant strides have been made in tackling this issue (such as Mobilian's TrueRadio™ solution) clearly it is a concern that has been a major thorn in the side of manufacturers who have often

---

[20] Source: Cahners In-Stat Group, *Bluetooth & WiFi: The Crusade for Coexistence*, February 2001.

been forced to battle for supremacy rather than being allowed to promote those individual strengths that complement rather than collide with their fellow technologies. In Chapter 5, we examine an effective marketing philosophy, which undoubtedly shifts the emphasis away from WLAN vs. Bluetooth technology and refocuses the marketing emphasis from *competing* to *complementary*. As we observe the evolution of new wireless technologies, it becomes more evident that the wireless standards bodies are indeed marketing their respective technologies as complementary. For example, many papers examine ZigBee and Bluetooth technology. These papers exist to provide reflection on what both the technologies offer and where they differ in terms of application potential. As we touched upon in Chapter 2, the overlapping Bluetooth applications that were originally offered in the first specification are now being disbanded and replaced with newer specifications. But we are still left with one common theme running through all these major technologies and that is coexistence. It is not surprising to note that new revisions of the Bluetooth specification introduce a scheme that overcomes coexistence issues experienced when WLAN and Bluetooth cohabit the same location, and this is discussed in further detail in Chapter 5.

With the introduction of ZigBee and its potential proliferation into a larger range of products, surely this will affect existing wireless infrastructures either in the home or office. ZigBee is marketed as a low-data-rate technology and, as such, its usage is not as prolific as say WiFi or Bluetooth. For example, with WiFi, it's easy to imagine large amounts of information being transferred between an access point and a notebook. ZigBee categorizes three traffic models: *periodic* (such as alarm sensors), *intermittent* (such as light switches) and *repetitive* (such as mice). Due to the infrequent nature of communication, it may well be the case that ZigBee-enabled products will not interfere with other wireless-enabled devices that are sharing the same frequency.

Another wireless technology that has been around for some time is WirelessUSB. Introduced by Cypress Semiconductors, the company identified shortcomings in the marketplace for Bluetooth. Primarily, Bluetooth was still in its infancy and WirelessUSB addressed an immediate need. Incorporating WirelessUSB into mice, keyboards and notebooks, the technology provided cable replacement solutions. More importantly, the technology also addressed power usage scenarios (i.e. sustaining longer battery life for mice and keyboards), offered rapid product development and resolved latency[21] issues. The technology also operates within the 2.4 GHz spectrum using a frequency hopping[22] scheme.

The following sections will help you to gain a better understanding of which type of wireless technology is best suited to which type of product by providing an appraisal of the various wireless technologies available, along with examples of their individual strengths and weaknesses and their suitability towards particular applications.

WiFi

Purpose

The first WLAN standard offering the ability for users to connect wirelessly to their LAN. The technology has evolved rapidly, offering increasingly greater bandwidth. Primarily, its deployment has allowed companies to expand their network infrastructure without the need to spend capital on wired infrastructures. Similarly, home users are able to equip their home with a wireless network, allowing individual family members to access the Internet and data from other computers.

Strengths

- Expanding existing networks without the need for cables.
- Expanding networks where cables are difficult to install.
- Evolving rapidly in accordance with consumer needs.

---

[21] Latency is the time it takes for information to be sent from one device to another – for example, the time it takes for a wireless-enabled mouse to communicate with a wireless-enabled notebook. If there are issues surrounding latency within these products, then the user will observe, as he or she moves the mouse around, that the screen pointer does not correspond to the movement on the mouse pad.

[22] This scheme attempts to overcome coexistence issues when devices using the same frequency are located in the same proximity. It randomly changes the channels when communicating with another device in the hope that other wireless-enabled devices are using alternative methods – for example, Bluetooth wireless technology also uses a frequency hopping scheme.

- Widely used and available.
- Is one of the fastest wireless technologies available.
- Providing home users and small businesses with greater flexibility.

Weaknesses

- Niche application.
- Can be difficult to set up and configure.

Competition

HiperLAN.

Complements

Bluetooth, WirelessUSB and ZigBee.

HiperLAN

Purpose

This wireless technology is largely used in Europe and offers various sets of wireless communication specifications that also provide WLAN support. The applications offered are similar to WiFi, but HiperLAN is also compatible with third-generation (3G) technologies. This allows it to support applications that utilize imaging and voice communications.

Strengths

- Offers WLAN support.
- Capable of supporting 3G applications for imaging and voice.
- Has a data rate of 54 Mbps.

Weakness

Restricted to Europe.

Competition

WiFi.

Complements

Bluetooth, WirelessUSB and ZigBee.

Bluetooth

Purpose

Bluetooth technology is a cable replacement technology; its initial introduction was to replace the cumbersome cables that sat around your notebook or desktop. Infrared[23] was also engineered to undertake a similar theme, but the disadvantage of infrared was that you would have to place the device right next to your notebook, within line of sight.

Strengths

- Capable of being incorporated into many products.
- Low cost, resulting in cheaper products.
- Evolving rapidly in accordance with consumer needs.

[23] Infrared can be seen in a wide range of products, ranging from TV remote controls to mobile phones; it can also be considered a cable replacement technology.

- Uses frequency hopping to help overcome coexistence issues.
- Can make use of effective low-power schemes.
- Encourages simplicity for consumers.

Weaknesses

- Attempts to resolve all wireless problems.
- Small data rate available, but applications seem well suited.
- Uses the same frequency as many other popular technologies.

Competition

WirelessUSB, possibly some overlap with ZigBee.

Complements

WiFi, HiperLAN.

ZigBee

Purpose

Introduced to proliferate a larger range of products and targeted at companies who wish to rapidly develop wireless-enabled products. Working closely with the IEEE to establish a new wireless standard.

Strengths

- Low power consumption.
- Low cost, resulting in cheaper products.

- Affordable wireless solution.
- Applications specifically addressed.
- Uses low-data-rate topologies to help overcome coexistence issues.
- Effective low-power schemes.
- Allows rapid wireless development.

Weaknesses

- Uses the same frequency as many other popular technologies.
- May overlap solutions provided by Bluetooth.

Competition

WirelessUSB, possibly some overlap with Bluetooth.

Complements

WiFi, HiperLAN.

WirelessUSB

Purpose

WirelessUSB is a short-range wireless technology that operates in the 2.4 GHz unlicensed spectrum. It was introduced by Cypress Semiconductors to resolve initial shortcomings of Bluetooth and addressed an immediate need.

Strengths

- Low power consumption.
- Affordable wireless solution.

- Uses frequency hopping to help overcome coexistence issues.
- Allows rapid wireless development.

Weaknesses

- Restricted number of applications.
- Uses the same frequency as many other popular technologies.
- Not widely available or known.

Competition

Bluetooth, possibly some overlap with ZigBee.

Complements

WiFi, HiperLAN.

Ultra Wide Band

Purpose

The FCC in the USA has only recently approved this technology. UWB is similar to Bluetooth technology, although it does boast an incredible bandwidth and can travel distances of up to 230 feet through most obstacles, using only minimal power. At this very early stage, only two types of application have been proposed. These are: radar, where objects can be detected behind walls; and voice and data communication, which can be achieved at a high data rate and at very low power.

Strengths

- Low power consumption.
- Radio waves travel further.
- Can travel though most obstacles.

Weaknesses

- In its early stages of development.
- Not widely available or known.

Competition

HiperLAN.

Complements

Too early to say.

Part II

Leading Perspectives

Chapter 5

The birth of an idea

Johan Åkesson

Marketing Director, Ericsson Technology Licensing

Good ideas are often born in the minds of people simply by coincidence, though nearly always in connection with something they are involved with. Such ideas may have something to do with boosting revenue or creating additional value for the users of those ideas, or they may just be interesting concepts worth looking into.

Our way of communicating with each other has changed dramatically since the arrival of mobile phones, not to mention the evolution of the Internet. Wireless phones, *Wide Area Networking* (WAN) and email are a few examples of so-called *new technology* that in fact is not all that new. The first car phones were already in use in the 1970s, and email has been around for more than 15 years. The way we now use these *tools* in our daily lives, however, both professionally and privately, has evolved over time. This evolution has brought us to the point today where we basically expect people to be accessible both around the clock and around the globe, either via a mobile phone or through an email address.

To come up with an idea that combines existing technologies is always challenging, but even more so when the technologies come from two completely different fields, such as the computer and telecom industries of the mid 1990s. In May 1998, a new promising initiative was launched – Bluetooth Wireless Technology – based on just such an idea. Aimed at uniting devices from both of these worlds using technologies such as those described above, the initiative would not only hook mobile phones up with PCs, but would also make it easy to communicate with a myriad of other devices, forming a close proximity network. And to make life even easier for the consumer, it would accomplish all of this without the use of cables.

Table 5.1 Typical PC and mobile phone data (1994)

Typical PC configuration in 1994	
Processor	Intel Pentium™
Address width	32-bit
CPU clock	75 MHz
RAM	32 MB
Hard disk size	1.0 GB
Modem speed	33.3 Kbps
Typical mobile phone battery in 1994	
Talk time	1–1.5 hours
Standby time	10–30 hours

This chapter will describe the challenges faced in marketing a new wireless technology as it is brought from the cradle to a mature stage ready for the mass market, a process driven not by any official standardization organization, but by the industry itself.

A retrospect

Back in 1994–95, mobile phones were still relatively large and cumbersome. They were also very inefficient in terms of energy use, draining batteries as if there were no tomorrow. At the same time, bulky laptop computers, predecessors to the notebook PC, were rapidly gaining in popularity (see Table 5.1). The PC market was experiencing unprecedented growth at a time when a 75 MHz processor was state-of-the-art, and 32 MB of RAM was more than one could ever dream of.

Adding value

Ericsson dominated the global mobile phone industry during that time and people within the company were becoming very mindful of the exploding PC market. Before long these people had come up with the idea of allowing mobile phone users to connect their phone to a PC or laptop in order to exchange data. Why?

It was all about *adding value*:

- Adding value for users of mobile phones.
- Adding new features and possibilities.
- Making the mobile phone the center of communication.

Of course, the whole reason for adding value was simply to sell more mobile phones, which at the time had a penetration of no more than 50 million subscribers worldwide. How, then, could this be accomplished so as to achieve maximum added value?

Maximizing the value of a simple idea

Connecting a mobile phone to a PC using standard cable technology would be relatively easy, but it also meant the usual limitations and inconveniences for the user that follow along with it, not to mention adding to the ever-increasing throng of cables already in place. Thanks to an earlier initiative that had led to the availability of infrared technology, wireless communication was suddenly an alternative. Certainly, by adding wireless connectivity to the equation the result would be even greater value, freeing users from the hassle of cables and greatly simplifying the interaction between user, phone and PC.

Infrared technology, however, which requires line-of-sight, was too limited for what the people at Ericsson had envisioned. They saw the possibility of completely new scenarios, with the mobile phone playing a central role. Some of the user scenarios first discussed within Ericsson's think-tank were:

- The headset – a wireless link to a headset for a true hands-free solution.
- Dial-up networking – accessing networks using a mobile phone as a gateway or modem.
- The 'magic wand' – using a mobile phone as an access device for various other devices.
- The 'bag trick' (later referred to as the 'briefcase trick') – automatic connection and synchronization of a mobile phone to a PC even when the PC is in standby or hibernating mode.
- Wireless workplace – achieving a clutter-free workplace with a wireless keyboard and mouse.
- Conference table – connectivity between all laptops in a meeting room, and even with a data projector.

Setting the wheels in motion

While walking through a wooded area on the outskirts of Lund, Sweden, two managers at Ericsson discussed how to go about turning these ideas into reality. The challenge was to replace a cable with a radio-based link at the same cost as the cable, i.e. US $5. The work was soon handed over to the engineering team at Ericsson and two pioneers in the field managed to take the initiative far beyond the expectations of the time.

Ericsson's team became the first to develop a technical solution for the purpose. The undertaking, originally known as the *Multi-Communicator Link* project, or MC-Link, was capable of communicating with up to seven devices simultaneously.

By 1996, Ericsson felt it was time to make this proprietary technology available to the awaiting mass market. A novel idea using MC-Link to create a wireless headset called 'Cornelius' was taking shape and it promised to rid headset users of bothersome cables. An adaptor was designed for use with Ericsson phones and preparations were made to launch the groundbreaking technology. At the same time, the idea of expanding the realm of wireless connectivity to allow what is today called Wireless *Personal Area Network* (PAN) was conceived. The idea was based on the technology behind MC-Link, and would soon come to be known as *Bluetooth*.

Proprietary rights or open global standard

Making a choice

Ericsson had already developed MC-Link, a radio-based technology that was well on the way to becoming Bluetooth. Furthermore, the first product based on this technology, the Cornelius headset, was ready for launch. At the same time, people at Ericsson began discussing whether or not it would be a good idea to turn this new technology into a global standard, which gave rise to some interesting questions:

- What would happen if Cornelius could communicate with phones from Nokia and other competitors?
- What would it mean to the technology if vendors of PCs and laptops could promote MC-Link?

At that point, Ericsson could very easily have kept the idea and the technology for itself. MC-Link would have worked with all Ericsson mobile phones and with all accessories bearing the Ericsson label. This would have given users of the company's mobile phones a convenient means of connecting the phone to any number of various devices supplied with Ericsson wireless technology. Eventually, however, competitors were certain to come up with similar ideas and technologies.

Discussing the pros and cons

The question of whether to turn the technology into an open, worldwide standard as opposed to keeping it as a proprietary asset is an excellent subject for debate.

The pros

- Easier adoption of the technology.
- Lightening the load by sharing the burden with other companies.
- Bringing a wide variety of companies and products to the market.

By assembling a united group of strong leaders from within the industry, it would be much easier to persuade most, if not all, of the industry players to follow suit and to adopt the technology. This would bring with it worldwide industry support, not only from the mobile phone industry, but also from players in other fields of the market.

Ericsson would benefit by persuading others to work ardently towards the advancement of the technology and contributing to the development of the specification. And still the company would be able to assert: 'Bluetooth was our idea.' Through its own heavy involvement Ericsson could continue to maintain a leading position.

The fact that a large number of companies would become involved virtually guaranteed that a wide variety of products would be developed and brought to the market. Though not all of these products would be based on 'original Ericsson solutions', they would still serve to further advance the technology and the market as a whole.

The cons

- Other companies would be empowered to build products that could communicate with Ericsson products. (Note: This point elicits further discussion as to whether or not this is actually a negative issue. Certainly from a user's point of view this would be listed as a pro.)
- Giving up total control over the evolution of the technology.
- Making it more difficult to take advantage of 'inventor' status.

By giving up exclusive 'rights' to the technology, Ericsson would be opening itself up for, and perhaps making itself vulnerable to, its competitors. The company would also be sacrificing control over the development of the technology. And, from a marketing point of view, sharing the credit with others would remove some of the edge in the inventor's own message.

Turning disadvantages into advantages

While it is always better to be in direct control of the development of one's own idea, it is still possible to be very influential, even without total control. A leading political and/or technical role can be very important. By exerting leadership regarding technology and business opportunities, significant returns can be anticipated from making the *core technology* available.

For marketers, however, the situation becomes less than ideal when trying to point the spotlight at one's own position as inventor, while at the same time having to share center stage with several others. Still, with a consistent message and a certain amount of maneuvering, this disadvantage can be compensated for. The following comparison to a similar situation serves as a case in point.

Comparison with CDMA

In the mid 1990s, San Diego-based Qualcomm Incorporated commercialized a wireless technology for cellular networks known as Code Division Multiple Access, or CDMA. Qualcomm owns certain basic patents behind CDMA and has adopted a business model combining the sale of IPRs and chipsets to vendors of CDMA equipment.

The CDMA technology is not proprietary to Qualcomm, but is fully adopted by all relevant international standards bodies in the same manner as, for example, GSM and WCDMA. Qualcomm has been uniquely successful thanks to its focus on providing an enabling technology without engaging in the equipment market and thus competing with its customers. One might wonder whether or not Ericsson could have accomplished the same feat with Bluetooth.

One way to examine this is to compare how the relevant target groups perceive the identities of these technologies and their respective founders:

CDMA as viewed from an industry perspective:

- Who invented CDMA?   Qualcomm.
- Who is Qualcomm?   CDMA supplier.
- Who is CDMA?   Qualcomm.

Bluetooth as viewed from a Bluetooth industry perspective:

- Who invented Bluetooth?   Ericsson.
- Who is Ericsson?   Bluetooth.
- Who is Bluetooth?   Ericsson.

The two appear quite similar, so what is the difference?

Ericsson has still managed to enjoy significant recognition for its role in the invention and development of Bluetooth, despite opting to share both the credit and the burden with others. Many players were invited to take part and, though some of them may have been less desirable partners, for competitive or other reasons, even these were most likely essential to the evolution of Bluetooth.

From a marketing point of view, it would appear that the strategy of open standards, as opposed to exclusivity, has paid off, not only for Ericsson, but also for many of those who contribute in such a large way to the further development of Bluetooth.

All things considered, what significance does this have for Ericsson as a whole?

- The addition of an important technology standard invented by Ericsson to the Ericsson brand, a brand already identified with GSM, WAP, GPRS and 3G, among others, which Ericsson has helped to create.
- Putting Ericsson in a position either to take full advantage of the undertaking should it prove successful, or to share the burden of a possible failure, though at the cost of full control.

- Allowing advantage to be taken of the company's core competency – wireless communication.
- Allowing advantage to be taken of the 'perceived ownership' and initiative for this new, emerging technology from a marketing standpoint.
- The ability to market Ericsson's inventor status, e.g. 'Bluetooth was our idea – now lets focus on yours.'
- The ability to gain an 'advantage' for capitalizing on business opportunities by exploiting Ericsson's early insight into the continued development of Bluetooth.
- The inconvenience of having to share the credit with others. As pointed out above, however, this is actually more of an advantage than a disadvantage. Bluetooth is currently mentioned in hundreds of articles appearing each day in various publications, providing broader exposure for the technology than ever expected. And, with an ever-increasing variety of emerging Bluetooth applications, the amount of attention given to the issue of 'sharing the spotlight' is likely to dwindle.

Still Qualcomm continues to maintain its monopoly standpoint. Their control over the specification for the interface to their proprietary CDMA baseband has had an impact even on Bluetooth and on the silicon market as a whole. In fact, they took this exclusivity a step further by developing a proprietary interface called 'BlueQ', which Qualcomm requires in order for a Bluetooth radio to operate with the CDMA baseband. Naturally this affected many silicon suppliers in the Bluetooth RF market, who suddenly found themselves having to adapt to a new proprietary interface controlled by Qualcomm.

In a world that is opening up standards more and more, it is rather noteworthy that Qualcomm can maintain this position. The reason they can, of course, is that they still own the rights to CDMA technology.

Approaching the industry

Any one of a number of recognized industry organizations such as the IEEE, ANSI, GSMA and others would have been a natural choice for establishing the new Bluetooth standard. The original Bluetooth group, however, decided that it would be better to go its own way by creating a new organization.

During the latter part of 1997, Ericsson approached leading suppliers of mobile phones and laptops, as well as the world-leading chip supplier, to discuss its idea. This group was selected based on the assumption that mobile phones and laptops were vital to the deployment of such technology. Provided that manufacturers could be convinced to integrate the technology in their laptop and mobile phone products, these two segments alone would be sufficient to achieve the necessary volumes. They would also provide a likely spin-off into other closely related segments.

In order to create the new organization, it was crucial that the dominant market players be brought on board. The combined force of these players would be far more powerful and expeditious than that of any standardization body. In fact, organizations such as the IEEE operate in effect by simply taking existing technology inventions and ideas and putting them into a context in order to establish a standard (e.g. USB, IRDA). The strong support evidenced throughout the industry for Bluetooth made it possible to accelerate the development of the specification initially, and then to slow it down once Bluetooth products began rolling out. It is, after all, in the best interest of those involved that the specification be stabilized as quickly as possible by not being revised all too frequently.

Conclusion

Would the 'Qualcomm approach' have been the right way to achieve successful business with Bluetooth?

Some will argue that Ericsson, by 'giving it all up' in order to establish a worldwide open standard, may have paid too high a price, especially considering the short-term advantages of exclusivity, which can be quite alluring. When embarking on the path chosen by Ericsson, one must be clear over one very important truth: a long-term commitment will be required before the harvest can be reaped.

In the modern world of technology, however, *open standards* have become buzzwords when discussing the economics of new technology. The proprietary path appears less successful today than it used to be. And once a global standard is established, proprietary standards are eventually phased out, a development that always benefits the users.

Setting up the Bluetooth SIG

The Bluetooth beginning

Bluetooth began at Ericsson in 1994 with a study of a short-range radio link, the MC-Link project that we introduced earlier in this chapter. Later, Ericsson approached Intel, who were developing a similar idea, to discuss making the new technology into an industry standard. The joint project came to be known as Bluetooth following a social meeting at a Canadian bar, where people from Ericsson and Intel engaged in a discussion concerning the Vikings.

As legend has it, the Viking King Harald Bluetooth wanted to unite the two separate kingdoms over which he ruled, Denmark and Norway. In the same way, Ericsson and Intel hoped that the technology they were to promote together would unite the two separate worlds of telecommunications and computing. In other words, Bluetooth was a very fitting name for the joint project.

Why was the name of the project also chosen as the name of the standard? The intention was to come up with an appealing name for the standard. In 1998, when Bluetooth was announced as an open technology, the trend was to use a three/four-letter acronym instead of a longer generic description of the technology. Examples of such abbreviations include WAP and GSM.

With a focus on the concept of a PAN, it was quite natural that the first choice concerning an appropriate name for the standard was PAN, a name agreed upon by the founders of the Bluetooth *Special Interest Group* (SIG). When 'PAN' was investigated for trademark protection, however, identical and similar trademarks were found. Time was running out and a name was needed quickly, so 'Bluetooth' was investigated. Fortunately, no such conflicts were found anywhere in the world. The Bluetooth SIG discussed the new name and decided it was a good time to be truly groundbreaking, not only with the technology, but with the name as well. The SIG also felt that a 'real' name such as 'Bluetooth' would be easier to remember and perhaps even generate extra interest in the technology.

A logo for Bluetooth was created and submitted for trademark protection as well, and once again the Bluetooth SIG stumbled over a major obstacle. As it turned out, the logo bore too close a resemblance to another logo submitted just three weeks earlier by another company in a different line of business.

Figure 5.1

A revised logo was subsequently created based on the initials of Harald Bluetooth and using runic characters. This logo was submitted for registration and finally approved. Today it is a well-known figure mark.

Is a protected brand necessary?

This question is still being debated. Standards are generally given a generic name – for example, IRDA, GSM, etc. However, there have been situations where a technology has had protected trademarks, such as Dolby.

The Bluetooth SIG realized that an open standard could also create problems, as many different manufacturers would be interpreting the open Bluetooth Specification. The whole idea of Bluetooth was an out-of-the-box experience where the consumer could easily connect two Bluetooth devices from two different manufacturers. But, in order to make sure this would happen, testing was required. Thus, the Bluetooth SIG set up the Bluetooth Qualification program, where only those who qualified their products would be allowed to use the Bluetooth brand. A protected trademark was therefore necessary.

What is a 'degenerated' trademark?

In order to achieve proper trademark protection, both a generic name and a brand name are essential. For example, 'Volvo', 'Ford', 'Fiat', 'Toyota', etc. are all examples of well-protected trademarks for basically the same product – an automobile. Here, 'automobile' is the generic name without which these brand names would run the risk of degenerating.

A degenerated trademark means that the brand loses its distinctiveness and instead becomes a general term within the language. Common examples of such degeneration are words like dynamite, windsurfer, vespa, insulin, gramophone, nylon and teflon, to name just a few. The problem is that once a brand degenerates it ceases to be the exclusive legal property of a certain company.

The people who were establishing Bluetooth were breaking new ground and were no brand experts. As a result, the need to produce a generic name was overlooked. When trademark specialists raised the issue, an appropriate generic name was created: 'wireless technology'. Great efforts were thereafter required to educate Bluetooth SIG members of the difference between the brand name and the generic name. One of the measures taken by the Bluetooth SIG was to issue a brand book, laying down strict rules and guidelines for the correct usage of both the brand name and the generic name. The ultimate purpose of the brand book is to protect the Bluetooth brand.

Why, then, is a logo needed?

The brand name is likely to be much more important than the brand mark, as the examples of well-established names listed in Table 5.2 clearly show.

The Bluetooth SIG realized that the Bluetooth name was in danger of degenerating, despite the efforts being made to protect it. If it did, there would then be products on the market labeled 'Bluetooth' which indeed did not comply with the standard. This in turn would destroy the aim of the Bluetooth brand.

It is much easier to protect a symbol than a name. A symbol has to be used exactly as specified graphically. Since Bluetooth development

Table 5.2 Well-known logos and brands

Name	Well-known logo	Well-known name/brand
CDMA	No	Yes
GSM	No	Yes
IRDA	No	Yes
USB	No	Yes
WiFi	No	Yes
Hi8	Yes	Yes
VHS	Yes	Yes

was so rapid, it was only natural that a logo be created just to be on the safe side. Furthermore, the bonus of having a logo was a visually appealing symbol to be used consistently, one that people could easily remember. In other words, a symbol would strengthen the Bluetooth brand.

Trademark ownership

In order for a trademark to remain protected, it must be easily identifiable with a specific company. Ericsson did not hand over the Bluetooth brand to the Bluetooth SIG until February 2001, when the Bluetooth SIG became incorporated.

Still, most people continue to identify 'Bluetooth' with Ericsson. In fact, a brand recognition survey performed by Frost and Sullivan in August–September 2002 showed that: 'when respondents were asked what vendors they were currently using or planning to use for Bluetooth products, 40% of responses were allocated to Ericsson, more than double that of the second highest scoring vendor.'

The Bluetooth Special Interest Group

A founding group consisting of Ericsson, Intel, Toshiba, Nokia and IBM carried out the groundwork that eventually led to the establishment of Bluetooth wireless technology and of the Bluetooth SIG. Assisted by a number of so-called *Adopter Members*, i.e. companies with limited participation and access, the complete SIG possessed unprecedented support and power to assert the Bluetooth message and to drive the specification work.

A few of the world's market leaders in mobile phones, PC software, PC accessories and chips were initially outside the inner circle. In 2000, the Bluetooth *Promoter Group* was expanded to include Microsoft, Motorola, Lucent and 3Com. At the same time, Adopter Members were offered the opportunity to upgrade their membership to that of *Associate* status. In doing so, they could raise their level of involvement and provide input during earlier stages of the development process. The four new additions to the Promoter Group, together with a number of new Associate members, meant additional resources for further development of the technology.

Bluetooth has indeed succeeded in uniting the worlds of telecom and datacom though, from time to time, the technology may appear to drift more towards telecom than towards datacom and vice versa. In the end, however, both industries have benefitted greatly from this course of convergence and will continue to do so.

Technology marketing – a necessary ingredient?

The ups and downs of technology marketing

Launching new technology, wireless or otherwise, always requires a major marketing push. Of course, target audiences may differ somewhat, at least initially.

Bluetooth is aimed at the mass market, with the target audience being consumers of electronic devices. But because of the diversity of Bluetooth applications, a campaign to reach all the potentially strong market segments for Bluetooth would have to be massive. The fact that some 40–50 million products have reached the market just five years after Bluetooth was launched is evidence of the enormous task that promoters of the technology were faced with. This is particularly impressive, considering that most of the major global economies were in recession during three of those five years.

The recognition and acceptance of Bluetooth five years after its introduction is rather widespread, although not to the extent that

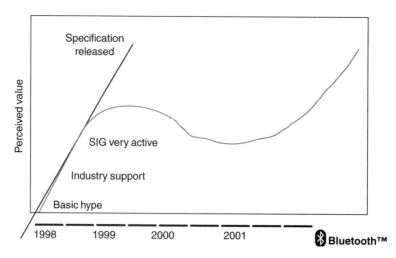

Figure 5.2

was foreseen in the early days. The development curve for most new technologies closely resembles the angles of a hockey stick, pointing sharply upwards at first, only to turn downward for a short while before once again rising upward for an extended period of time. Bluetooth is no exception.

The hype that eventually made 'Bluetooth' a well-known buzzword grew steadily early on. By the start of 2000, however, disappointment began to set in. A lack of products, numerous delays and various imminent battles stalled Bluetooth's stardom.

Could the ensuing downfall have been avoided? Not completely, but had initial predictions been more realistic, perhaps the fall could have been softened.

Would the enormous interest generated around Bluetooth have reached the same pinnacle without the aid of heavy 'over-marketing'? Probably not.

The lesson that was learned here was that initial hype, created through intense marketing efforts, is necessary. Although there is a clear risk for disillusionment that may result from unfulfilled expectations, advance awareness of this problem can alleviate the situation.

In Bluetooth's case, there were a number of circumstances that led to the downturn in 2000:

- No products were being delivered.
- Surveys failed to predict this, damaging their credibility.
- Technical issues with the specification delayed the rollout of products.

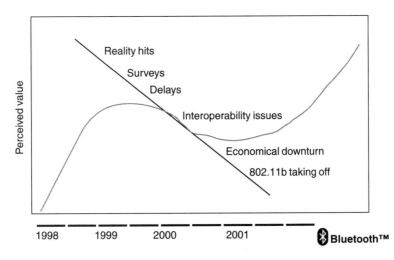

Figure 5.3

- The interoperability program was delayed, making it impossible to properly qualify products. As a result, interoperability problems occurred, leading to a significant amount of bad press.
- The world economy was entering into a recession and the telecom industry suffered from carriers scaling down their investments.
- After 10 years of development IEEE 802.11, a technology for Wireless Local Area Networks (WLAN), was finally starting to take off. In contrast to Bluetooth, the development of IEEE 802.11 was being driven by a standardization body rather than by the industry itself.
- WLAN was perceived as a competing technology and a 'WLAN vs. Bluetooth' debate was gaining momentum, particularly in the US.

Would Bluetooth have experienced such a decline even in the absence of the above circumstances? Most probably. While some of these circumstances could have been avoided, the 'hockey stick' development curve is generally considered inherent to the nature of developing a new technology standard. Still, proper measures must be taken to ensure that the curve rebounds from the seemingly predetermined fall.

Making a rebound

Bluetooth v1.1 was released early in 2001, solving the interoperability issues caused by ambiguity in the previous specification. Eventually,

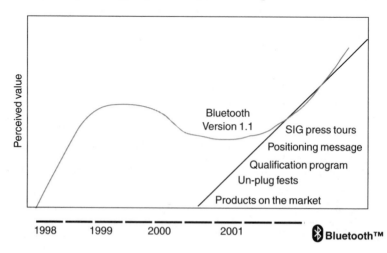

Figure 5.4

Bluetooth mobile phones, headsets and other connectivity products that had been unveiled months earlier were being brought to the market.

The SIG took measures to counter the negative fallout surrounding Bluetooth, including the launching of several marketing initiatives:

- Marketing messages to position Bluetooth and WLAN were developed and communicated.
- A major press tour was organized to explain Bluetooth's positioning and the Bluetooth products that were soon to hit the market.
- The qualification program was finalized and the SIG initiated 'unplug fests' for unofficial testing of products prior to undergoing official, SIG-controlled Bluetooth qualification.
- The Bluetooth consortium voted to create the Bluetooth SIG Inc., a corporation with full-time employees dedicated to the advancement of the technology.

Two very important lessons were learned here. The first was that marketing messages aimed at positioning the technology become increasingly important when other technologies are perceived as competitors. The SIG managed to change the perception of 'WLAN vs. Bluetooth' from 'competing technologies' to 'complementing technologies'.

The second lesson was that it is of great importance to spread the word concerning the efforts taken to fix the problems being addressed in the public arena and in the press. In the case of Bluetooth,

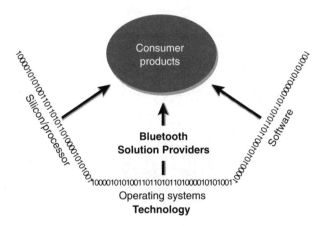

Figure 5.5

this was about finalizing the qualification program and initiating the 'unplug fests'.

Building the foundations

The initial group that convened to form the development of Bluetooth was selected from leading manufacturers of mobile phones, PCs and chipsets. Would this limited group be enough to bring Bluetooth to the market?

No. Additional 'supporting' players would be needed to comprise all the necessary cornerstones upon which the standard was to be built. These would have to include:

- Operating system suppliers.
- Software suppliers.
- Silicon suppliers.

Heavy marketing towards each of these 'segments' was therefore required in order to create a 'pull' effect and to attract vital industry support by recruiting key industry players.

The next step would be to address the ingredient brand. The trademark logo and its value arguments are extremely important. Firstly, there is the matter of the vision with which the brand is to be associated. Are the values and the visions of the brand well addressed?

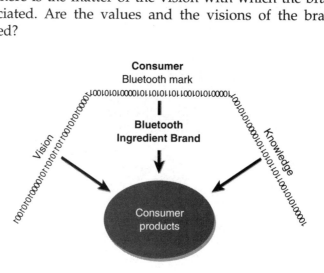

Figure 5.6

Secondly, there is the question of knowledge – what can the technology do? Providing 'user cases' is an excellent means of explaining the various possibilities presented by this new technology.

A miscalculation

Marketing to the consumer segment is a very strenuous task and a very expensive one, and so little effort was made to push the technology among consumers. It was generally assumed that the operators would eventually provide far more push than they actually have and that this would be sufficient.

Now, a few years later, it is quite clear that the Bluetooth community somewhat misjudged the operators' willingness to promote the technology. Had the Bluetooth SIG instead made a greater effort to promote Bluetooth among consumers, then there would be far greater Bluetooth *penetration* today. Many consumers know what Bluetooth is, but the anticipated rush to purchase Bluetooth devices has yet to occur. It will eventually happen, but a marketing push aimed at the consumer would have made it happen sooner.

The complete market dynamics addressing both the technology and consumer markets can be seen in Figure 5.7.

Technology marketing channels

Introducing new technology requires extensive marketing efforts, and Bluetooth is no exception. In fact, the SIG and the companies within the Bluetooth community have worked arduously to market the technology.

Technology marketing focuses on key messages concerning:

- The technology.
- The future of the technology.
- User cases.

The various channels and methods used for technology marketing include:

- Conferences.
- Tradeshows.

- Public Relations/media.
- Training.
- Universities.
- Demos.
- Web.

Conferences

As new technology progresses, it usually becomes more and more interesting over a period of time. Event and conference organizers can easily add interesting topics to already existing and established events/conferences.

During the 'build-up phase' technologies such as GSM, GPRS, WAP and others started out taking up a few 'slots' at already established conferences. Eventually, each of these technologies began hosting complete new events and tradeshows of their own. The Bluetooth SIG has followed suit, actively seeking out and accepting speaking opportunities in order to convey the 'Bluetooth message'.

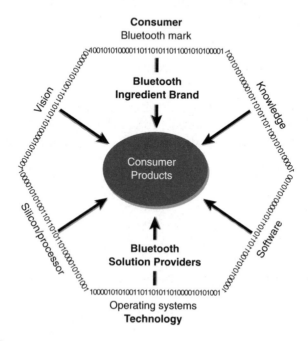

Figure 5.7

Tradeshows

Even today, old-fashioned tradeshows are an important channel for broadcasting a marketing message. Such events are useful for showcasing not only new products, but also the technology behind them. The best way to demonstrate a technology is to demonstrate how it benefits the user, i.e. use cases. Initial use cases for Bluetooth include:

- Headset.
- Dial-up networking.
- Instant imaging.
- Synchronization.

All of these use cases have been demonstrated at numerous tradeshows, taking care to explain to visitors that these were technology demos, not ready-to-go products.

Public Relations/media

Various newspapers and other media are vital channels when attempting to reach the mass market. The SIG did not invest in advertisements, but did make a massive commitment to Public Relations (PR) efforts. Members of the SIG continually contacted hundreds of journalists and invited them to see for themselves just how Bluetooth worked and to ask as many questions as they liked.

It was not only hard work, however, that drew the media's attention to Bluetooth. The technology was, in itself, newsworthy. As opposed to many other technologies, Bluetooth solved a real problem: everyone gets annoyed with the hassle of cables from time to time. Therefore, it was relatively easy to attract the interest of the media.

A newsletter dedicated to Bluetooth, *Incisor*, was issued early on and was very instrumental in conveying the message both to the media and to possible customers as well.

Training

Training is a vital part of 'technology marketing'. The need for information and knowledge about the new technology was enormous in the beginning. Even here, there was the possibility of using marketing messages to gain an advantageous position, but product marketing messages could also be used to inform about the benefits of a particular solution.

Training material was targeted towards different areas and different classes of participants:

- Technology developers.
- How to implement the technology.
- What supplier to choose.
- Telecom operators.
- Use cases featuring mobile phones with Bluetooth connectivity.
- Business case.
- Universities.
- Promote a certain solution tailored for students.
- Train the trainers – get the universities to offer Bluetooth courses.

Universities

A Bluetooth contest was launched jointly by CSIDC, a suborganization within the IEEE, and Ericsson, Toshiba and Intel. Nearly 80 universities around the world were invited to participate by creating appealing Bluetooth applications. The initiators of the contest helped out by providing these institutions with PCs and other hardware for the purpose. The intention was to plant knowledge about Bluetooth in the minds of the students.

Demos

Among the Bluetooth demos prepared and used by Ericsson were a headset, dial-up networking and synchronization. The Ericsson headset demo used at early tradeshows featured a blue, pen-like design.

Figure 5.8

In the case of dial-up networking, which was also demoed at various shows and events, adaptors had to be developed for use with existing phones. The reason for this was that at the time there were no mobile phones with built-in Bluetooth functionality. This called for some explanation to the audience: 'This is not an actual product that will be coming to the market, but rather a demo used to illustrate what is possible with Bluetooth technology.'

Synchronization was shown using a device resembling a pager. It included a mail client and various 'PIM' (Personal Information Management) functions. Again, this was another example of a very interesting 'product' that was never intended to be put on the market.

These early demonstration devices were instrumental in breathing life into Bluetooth. They provided clear, hands-on examples of the types of user benefits that could be expected from the technology. The overall message they conveyed was:

- These are the types of solutions that will be on the market and this is how they will work.
- All kinds of devices will be able to communicate with each other using Bluetooth wireless technology.

In the final analysis the technology demos were a vital component in the marketing phase of Bluetooth. Put simply, *seeing is believing*.

Figure 5.9

Web

A website was established early on at www.bluetooth.com, which provided a wide-reaching medium for broadcasting key marketing messages.

Where is Bluetooth headed?

Market predictions

When Bluetooth first appeared it was surrounded by a great deal of hype. Analysts and IT people in general, not to mention the Bluetooth community, were all convinced that Bluetooth would conquer the world after just a couple of years. Of course, they would all be proven wrong. Development proceeded at a slower pace than anticipated and the market was not quite ready. It is only in the last couple of years that major advances have been made in terms of the numbers and types of Bluetooth products making it to the market. Although progress has been slower than originally predicted in the mid 1990s, it has nonetheless advanced at a faster pace than virtually any other technology thus far.

Today, predictions are made based on facts rather than on wishful thinking or typical IT hype. One such fact is that the Bluetooth market is growing rapidly – currently between 200 and 300 percent annually. Due in part to falling Bluetooth chip prices (now below the magic $5 mark), this enormous growth is likely to continue over the next couple of years.

The mobile phone segment will continue to be a driving force for Bluetooth chips according to various analysts, who predict penetration levels of anywhere from 50 to 80 percent of all mobile phones in just a few years. Other key devices for the Bluetooth market will be headsets, PDAs and connectivity products. And a new group of products likely to evolve into an important segment as the technology evolves includes audio-centric devices such as headphones and MP3 players.

New requirements

The Bluetooth SIG is constantly working to further develop the Bluetooth specification. For example, in order for Bluetooth to work in audio products, new profiles and protocols for audio had to be developed.

Another such example is coexistence with WLAN. The market and the fast-paced technological environment had quickly presented Bluetooth with additional requirements aimed at improving coexistence in the unlicensed ISM band. As both Bluetooth and WLAN grew rapidly in popularity, a sudden urgency arose to find a way to deal with the interference caused when these two technologies operate in the same environment. For this purpose, the Bluetooth SIG decided to incorporate a technique known as Adaptive Frequency Hopping (AFH) in a subsequent version of the Bluetooth specification. AFH is further evidence of the work carried out by the Bluetooth SIG for the evolution of the technology.

New requirements will continue to pop up as the technological environment changes and the market demands newer or better functionality. One idea currently being discussed is the possibility of different communication speeds for different applications. So, in the future there may very well be high-, mid- and low-rate Bluetooth solutions available, allowing for faster, cheaper and more advanced Bluetooth functionality.

Staying ahead

Ericsson not only invented Bluetooth technology, but it also dedicated an entire company to the development of Bluetooth solutions: Ericsson Technology Licensing. For Ericsson, it is important to remain a major player in the world of Bluetooth. As a leading member of the Bluetooth SIG, Ericsson Technology Licensing has strategically positioned itself so as to ensure quick adaptation to any new developments, trends or modifications in the Bluetooth specification. In doing so, Ericsson will continue to be a frontrunner in the ever-expanding Bluetooth market.

Chapter 6

Marketing IBM wireless leadership: technology, inhibitors, strategy and solutions

Dr Ronald Sperano

Program Director for Mobile Market Development,
IBM Personal Computer Division

Recently I took a business trip to California from the east coast. That morning I turned on my ThinkPad® notebook, which automatically connected to my home Wireless Local Area Network (WLAN) via IBM Access Connections, a pre-loaded connectivity software utility. My Virtual Private Network (VPN) client application popped up and with one click I securely accessed my Lotus® Notes® email on the IBM Intranet as if I were sitting in my office. I checked email for urgent messages and my calendar for any new meetings. I printed the day's calendar on my home printer, which defaulted automatically, and prepared for work. I logged off email, exited the VPN application, closed the lid on my notebook, placing it into suspend mode, and left for work.

At the office, I opened my notebook and docked it to my docking station, which provides peripheral connectivity as well as wired

Ethernet. Within seconds the notebook was connected to the IBM LAN and the printer defaulted to the office LAN-based color printer. I logged on to Notes, replicated the server copy of email to my local copy, undocked the notebook and left for the day's first meeting with notebook in hand. At the meeting, a few offices away, the notebook automatically and securely connected to the IBM wireless LAN using IEEE 802.1x authentication.

During the meeting I instant messaged my administrative assistant (AA) to check my flight schedule using Sametime, Notes' version of instant messaging. My AA responded, indicating that I had three hours before liftoff. During some meeting 'down time' I answered email, edited the presentation I needed for my trip, sent the presentation to the LAN printer and replicated email one more time. When the meeting adjourned, I suspended my notebook and left for the airport, picking up the hard copy of my presentation from the printer.

At my seat at the gate I opened my notebook and within seconds I was connected to the T-Mobile Public Wireless Local Area Network (PWLAN), which is available in the Admirals Club (I'm not a member of the Admirals Club but remember radio waves penetrate walls!). I logged in, connected to Notes through the VPN, answered some email, checked the connecting flight status in Dallas and replicated one more time before boarding. During the flight I answered more email from my local copy.

With a two-hour layover in Dallas I opened my notebook and, as expected, within seconds was connected to the Wayport® PWLAN that is available throughout the Dallas airport. I logged in, connected to Notes, Sametimed staff and answered email. My AA Sametimed me for a copy of my itinerary, which I sent to the IBM LAN printer for pick-up. I replicated email and boarded the flight to San Jose. At cruising altitude I answered more email until landing at the San Jose airport, where I logged in to the Wayport PWLAN and replicated email as I waited for my luggage.

In the hotel room I plugged my notebook into the Ethernet jack and connected to Notes through the VPN. I replicated email, unpacked, had supper and retired for the evening. The next morning I worked in the hotel room connected to Notes as if I were back at my office. Later that day at the customer site I connected my notebook, which has Bluetooth™ wireless capability, to the InFocus® projector, advancing the Microsoft PowerPoint® slides over the Bluetooth wireless connection using my Ericsson T39m cellular phone with Bluetooth wireless capability.

I presented IBM's wireless strategy, which included IBM personal computers as well as tools and utilities designed to improve the user's connectivity experience. I used Access Connections to 'sniff' out any on-site WLANs. Since the WLAN was broadcasting access point IDs the access points were found by Access Connections. To the credit of the customer's WLAN administrator, I failed to connect because the WLAN was using encryption and I did not have the correct key. During the presentation the customer asked a question that neither the local IBM Marketing Representative nor I could answer. Instead of deferring to a later time, I inserted my Sprint® PCS wireless modem PC Card, selected the Sprint PCS profile from Access Connections and connected to the IBM Intranet through the VPN. I Sametimed one of my staff with the question, and during the presentation I received a Sametime response with the answer. The customer was impressed!

I not only presented IBM's wireless strategy, I demonstrated IBM's wireless objective: to provide easy and secure anytime, anywhere connectivity at high speeds. From the time I began the trip to the time I returned home I was securely connected to the IBM Intranet, either through a wired LAN, wireless LAN or cellular modem. Access Connections enabled the ThinkPad notebook to automatically connect to the most optimal connection, and when it did not all I had to do was click on the profile I wanted. One more thing, I never rebooted during the entire trip!

This chapter will show the strategy and tactics IBM employs to deliver on IBM's promise of providing users with easy and secure wireless connectivity. The chapter includes how to choose the right IEEE 802.11 WLAN technology, reviews the inhibitors to WLAN implementations, shows how IBM brings differentiation through IBM's ThinkVantage™ Technologies and Design, and details IBM's wireless marketing strategy. The objective of this chapter is to show how IBM brings value-add to the wireless LANscape.

Choosing the right WLAN technology: IEEE 802.11b, 802.11a or 802.11g

The factors to consider when choosing a WLAN technology range from technology attributes to customer size and characteristics. IBM categorizes customers into large enterprises (LE) with 1000 employees or more, middle markets (MM) with 100–999 employees and small businesses (SB) with 1–99 employees. The individual consumer makes up another category. Assuming the need for a WLAN is present (the question of need is discussed later in the chapter), the customer must explore these questions:

- Is the technology standards based?
- Will technology from multiple vendors interoperate?
- What will the actual throughput be?
- Will the technology allow for capacity growth (is it scalable)?
- What level of interference from non-WLAN devices will be present?
- What kind of range does the technology offer?
- What is the price of the technology?
- Can the technology be integrated into the existing WLAN infrastructure?
- What level of security does the technology offer?

Is the technology standards based?

At the time of writing there are three IEEE WLAN standards: the 802.11b, 802.11a and 802.11g specifications. IEEE 802.11b technology has been integrated into commercial notebook personal computers (PCs) since 2000. IEEE 802.11b technology is rapidly becoming a standard integrated feature in many notebook PCs. Consequently, 802.11b is more mature and has a large install base compared to 802.11a or 802.11g. IEEE 802.11a has been commercially available since early 2002 in the form of PC Cards and can also be found as an integrated feature in some notebook PCs. The IEEE 802.11g specification, which is the newest of the three, was ratified by the IEEE in June 2003, with industry certification beginning in August 2003. Customers, particularly LE and MM enterprises, must be leery of implementing any non-standard/non-certified WLAN technology, particularly any 802.11g product that shipped prior to IEEE ratification.

Will technology from multiple vendors interoperate?

The Wi-Fi Alliance (WFA) is a non-profit international association formed in 1999 to certify interoperability of WLAN products based on the family of 802.11 specifications. All three IEEE WLAN specifications – 802.11b, 802.11a and 802.11g – as well as dual-band and tri-mode technology, have received Wi-Fi certification. IBM offers select models of ThinkPad notebooks with integrated Wi-Fi 802.11b, 802.11a/b dual-band as well as 802.11a/b/g tri-mode technology.

Wi-Fi certification means that an 802.11b device from vendor X will communicate with an 802.11b device from vendor Y. The same is true for devices with 802.11a and 802.11g technology that have Wi-Fi certification. Without Wi-Fi certification the enterprise gambles that devices from multiple vendors will interoperate, or they must purchase devices from a single vendor to ensure interoperability.

What is the actual throughput?

The nominal data rate of 802.11b technology is 11 Mbps, while 802.11a and 802.11g technologies have a nominal data rate of 54 Mbps. WLAN bandwidth is shared among all users in the subnet. At the 2002 Microsoft Windows™ Hardware Engineering Conference (WinHEC) a paper was presented that documented the throughput of IEEE 802.11-based networks (Lansford and Gillham, 2002). According to Lansford and Gillham, the throughput of pure 802.11a or 802.11g networks was between 28 and 31 Mbps. An 802.11b WLAN had a throughput of 5–7 Mbps. In a mixed 802.11g and 802.11b environment (802.11g access points with 802.11b and 802.11g clients), the throughput was between 10 and 12 Mbps, indicating that a hybrid 802.11b and 802.11g WLAN will experience significant throughput deterioration for the 802.11g clients.

Will the technology allow for capacity growth (is it scalable?)

In an 802.11b WLAN, three non-overlapping channels (three access points) can be colocated for maximum capacity and minimum interference. This will create a WLAN segment with an aggregate capacity of 33 (11 × 3) Mbps distributed among the three access points. IEEE 802.11a technology supports eight indoor non-overlapping colocated channels with an aggregate capacity of 432 (54 × 8) Mbps.

IEEE 802.11g has a maximum data rate of 54 Mbps, but resides in the same frequency spectrum as 802.11b, so has an aggregate capacity of 162 (54 × 3) Mbps. IEEE 802.11a offers the most capacity and therefore is more scalable than either 802.11b or 802.11g.

What level of interference from non-WLAN devices will be present?

According to Flickenger (2002), the 2.4 GHz ISM (Industry, Scientific, Medical) band is saturated due to the proliferation of 802.11b WLAN devices, microwave ovens, cordless phones and other devices that operate in this band. Conover (2001) wrote that the steady availability of Bluetooth wireless devices will cause additional interference in the 2.4 GHz band. IEEE 802.11a technology runs in the less crowded 5 GHz U-NII (Unlicensed National Information Infrastructure) band and as such interference problems will be drastically reduced. Therefore, 802.11a running in the 5 GHz band will have less interference problems than 802.11b and 802.11g, which operate in the more crowed 2.4 GHz band.

What kind of range does the technology offer?

According to Lansford and Gillham (2002), holding power and throughput constant and assuming common environments and operating parameters, systems operating in the 2.4 GHz band offer roughly double the range of those operating in the 5 GHz band. Lansford and Gillham concluded that, with equal parameters, 802.11a WLANs require four times as many access points as do WLANs based on 802.11b or 802.11g to cover the same area. However, there is not a consensus on the range of 802.11a technology.

In a study conducted by Salvator (2002), 802.11a delivered higher data rates than either 802.11b or 802.11g up to 100 feet (ranges beyond 100 feet were not reported on). Proxim (2002) found that 802.11a WLANs retained consistently higher data rates than 802.11b at all distances. In a WLAN site survey performed by Geier (2002) for the Miami International Airport, it was found that in some areas, particularly baggage claims, 802.11a range was often better than 802.11b.

Geier also found that 802.11a nearly always operated at higher data rates than 802.11b, at all distances up until 802.11a became completely disassociated with the access point, which was about 30–50 feet less than 802.11b technology. Geier concluded that enterprises don't need more 802.11a than 802.11b access points to fully cover an area, assuming the goal is to support 11 Mbps or better data rates everywhere. In LE and MM environments, it is unlikely that 802.11a will replace 802.11b. Instead, 802.11a will augment the existing 802.11b network where high-speed, high-capacity hot spots are required. The answer to the question of 802.11a's range compared to 802.11b or 802.11g is: 'it depends'.

What is the price of the technology?

The consistent growth in 802.11b WLANs has lead to a steady decline in the average price of an 802.11b WLAN PC Card. A search of the Internet revealed a price range from $38 to $85 for an 802.11b WLAN PC Card (buy.com, 2003). IEEE 802.11a technology was ratified at the same time as 802.11b; however, due to difficulties in manufacturing 802.11a products and only recent Wi-Fi certification (early 2003), 802.11a PC Cards are priced between $80 and $107 (buy.com, 2003). IEEE 802.11a/b/g tri-mode PC Cards are priced under $100 (buy.com, 2003). The price to the end-user for WLAN technology integrated into the notebook PC, in the form of a miniPCI adaptor, is substantially lower across all the WLAN technologies.

Can the technology be integrated into the existing WLAN infrastructure?

IEEE 802.11b WLANs are found in homes, public locations such as airports, hotels and coffee shops, as well as education and business environments. Because of Wi-Fi a traveler is guaranteed that their Wi-Fi-enabled notebook can be used on the Wi-Fi WLAN in the office, at home or at the airport. For existing Wi-Fi networks it is crucial that new WLAN technology can be integrated with minimal impact.

IEEE 802.11g operates in the 2.4 GHz band, as does 802.11b, but uses a different modulation technique, so 802.11b and 802.11g should not be compatible. However, IEEE 802.11g maintains backwards compatibility to 802.11b networks by supporting 802.11b's modulation technique. This backwards compatibility does have limitations. In an 802.11b WLAN, 802.11g clients can only operate at 802.11b speeds. In an 802.11 g WLAN, maximum throughput can only be achieved if all the access points and clients use 802.11g technology.

Since 802.11a technology operates in a different frequency band than both 802.11b and 802.11g, 802.11a technology is not compatible with either 802.11b or 802.11g. This non-compatibility also means that 802.11a WLANs can be colocated with either 802.11b or 802.11g WLANs without interference. However, inter-band compatibility between 5 and 2.4 GHz products is achievable. A ThinkPad notebook with an 802.11a/b/g tri-mode miniPCI adaptor card can communicate with any IEEE 802.11 WLAN: 802.11a and 802.11g at speeds up to 54 Mbps, and 802.11b at speeds up to 11 Mbps. Since 802.11a and 802.11b/g operate at different frequencies there is no throughput degradation for 802.11a clients in a hybrid 802.11a/b/g network.

What level of security does the technology offer?

All three technologies – 802.11a, 802.11b and 802.11g – support the standard security features contained in the 802.11 specifications: access point identification, data encryption and network interface card (NIC) address filtering. The technologies will also support the Wi-Fi Protected Access (WPA) security protocols and the IEEE 802.11i security standard, when it becomes ratified. The standard 802.11 security features, along with WPA and 802.11i, are discussed later in the chapter.

It is interesting to note that 802.11a technology may provide an added level of security due to the technology's reduced range. WLAN technology penetrates walls and if access points are placed too near the periphery of the building, the signal will leak beyond the physical boundaries into parking lots and adjacent buildings. To reduce this security breach, IT managers may choose to place 802.11a access points along the periphery. Table 6.1 summarizes similarities and differences between the 802.11-based WLAN technologies.

Table 6.1 IEEE WLAN technology comparison

Attributes	802.11b	802.11a	802.11g	802.11a/b/g
Ratified IEEE standard	Yes	Yes	Yes	Yes
WFA certified	Yes	Yes	Yes	Yes
Maximum data rate (Mbps)	11	54	54	11b: 11 Mbps 11a: 54 Mbps 11g: 54 Mbps
Actual throughput* (Mbps)	5–7	28–31	28–31 (all 11g environment) 10–12 (mixed environment with 11b clients)	11b: 5–7 Mbps 11a: 28–31 Mbps (11b/g technology has no impact on 11a technology) 11g: 28–31 Mbps (all 11g environment) 10–12 Mbps (mixed environment with 11b clients)
Maximum capacity (Mbps)	33 (3 channels × 11)	432 (8 channels × 54)	162 (3 channels × 54)	465 (8 channels × 54, plus 3 channels × 11 assuming a mixed 11b and 11g environment)
Modulation technique	2.4 GHz CCK	5 GHz OFDM	2.4 GHz OFDM CCK	5 GHz: 11a-OFDM 2.4 GHz: 11b-CCK 2.4 GHz: 11g-OFDM
Backwards compatibility	Yes (client operates at 11b speeds on 11g and 11b APs)	No	Yes (client operates at 11b speeds on 11b APs and 11g speeds on 11g APs)	Yes (11b client operates at 11b speeds on 11b or 11g APs, while 11a client operates at 11a speeds on 11a APs. 11g client speeds depend on make-up of network)

Table 6.1 (continued)

Attributes	802.11b	802.11a	802.11g	802.11a/b/g
Interference with other devices	Yes (cordless phones, Bluetooth, microwave ovens)	No	Yes (cordless phones, Bluetooth, microwave ovens)	11b: Yes 11g: Yes 11a: No
Indoor range[†]	100 feet as the base case	Faster speeds at 100 feet compared to 11b and 11g	Faster speeds at 100 feet compared to 11b	Comparable to 11b WLAN
Price ($ US)[‡]	38–85	80–107	70	100
Infrastructure impact	n/a	New access points must be installed	New access points must be installed to exploit full speed	New access points must be installed to exploit full speed of 11a and/or 11g
Security	WEP, VPN, WPA and 802.11i	WEP, VPN, WPA and 802.11i	WEP, VPN, WPA and 802.11i	WEP, VPN, WPA and 802.11i

*Microsoft Windows Hardware Engineering Conference (WinHEC, 2002).
[†]Test conducted by ExtremeTech: http://www.extremetech.com/print_article/0,3998, a=36375,00.asp
[‡]Prices of PC Cards obtained from buy.com on 26 January 2003.

Inhibitors to WLAN implementations

Quantifying return on investment for WLANs

Before customers commit to deploying a WLAN, the cost of implementation must be recoverable. Customers must be shown that
savings relative to WLAN deployments can be realized by avoiding
the cost of cabling and its associated maintenance. Customers may

also need convincing that improved productivity due to employee access to the company LAN anywhere on campus, at home or while traveling is quantifiable.

According to the Wireless LAN Association (WLANA), the cost of installing and maintaining a WLAN is generally lower than the cost of installing and maintaining a wired LAN for two reasons. First, a WLAN eliminates the direct costs of cabling and the labor associated with installation and repair. Second, because WLANs simplify moves, adds and changes, WLANs reduce the indirect costs of user downtime and administrative overhead (WLANA, 2001). Depending on the WLAN size, substantial savings can accrue by avoiding the costs related to cabling client devices.

There have been a number of studies quantifying the productivity improvements resulting from WLAN deployments. Gartner (2001), the Kellogg School of Management (Intel, 2002a), NOP World (2001), Intel (2002b) and a consolidated report from Gartner Group, Yankee Group and Sage Research (Intel, 2001) have documented monetary benefits due to productivity improvements from WLAN deployments. An analysis of these studies shows that five to eight hours per week per employee can be gained due to implementing a WLAN. IBM helps customers to overcome the WLAN return-on-investment inhibitor with software tools, discussed later in the chapter, designed to quantify WLAN savings and productivity benefits.

Security issues regarding IEEE 802.11 WLAN deployments

Published incidents have highlighted the inadequate security mechanisms of the IEEE 802.11-based WLAN standards. The standard defines three mechanisms to provide access control and privacy on WLANs: Service Set Identifiers (SSIDs); Media Access Control (MAC) filtering; and encryption with the Wired Equivalent Privacy (WEP) protocol. The SSID is the name used by the access point to allow client devices configured with the proper SSID to gain access. Using SSIDs provides a rudimentary level of access control and serves to logically segment the WLAN. The use of SSIDs for access control is not secure because the access point can broadcast the SSID to all users. However, the broadcasting feature can be turned off, requiring users to know the SSID. To address the problem of data privacy the WEP cryptographic system is employed.

WEP allows up to four shared and static WEP keys to be configured on all client devices and access points in the WLAN. When a client device presents the correct WEP key to the access point, the client device can communicate securely with other client devices on the WLAN. One problem with WEP is that the keys can be compromised through wide distribution, which is necessary for large WLAN implementations. Also, the WEP system does not define how the shared keys are established or how the keys are distributed. WEP is an optional feature and must be enabled by the WLAN administrator. The WEP system uses a 64-bit RC4 stream cipher. RC4 is a symmetric encryption algorithm where the same key is used to both encrypt and decrypt the data. Although not part of the 802.11 specifications, many 802.11b, 802.11g and 802.11a products support 128-bit RC4 encryption.

The third security feature describes a rudimentary form of network authentication by using MAC (Media Access Control) filtering. Every Ethernet device has a unique physical address called the MAC address. Only clients listed on the MAC authentication table loaded in the access point will have access to the WLAN. This method works well with a small number of users, but as the number of users increases, maintaining the MAC authentication table is burdensome. Also, with the right equipment, a MAC address of a legitimate client device can be duplicated, allowing unauthorized network access.

According to Borisov et al. (2001) there are a number of flaws in the WEP algorithm that undermine the security of IEEE 802.11-based WLANs. Borisov et al. identified the following potential attacks on WEP:

- Passive attacks to decrypt traffic, based on statistical analysis.
- Active attacks to inject new traffic from unauthorized mobile stations, based on known plain text.
- Active attacks to decrypt traffic, based on tricking the access point.
- Dictionary-building attacks that analyze transmitted traffic, allowing real-time automated decryption of the traffic.

Borisov et al. wrote that, with sufficient time and resources, active interception and decryption of 802.11 traffic is possible and concluded that 'WEP fails to achieve its security goals'.

Another attack on WEP was documented by Fluhrer et al. (2001). Fluhrer et al. performed a passive network attack that took advantage of several weaknesses in the key-scheduling algorithm of RC4. According to Mannion (2001), unlike the attack performed by Borisov et al., the attack on WEP performed by Fluhrer et al. was passive as opposed to active, took minutes to complete as compared to days, and compromised the WEP key as opposed to capturing finite amounts of network traffic, making the need to improve the security of 802.11 WLANs more immediate.

To address the concerns of inadequate security of the 802.11 standards, the IEEE established the IEEE 802.11i Task Group (TGi). The four major deficiencies of WEP to be addressed by 802.11i are authentication, encryption key management, the static nature of the WEP key, and the WEP encryption algorithm. The current 802.11i draft specification addresses these deficiencies with 128-bit WEP in association with TKIP (Temporal Key Integrity Protocol), MIC (Message Integrity Checking), 802.1x authentication and AES (Advanced Encryption Standard) cryptography. TKIP is a suite of software algorithms that enhances WEP, without breaking compatibility, by surrounding WEP with new algorithms. For legacy devices 802.11i will mandate that 128-bit WEP be implemented, in addition to adding TKIP, MIC and 802.1x authentication. For new devices 802.11i will mandate the use of 802.1x authentication, as well as replace RC4-based WEP with AES, which is a more secure block cipher cryptographic system.

IEEE 802.1x is a network access control mechanism for wired and wireless networks. In a WLAN environment the 802.1x authentication scheme allows the client device to send authentication credentials, such as user name and password or digital certificate, to a back-end authentication server through the WLAN access point. The authentication server checks the validity of the information and authorizes or denies access to the network, as well as issuing dynamic WEP keys on a per-user/per-session basis. At the time of writing, TGi has not completed its work so there is no replacement for the current 802.11 security features that are accepted by the WFA. To address the current need for improved security, the WFA has proposed a solution, called Wi-Fi-Protected Access (WPA), which is a subset of the proposed 802.11i standard, but is available now.

To satisfy the immediate security concerns, the WFA announced, on 31 October 2002, the WPA protocols. WPA products must support 128-bit WEP with TKIP, MIC and 802.1x authentication. The one

802.11i major component not incorporated in WPA is AES. AES will eventually replace WEP; however, to fully exploit AES, new client and access point hardware may be required. Legacy hardware will only require a software upgrade to support WPA. The WFA began WPA interoperability certification in February 2003.

Perceived lack of security is the number one inhibitor for rolling out WLANs in large and middle-market enterprises. In a survey performed by *Network World* magazine, 74 percent of respondents indicated that security was their number one issue relative to WLAN implementations (Messmer et al., 2002). There is no doubt that the security features included in the IEEE 802.11 WLAN specifications, particularly WEP, are weak at best, as well as not scalable. However, as weak as WEP is, WEP is better than nothing and does offer protection against the casual attack. There may be many reasons for not implementing a WLAN, including the lack of need for mobility or even the inability to provide convincing ROI data, but lack of security is not one of them. In today's environment, large and middle-market enterprises can implement a number of security features, including WPA and VPNs, that will make WLANs very secure. However, it is virtually impossible to guarantee that a WLAN or any network is invulnerable to security breaches.

The IBM Think strategy

For years computer manufacturers have been struggling to prevent their products from becoming commoditized. Differentiating on attributes such as processor speed, memory, hard-disk drive capacity and display resolution is counter-productive. The personal computer industry has reached the point at which component differences are becoming less important to the average computer user. Over the years, IBM has been very successful in selling solutions that are comprised of hardware, software and services addressing the customer's needs holistically. To further advance the concept of solution selling, IBM's Personal Computer Division (PCD) has developed a new strategy, called 'Think', to deliver value that extends beyond the speeds and feeds of yesterday.

PCD's Think strategy addresses complex business challenges by designing technology that's easier to use, more intuitive and more secure. PCD no longer simply offers customers desktop or notebook personal computers. PCD now offers solutions that allow customers to be more efficient and productive. Two cornerstones of the Think strategy are ThinkVantage™ Technologies and ThinkVantage Design. Together, they demonstrate the IBM philosophy of innovation for business advantage.

What is an IBM ThinkVantage Technology?

IBM developed ThinkVantage Technologies to make IBM personal systems less dependent on IT staff or user intervention for basic tasks like deployment, backup, security and connectivity, thereby freeing users and IT staff to focus on business success. IBM currently offers 11 ThinkVantage Technologies in four categories – Wireless Computing, Security, Migration, and Access to Capabilities – that make computing simpler and more secure. There are two Think-Vantage Technologies relative to networking designed to make connectivity easier and more secure: IBM Access Connections and Embedded Security Subsystem (ESS).

IBM Access Connections: a ThinkVantage Technology

Access Connections addresses the difficulties of connecting to wired and wireless networks. There are a variety of network adaptors, including Ethernet, token-ring, modem, cellular, Bluetooth and WLAN, that can be used at different venues, such as home, office and on the road. Selecting the right adaptor for the current venue can be a challenging task for many users, especially for users who travel. For WLANs the user might have to know the correct SSID, WEP key and 802.1x authentication parameters, along with the standard network parameters.

In the office, most users connect via a TCP/IP (Transmission Control Protocol/Internet Protocol) connection to a DNS (Domain Name System or Server) using DHCP (Dynamic Host Configuration Protocol) and perhaps a proxy server (a server that sits between a client application and the actual real enterprise server). In some cases, on the road or at home, the same network adaptor is also configured with a static IP address to an ISP (Internet Service Provider) without using proxy settings, but requires the use of a VPN (Virtual Private Network), allowing the user to access the private corporate LAN from the Internet. Depending on venue, different Windows-based security features may also be implemented.

Access Connections has three goals: ease of use for quickly switching between various network topologies, a repository for all critical network parameters, and a tool to quickly troubleshoot connectivity problems. Access Connections is a pre-loaded software utility on ThinkPad notebooks to aid users and IT administrators with setting up networking on Windows-based systems. Access Connections uses 'location profiles' that define the network adaptor to be used, as well as networking and other system parameters associated with that adaptor and venue.

Figure 6.1 is a screen shot of the Access Connection's primary graphical user interface (GUI) that shows which profile is in use, the WLAN signal strength and adaptor speed, which NIC is active, the IP address, the connection status and the default printer. By moving the cursor over the icons in the GUI panel, more information is displayed that can be used in consultation with help desk personnel to troubleshoot connectivity problems. In addition, by accessing various menus from the main GUI the user has the ability to execute Window's DOS commands, such as releasing and renewing IP, or

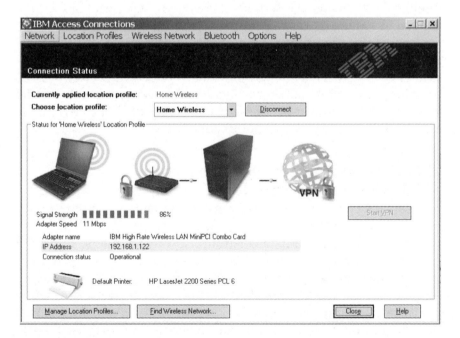

Figure 6.1   IBM Access Connection

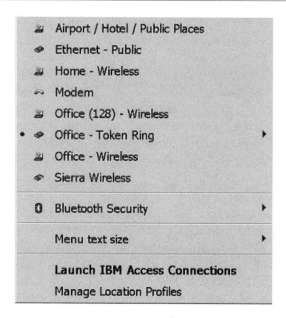

Figure 6.2   IBM Access Connections Location Profile menu

pinging a gateway, by simply clicking on the desired function instead of having to know the correct command syntax.

Once the location profile is created, the user switches profiles by clicking the Access Connections task tray icon and selecting a profile, as shown in Figure 6.2. In addition, once configured, WLAN roaming on or off campus or switching between a wired LAN and WLAN connection can be accomplished without user intervention: the ThinkPad notebook will automatically switch!

IBM Embedded Security Subsystem: a ThinkVantage Technology

As users rely on the speed and ease of intranet and Internet communications, the threats of network infiltration, data theft, client theft, identity theft and data corruption are real dangers. To protect information from costly exposures, users need security offerings that will help protect data, prevent unauthorized users from learning and using your digital identification, and create secure wired and wireless communications.

Only IBM offers select ThinkPad notebooks and NetVista® desktop systems with the IBM Embedded Security Subsystem (ESS), a

ThinkVantage Technology that is a hardware- and software-based solution. Select models now feature the TCPA-and TCG-compliant Embedded Security Subsystem 2.0 to provide the highest level of industry-standard PC security. The TCPA (Trusted Computing Platform Alliance: http://www.trustedcomputing.org/home) and the TCG (Trusted Computer Group: http://www.trustedcomputing-group.org) are alliances of hardware, software, communications and technology vendors, including IBM, with the mission to enhance security on client, server, networking and communication platforms.

The hardware portion, an integrated security chip, is a cryptographic microprocessor that is embedded in the system board of select IBM client devices. In addition, IBM has developed the Client Security Software (CSS) suite specially designed for the integrated security chip. The CSS consists of multiple software components that support cryptographic and identification services, which strengthen the security of the IBM client device. The core of the CSS is the User Verification Manager (UVM), which is software that can use multiple, configurable security mechanisms to identify a user and determine access rights and privileges.

The ESS is included on all ThinkPad notebooks that have integrated WLAN technology. The ESS can be thought of as an integrated 'lock-box' that can be used to protect 'valuables'. One way to secure a WLAN is to use client authentication, such as 802.1x. Authentication credentials such as user name/password or digital certificates can be securely stored with the ESS, which is an IBM exclusive. To the extent your WLAN authentication credentials are more secure, your WLAN is more secure.

What is an IBM ThinkVantage Design?

IBM's ThinkVantage Design encompasses the unique design elements that make IBM personal systems more comfortable, more intuitive and easier to use. ThinkVantage Design attributes enhance the user experience with innovations that make systems work better and feel better. Every ThinkVantage Design element is developed with a specific purpose in mind. ThinkVantage Design lets users focus on the task at hand and forget the technology behind it. When the user is forced to configure, initialize or optimize a technology, it adds time and frustration.

Figure 6.3   Placement of IBM UltraConnect antenna

Customers have been able to tell a ThinkPad notebook apart from the competition for more than 10 years. That's because ThinkPad notebooks feature signature styling that is distinctly IBM. Details like the black color, angular shape, efficient form, ThinkLight™ for illuminating the keyboard in low light and punctuating red TrackPoint™ pointing device let the user know at a glance that this product features ThinkVantage Design attributes.

IBM UltraConnect™ antenna: a ThinkVantage Design

Relating to wireless computing, there is one ThinkVantage Design attribute that is not obvious: The IBM UltraConnect antenna. The UltraConnect diversity antennas are purposely located near the top of the screen rather than in the base because the higher location delivers superior performance, gain and clearer reception (see Figure 6.3). The UltraConnect antenna supports multiple frequencies for 802.11a, 802.11b and 802.11g technologies, optimizing coverage and performance for improved wireless LAN connectivity worldwide.

IBM commissioned VeriTest to test the network performance of the IBM integrated antenna on an 802.11b WLAN. The ThinkPad notebook was tested against eight competitive systems with integrated Wi-Fi radio technology and was found to provide the best 802.11b wireless solution (VeriTest, 2002).

Marketing wireless LANs

In 2000, IBM announced the ThinkPad i Series, which was the first WinTel-based notebook computer with an integrated antenna and

802.11b Wi-Fi certified WLAN radio (WinTel refers to a system running the Windows operating system and an Intel microprocessor). Today IBM ThinkPad notebooks have various communications technologies integrated into select models, including 802.11b, 802.11a/b/g, infrared (IR), Bluetooth wireless communications, Giga-bit Ethernet and modem technology. Many ThinkPad models have all five connectivity technologies integrated. IBM rounds out its communication offerings with CDMA (Code-Division Multiple Access) and GSM/GPRS (Global Systems for Mobile Communications/General Packet Radio Service) cellular PC Cards for connectivity wherever CDMA or GSM/GPRS networks are available. The following is a five-step approach for IBM marketing representatives to follow when marketing WLAN solutions:

1 Determine the customer's need for mobility.
2 Select the right WLAN technology based on the mobility need.
3 Calculate the potential WLAN savings and benefits.
4 Address the customer's security concerns.
5 Demonstrate IBM's differentiation with ThinkVantage Technologies and Design.

Determine the customer's need for mobility

Organizations need to enable users to work at different venues such as home, on the road and throughout the corporate campus. This new untethered paradigm will facilitate faster collaboration, better decision-making, more customer 'face time' and faster response to customer requirements. The wireless industry has emerged as one of the fastest-growing segments of the communications industry. The demand for wireless devices, particularly WLAN devices, is growing rapidly. The IDC predicts that the worldwide market for WLAN devices will grow to $1.6 billion in 2004, up from $785 million in 2000 (as cited in Intel, 2003).

IBM marketing representatives are armed with a list of questions to be discussed with customers who are looking to improve the way their employees work. The questions, detailed in Table 6.2, address four areas: current network background, connectivity problems, effects of not being connected and value of improved connectivity (Dugger, 2003).

Table 6.2 Qualifying the value of mobility

Background	• Are you currently using wireless technology in your business? • How many hours a week do your employees spend working away from the office or their desks where they require a network connection? • How many of your offices are difficult to wire for networks? • How many of your offices have PCs that are not networked together?
Problem	• What obstacles have you encountered in trying to network together PCs? • What has prevented you from implementing wireless technology in your company?
Effect	• How many hours a week do your employees waste because they are working away from the office or their desks and cannot access data? • How much sales revenue have you lost because your reps can't access data remotely? • How much would you need to spend to add infrastructure for a wired network? • If you implemented a wired network, who would install your wiring? If your own IT staff installs it, what other projects will be delayed while they are installing the LAN? How will delays in these other projects affect your business?
Value	• How much faster would your reps close sales if they could access data from remote locations? How much additional revenue would this translate into? • How much faster would your employees be able to make important decisions if they could access critical data from anywhere on the corporate campus? What would productivity savings be? • How else would you benefit from accessing data from anywhere at anytime? • How much money would you save if you didn't have to add to your installed wired infrastructure?

The purpose of these questions is to establish the fact that implementing a WLAN has benefits above and beyond merely extending the current wired infrastructure, both in terms of monetary savings (cable vs. no cable) and improved productivity benefits (connected vs. not connected). Once the customer is convinced that WLANs have advantages over wired LANs, a discussion of which WLAN technology to choose should follow.

Select the right WLAN technology based on the mobility need

For individuals and small to middle-market enterprises that are just implementing WLAN solutions (no existing WLAN infrastructure), either 802.11b or the nascent 802.11g specifications are appropriate (remember 802.11g is backwards compatible with 802.11b WLANs). IEEE 802.11b may be the 'safer' choice for these customers, since 802.11b has been on the market since 2000, which has created a wealth of knowledge relative to 'Best Practices' procedures. However, if the relative slow speed of 802.11b (up to 11 Mbps) is a concern, then these customers should investigate implementing the faster (up to 54 Mbps) 802.11g specification.

For the middle-market to large enterprises with an existing 802.11b WLAN infrastructure experiencing throughput and capacity issues or enterprises without any existing WLAN infrastructure but with mobility needs, a serious evaluation of 802.11a/b/g tri-mode technology is recommended. For the client side, IBM recommends ThinkPad notebooks with integrated 802.11a/b/g tri-mode technology. For the infrastructure side, open-slot access points are recommended. One slot of the access point can be populated with 802.11a technology while the other slot remains open. These 802.11a populated access points can be overlaid on the existing 802.11b WLAN without impacting the 802.11b network. This will allow the ThinkPad notebooks with 802.11a/b/g tri-mode technology to connect to either the 802.11b or 802.11a access points. The 802.11a/b/g tri-mode ThinkPad notebooks and open-slot access points should be used in areas of high WLAN usage. The open-slot access points afford the customer the flexibility to choose which technology to place in the other open slot: either 802.11g or remain with the current 802.11b technology. Table 6.3 summarizes the available WLAN technologies and reasons to choose that particular technology.

Calculate the potential WLAN savings and benefits

Once the need for mobility is established and the correct WLAN technology chosen, then the next step is to use the IBM WLAN savings

Table 6.3 Reasons to choose which WLAN technology

WLAN technology	Reasons to choose
802.11b	• Ubiquitous availability: home, office, public locations such as airports and hotels. • Lowest cost WLAN technology. • An existing 802.11b corporate WLAN is in place. • Throughput and capacity are adequate for the near future. • Connection to public WLANs is required.
802.11a	• Offers the highest speed (54 Mbps) and most capacity (432 Mbps). • No existing WLAN infrastructure. • Will only be used in a single location: office or home. • Connection to public WLANs is *not* required.
802.11a/b/g	• Investment protection. • Ubiquitous availability: home, office, public locations such as airports and hotels. • Reasonably priced for most flexibility (connects to any IEEE 802.11 WLAN). • Offers the highest speed (54 Mbps) and most capacity (465 Mbps). • An existing 802.11b corporate WLAN is in place. • Throughput and capacity of both 802.11b and 802.11g are an issue.
802.11g	• Low-cost WLAN technology. • 802.11b capacity and throughput are not enough. • Connection to public WLANs is required. • 802.11g throughput and capacity are adequate for the near future.

and benefits calculators to formulate a sizing of what the WLAN benefits may be. The calculators should be used with the help of trained IBM Marketing Representatives, but with as much customer-specific data as can be made available. The default values and customer scenarios, while based on industry data, are included in the tools to provide a reference point. The real value of the tools, the Wired vs. WLAN Cost Calculator and the WLAN Productivity Benefits Calculator, is the ability to customize them with customer-specific data that better reflects the customer's unique environment.

The purpose of the Wired vs. Wireless LAN Cost Calculator is to show customers potential financial savings relative to WLANs (see

Appendix A, Exhibit 1). The tool is the result of interviews with 2000 enterprise customers of all sizes. Ziff Davis Media Inc. conducted the interviews on behalf of IBM. Most respondents were CIOs, IT managers and LAN managers. The survey establishes estimates from the average response of those interviewed. The estimates change with size of enterprise, where economies of scale are an advantage for larger enterprises.

The tool was built as a Microsoft Access database and is presented to the user in three sections:

1 Category-5 Wired LAN Costs.
2 Wireless LAN Costs.
3 Cost Savings for Wireless vs. Wired Based on Number of New Nodes.

The customer begins by entering the total number of employees at the site as well as the number of existing Ethernet nodes (there may not be a 1:1 correlation). Based on this information, the survey displays estimates in the following categories:

* Average moves each year for:
  − Staff.
  − Printers.
  − PCs.
* Discrete costs:
  − Average cost to move a Cat-5 tap.
  − Number of full-time staff dealing with cable issues.
  − Average cost to add a Cat-5 tap.
* Budgets for:
  − Cat-5 cable certification.
  − Repairing/changing cabling infrastructure.
  − LAN wiring and installation.
  − Tracking physical Cat-5 tap location.
  − Outsourcing costs for remote locations.

To compare the costs of wired versus wireless LANs, the cost of an installed access point and cost differential between a wired and wireless LAN NIC are entered in Section 2, or the survey generated values may be used. To complete Section 2 the number of client devices (or nodes) per access point is entered. Section 3, Cost Savings for Wireless vs. Wired Based on Number of New Nodes, is where the tool performs the final calculations. The saving per node is multiplied by the number of new nodes, which yields the total savings from augmenting a wired LAN with a wireless LAN.

To aid customers in quantifying increases in productivity due to WLANs, IBM created the WLAN Productivity Benefits Calculator (see Appendix A, Exhibit 2). The tool is written as a Microsoft Excel Spreadsheet and has seven sections:

1 Welcome and Instructions.
2 Customer Data.
3 WLAN.
4 ThinkPad.
5 Access Connections.
6 Summary.
7 Help.

Section 1 explains the intent of the tool and how to get started. Section 2 is where vital customer data is entered as follows:

• Total number of employees.
• Percentage of employees using PCs.
• Percentage of employees using notebook PCs.
• Percentage of notebook users requiring WLAN.
• Average notebook PC lifespan in years.
• Percentage of integrated WLAN NIC clients vs. PC Cards.
• Number of sites requiring WLAN infrastructure.

The tool looks at three areas of productivity improvements: baseline productivity improvements accruing from ubiquitous connectivity provided by a WLAN; improvements from using IBM ThinkPad notebooks; and additional improvements from using IBM Access Connections.

Section 3 is where the costs of a WLAN are inputted, as well as where generic productivity improvements and payback are calculated. The calculations are based on data entered in Sections 2 and 3 applied against average data accumulated from a number of industry studies. The output of Section 3 will be payback in terms of months and annual per-user benefits in terms of dollars. For example, using a default customer scenario for 250 WLAN users, the number of months it may take to recoup the cost of implementing a WLAN comes to 10.3 months with a potential per-user annual savings of $505. Sections 4 and 5 are used to fine-tune the calculations based on using ThinkPad notebooks with the UltraConnect antenna and Access Connections. Based on productivity improvements due to optimal performance provided by the UltraConnect antenna and ease-of-use provided by Access Connections, calculations can be made reducing the number of payback months and increasing per-user annual savings. The calculations in Sections 4 and 5 are based on IBM estimates that are, in some instances, backed by independent industry studies (VeriTest, 2002). Section 6 summarizes the data while Section 7 provides the user with additional help text.

The IBM WLAN Productivity Benefits Calculator has proved to be a very popular tool for IBM customers looking to implement a WLAN. For non-IBM customers a version of the IBM tool can be downloaded from the Quick Links section (look for WLAN Benefits Calculator) on the home page of the WFA website (http://www.wi-fi.org/OpenSection/index.asp).

Address the customer's security concerns

There are four levels of WLAN security: none, basic, enhanced and specialized. With no security the default access point name (SSID) is broadcasted, no encryption is used (WEP is disabled) and access controls are not used (MAC filtering is disabled). With no security anyone can access the WLAN. For Public Wireless Local Area Networks (PWLANs) in airports and hotels, no security is the default because it facilitates the easy connection to the PWLAN.

A WLAN with basic security will use a unique SSID with broadcasting turned off, have WEP (128-bit) enabled and use an MAC filtering table for access control. To access a WLAN with basic security, the user must know the SSID, have the correct WEP key and be listed on the MAC filter table. Basic security will most likely deter all but the most dedicated hacker, and as a result may be enough security for a home WLAN or a WLAN in a small business.

Enhanced security addresses the static nature of the WEP key and improves network authentication by utilizing the 802.1x port-based authentication system. Enhanced security can also be obtained by using security features from companies such as Cisco, who license a form of 802.1x authentication referred to as LEAP (which stands for Light Extensible Authentication Protocol). Over time, enhanced security will evolve to the WPA security protocol and eventually to the 802.11i WLAN security standard, once the standard becomes available.

Specialized security is the highest level of security because it incorporates Virtual Private Network (VPN) technology. VPNs are constructed by using public infrastructure (the Internet) to connect to a private corporate network. The terminology used is 'VPN tunneling', which means that once the VPN application is activated only authenticated users can access the private network and the data is encrypted from the client device all the way through to the corporate server. End-to-end traffic encryption is not provided with enhanced security. To implement VPN technology the WLAN is treated as an untrusted network and installed outside of the corporate firewall, even though it is still on-campus.

The level of security that is right for a given situation depends on what is being protected. In small businesses without an IT infrastructure and home WLANs, basic security should be sufficient to deter the casual hacker. Following a regime that changes the WEP key on a periodic basis can augment basic security, as long as the number of users is manageable. Enhanced and specialized security are more applicable for the larger and middle-market customers because an IT infrastructure is required to support 802.1x authentication or VPN technology. The more secure the WLAN, the more expertise and resource required for implementation. Wireless LANs can be made very secure today. Not being able to secure a WLAN should not be justification for not implementing one, given that the need for mobility and ROI has been established. In addition to basic, enhanced and specialized security, the following suggestions are offered to further ensure the security of your WLAN:

- Choose an SSID that is not reflective of your company name or location.
- Place access points towards the center of the facility, not on the periphery.
- Monitor the immediate exterior of the buildings and parking lots for leakage of WLAN signals.
- Do periodic 'sniffs' for rogue access points.
- Use static IP instead of DHCP (if appropriate).
- Install and activate personal firewalls.
- Turn all sharing off – Internet/files/printers.

Demonstrate IBM's differentiation with ThinkVantage Technology and Design

Whether you need to connect via a modem, Ethernet, cellular data modem or WLAN at home, in the office or on the road, IBM has the solution. IBM provides differentiated value-add by getting the user connected easier, at optimal speeds and more securely. Access Connections can automatically connect the user to wired and wireless networks based on pre-configured 'profiles', taking the guesswork out of connectivity. The UltraConnect antenna coupled with an integrated 802.11a/b/g tri-mode minPCI adaptor makes it possible for users to connect to any IEEE 802.11 network seamlessly and at optimal speeds worldwide. Finally, IBM's Embedded Security Subsystem (ESS) adds an additional level of security on top of 802.1x authentication by securely storing authentication credentials. Tables 6.4–6.6 list some questions that IBM Marketing Representatives can use with customers to qualify the value of Access Connections, the UltraConnect antenna and the ESS (Dugger, 2003).

Table 6.4 Qualifying IBM Access Connection benefits

Background questions	• How many employees use their computers at home or while traveling and need to switch their network connection settings each time? • How many different connectivity settings does your average mobile worker use?
Problem questions	• What difficulties do your users/employees have managing and using multiple modes of connectivity and different communication software settings? • What challenges does your help desk face supporting your mobile users' connectivity settings?
Effect questions	• How much time do your employees spend just trying to connect to different networks in different locations? • How much time does your IT department spend answering questions and solving problems related to connectivity settings for the mobile employees? • How is your business affected when end-users have trouble accessing the network due to problems with their network settings?
Value questions	• How much more productive would your users be if they didn't have to deal with disruptions caused by difficulties in managing multiple types of network connections? • How much more time could your sales reps spend with customers if they didn't have to deal with connectivity problems? How would this translate into increased sales revenue? • How much time would your IT department save on calls for help from the end-users?

Table 6.5 Qualifying IBM UltraConnect antenna design

Background questions	• What is the typical range you have experienced with the wireless client products you are currently using or with products you are considering purchasing? • What is the furthest distance away some of your users work from an access point? • What is your service level agreement with end-users for wireless computing?
Problem questions	• What problems would your end-users face if they experienced inconsistent and poor wireless networking performance? • What challenges have you experienced trying to get the required range for your wireless client systems? • What have you disliked about other vendors' wireless solutions? • How happy would users be if they often had to move the position of their system to get a strong wireless signal? • Have you had difficulties related to the placement of the wireless antenna in a notebook, such as in the palm rest or the back of the display? What problem has this created for performance or broadcast range?
Effect questions	• How much productivity would be lost if your users had to connect to the network at significantly slower speeds due to issues with transmission distances? • How much productivity would be lost if your users had to reconnect to the network when moving around the office? • If you implemented a non-IBM wireless solution, how many more access points would you need to satisfy both coverage and performance requirements? How much more would that cost in both initial acquisition costs and ongoing support? • How would inconsistent and poor WLAN performance impact your ability to meet your service levels? • How much time has your IT department spent on wireless performance issues? • How much more frustrated would your users be with inconsistent and poor wireless networking performance? How would this affect their job performance?
Value questions	• How much further could your users roam from an access point with an IBM wireless solution and still get excellent performance? How would this impact their productivity and morale? How many fewer access points would be required? How much money would be saved in initial acquisition costs? • How much more productive would your end-users be with consistent and high-speed wireless networking performance? How would this help the IT department?

Table 6.6 Qualifying IBM's enhanced security with ESS

Background questions	• How have security concerns inhibited your deployment of wireless technology? • What features do you currently use to secure systems and data associated with your wireless networks? What do you use with your wired networks? • What authentication and other security requirements must your organization meet? • What kind of data do you need to transmit securely over a wireless network?
Problem questions	• What difficulties are you experiencing with wireless security? • What concerns do you have with the security solutions you have seen? • What problems has the need for a VPN key fob created for IT support? For your users?
Effect questions	• What would be the cost to your business if an intruder hacked into your systems or accessed your data? What would be the impact on your department? On your customers? What would be the legal implications for your company? • How much support time is wasted each month because end-users lose their key fobs? • How much productivity is lost each year because your users lose or forget their key fobs?
Value questions	• How much time would your support group save if your users didn't need to use key fobs? • How much more productive would your users be if they could avoid the hassle of dealing with lost key fobs? Would your users be happier if they didn't have to worry about key fobs? • How could you improve the way your mobile users work if you had strong wireless security? What benefits would your business realize? Can you quantify these benefits?

Summary

Since 1911, when IBM adopted 'Think' as the corporate motto, IBM has focused on quality, design and service. Looking ahead, IBM continues to develop new concepts with Think as the watchword: ideas to help people get more out of their work, and more for their money, by enabling smarter, faster thinking. IBM believes that customer needs are no longer just about their systems: What's the latest processor? Can I buy it on the web? What's the cheapest price? Rather, customers are indicating that they need help managing the costs beyond the box, as well as expertise in enabling new technologies like wireless computing. The IBM Think strategy was implemented to provide customers a better ownership experience by offering total solutions to business problems, not just separate pieces of hardware and software elements. IBM ThinkVantage Technology and Design attributes are complementary proof points of this strategy. For example, WLAN-enabled ThinkPad notebooks are the easiest to use because of Access Connections, the most secure due to the Embedded Security Subsystem and provide optimal worldwide wireless performance because of the UltraConnect antenna.

Appendix A

Exhibit 1: Wired vs. Wireless LAN Cost Calculator

This tool provides examples of possible savings or efficiencies that may be realized by implementing a wireless LAN solution. Actual customer results will vary based on many factors. IBM makes no representations or warranties concerning the accuracy of this data or its applicability to a particular customer setting.

Exhibit 2: WLAN Productivity Benefits Calculator

This tool provides examples of possible savings or efficiencies that may be realized by implementing a wireless LAN solution. Actual customer results will vary based on many factors. IBM makes no representations or warranties concerning the accuracy of this data or its applicability to a particular customer setting.

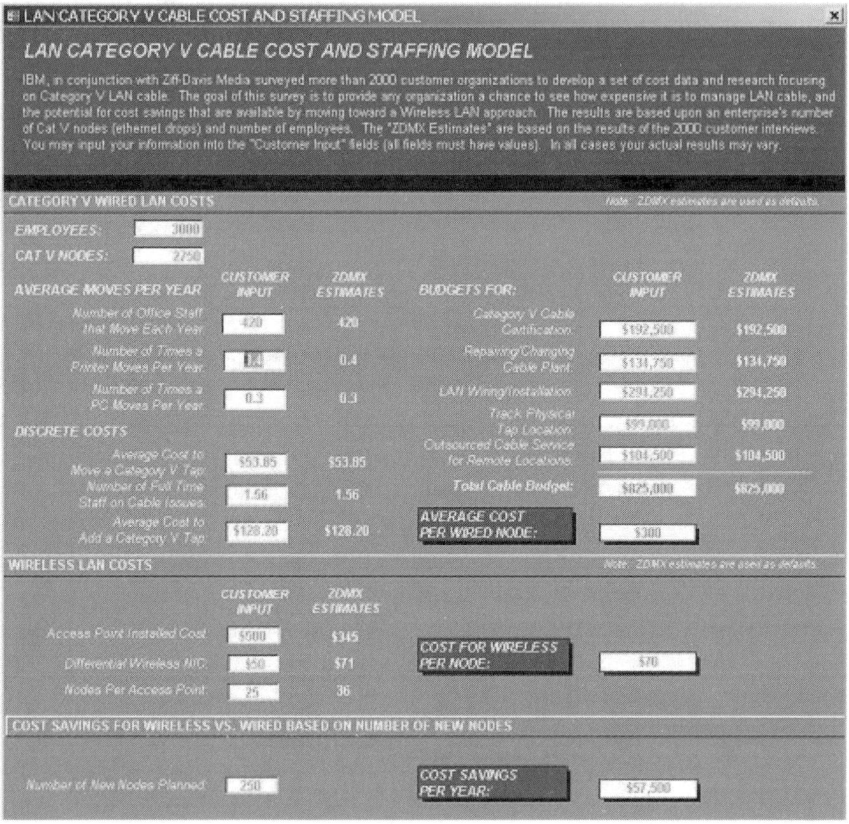

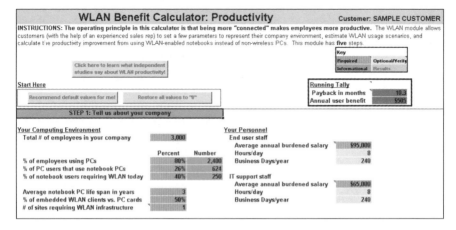

Figure 6.4

Figure 6.5

WLAN Network Cost			WLAN Network Benefit			
STEP 2: Calculate capitalized WLAN client/infrastructure costs			STEP 4: Compute productivity benefit from efficiency gains			
	Installed Cost/Unit	Quantity	Number of Employees in Scenario	250		
PC Card adapters	$250	125	The Working Environment			
Integrated WLAN notebooks	$100	125	Average burdened salary	$95,000		
			Hours/day	8		
Clients per Access Point		25	Business Days/year	240		
Access Points	$1,000	10				
				Daily	Monthly	Annually
Clients per Authentication Server		200	Average # of meetings per employee	2	40	480
Authentication Servers	$20,000	2	Average meeting duration (minutes)	60		
Other network administration/security tools	$0		Minutes employee spends in meetings	120	2,400	28,800
Network Drops	$250	10				
Power Drops	$200	10	% of "recoverable" meeting time	10%		
Site Surveys	$10,000	1	Recoverable meeting minutes / day	12		
			Recoup Factor	50%		
Estimated total cost of your IBM WLAN	$108,250		Increased efficiency gains (gross)	Per Day	Per Month	Per Year
			Benefit for one WLAN employee	$5	$99	$1,180
			Benefit for your WLAN install base	$1,237	$24,740	$296,875

Figure 6.6

STEP 3: Calculate recurring WLAN client/infrastructure expenses			STEP 5: Compute productivity benefit from increased connectivity			
Average burdened IT salary (per year)	$65,000		Daily employee time gain from using WLAN while out of primary office (minutes)	24		
Annual recurring costs	Per User	Total			Percent	Number
IT support staff and management	$1,068	$267,050				
Administration (financials and training)	$763	$190,750	Traveling employees who can benefit		50%	125
Additional hardware and software costs	$161	$40,250	from public WLAN access			
End-user operations	$916	$228,900			Per Month	Per Year
			Public WLAN subscription cost		$25	$300
Monthly recurring charges	$60,579		Company total subscription cost		$3,125	$37,500
NOTE: Recurring charges are subtracted from productivity gains to calculate total potential productivity gains			Recoup Factor	50%		
			Increased connectivity gains (gross)	Per Day	Per Month	Per Year
			Benefit average per WLAN employee	$9	$185	$2,225
			Benefit for your company	$2,318	$46,354	$556,250
			Total Productivity Benefits	Per Day	Per Month	Per Year
			WLAN benefit for one employee	$2	$42	$505
			WLAN benefit for your company	$526	$10,515	$126,175
			Estimated Payback (months)			
			10.3			

Figure 6.7

Chapter 7

From entrapment to freedom

Gary Evans

Head of Business Development, Toshiba Information Systems, UK

Little did Hisashige Tanaka or Ichisuke Fujioka, the founding fathers of what we know today as the Toshiba Corporation, as they manufactured everything from cannons to incandescent light-bulbs in the late 1800s, or Shogo Yamada, in postwar 1950s Japan, selling electric washing machines door to door, dream of the technologies that would shape the working norms of the early twenty-first century.

We live and operate in a global economy where working practices born in the Industrial Revolution are being systematically (albeit in some industries very slowly) dismantled. One only has to experience at first hand the efficiency of offshore software development to begin to appreciate the growing need to organize the incredibly flexible working hours that go with managing or participating in virtual teams spread as far apart as Brighton, Bangalore and Boston.

Mobility and flexibility, certainly in the context of the knowledge worker, are now well-worn (if not a little overused) words, hopelessly trying to convey the true meaning of making work an activity rather than a place. At Toshiba we have coined the phrase Freedom Computing to describe the application of *Information and Communication Technology* (ICT) to the mobile worker, whether highly mobile (the fabled and heroic 'road warrior') or sporadically so.

The ubiquity of the mobile phone, the commonplace notebook PC and the growing *Personal Digital Assistant* (PDA) population all point to a thirst for that 'always on' capability that can both liberate and

Figure 7.1   The T1100 – the first 'notebook'

burden at the same time. It is interesting that, with the proliferation of information delivery devices, the ability of the average user to find the on/off button has declined in equal measure (or so it would seem).

But as recently as 1984 the mobile phone was the size of a car battery and the portable computer was still on the drawing board, and the idea of people working from home raised howls of laughter in the smoking room.

In just short of 20 years, coincident with the change from industrial-age to information-age organizational structures and the resultant dispersal of people and information, we have gone from an era of knowledge-worker entrapment to one of liberation and one in which the mobile computer has progressed from a drawing-board concept toy to a two million unit[24] a year business essential?

Marketing the luggable

One thing that is certain is that, alongside the car, air travel and the Internet, mobile computing will be a major driver of fundamental change to work and play globally.

[24] UK only estimate at time of writing.

Until the advent of the 'notebook' form factor, mobile computers were, in reality, transportable desktop computers, which offered the relatively cash-rich user the ability to move his or her computer from place to place, but was trapped by the need to be physically connected to both the mains electricity supply and the cabled office network or the telephone system.

Many a happy hour was spent by road-weary professionals unscrewing the face plates off hotel room phone sockets, wielding crocodile-clip-equipped wires or fumbling with acoustic couplers to enable connection back to their office systems which were, to make life even more difficult, often remarkably unfriendly towards liaison with those upstart personal computer things which seemed to be proliferating at a remarkable pace.

Marketing the luggable was characterized by the classic early adoption strategies of:

- Evangelism.
- Education.
- Face-to-face selling to front-line business units where early return on investment was quickly achievable.
- Finding niche applications in vertical sectors (e.g. field-based engineers) easily enhanced through better mobility.
- Appealing to the 'must have' technophiles.
- Developing channels to market (retail, traditional reseller, mail order).

Even then, at the earliest points on the adoption curve, many regarded mobile (or perhaps portable) computing as a novelty.

Coupled with the additional costs associated with miniaturization and therefore the premium that had to be paid for a portable, many found it difficult to justify the added expense involved. For many IS departments, the spectre of loss of control also loomed large as corporate data could now easily walk out through the office doors. To say that there was reluctance to wholeheartedly embrace the mobile revolution would be a gross understatement, but armed with the knowledge that increasing mobility has a profoundly positive effect on an economy (whether the ability to move goods or people), and understanding that one of the most valuable commodities of the moment was information and its timely distribution, it comes as no surprise that data, its movement, delivery and application at the point of maximum benefit is key to the future health and growth of

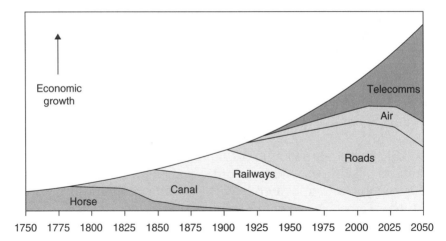

Figure 7.2 The impact of mobility on the economy: the chart shows the relative importance of communications to economic growth

the global economy. This also holds true at the micro-economic level of individuals and organizations.

The age of mobile computing was upon us – like it or not.

The world wakes up

It wasn't really until the advent of the battery-powered 'notebook' computer (1989) and, in truth, the delivery to market of the now ubiquitous A4 format notebook PC with its low-power processor, tightly integrated electronics and high-performance color displays (1991/2), that the world really woke up to the potential of truly mobile computing and the freedom to enhance productivity and even change working practices. Toshiba had a significant advantage at that time as it owned most of the specialist technology needed to manufacture the high-performance electronics suitable to be packed into the excruciatingly tight confines of the A4 footprint of the note-book PC. A good example was Toshiba's work in collaboration with Intel to develop the thermally efficient tab bonding technique that enabled the Pentium processor to be implemented in a low-profile portable platform.

Being a vertically integrated manufacturer helped a great deal because it allowed Toshiba to take a leading role in mobile computing

Table 7.1 Significant 'firsts' in Toshiba's portable PC manufacturing history

1986	First mobile PC with 286 processor
1988	First mobile PC with 386 processor
	First mobile PC with Power Management
	First mobile PC with Auto Resume
1989	First mobile battery-powered PC with 386 processor
	First mobile PC with TFT screen
	First mobile PC with 486 processor
1992	First notebook with TFT screen
1993	First notebook with lithium-ion batteries
1996	First notebook with full PCI docking
2000	World's highest resolution 10.4-inch TFT screen
2001	World's highest capacity HDD (1.8 inch/10 Gb)

development, and not only derive healthy sales revenues from selling componentry to other PC manufacturers, but also to design and market its own highly successful range of portable PCs. Table 7.1 shows some of the more significant 'firsts' in Toshiba's portable PC manufacturing history.

The significance of this is that at a time when the personal computer was displacing the thin client infrastructure inside large organizations and bringing computing power to the masses, technology was great for the marketeers to focus on. It was still possible to gain market advantage through the speedy introduction of latest and greatest whizzy technology. I still remember the halcyon days where six-month windows of opportunity were possible. Technology leadership and a reputation for superb quality invariably put Toshiba at the top of the worldwide rankings. Today, in direct contrast, we see the introduction of new technology in the personal computer space virtually simultaneously by all vendors and one of the main battlefields is price. Price erosion on the scale witnessed by the PC industry (in the region of 26 percent in the 18 months leading up to the end of 2002 and with no sign of slackening), whilst welcome news to the consumer and corporate buyer, leaves the marketeer having to be highly creative to find advantage in such an aggressive marketplace.

So, where have we got to? In the mid 1990s, portable PC performance was closing the gap on desktop technology which, up to this point, was usually a couple of generations ahead in terms of processor and hard disk technology. The timeline, to put this all into perspective, is shown in Figure 7.3.

Year	1985	1990	1995	1997	2000	2003
Form factor	Luggable	Notebook	Notebook	Ultra	Ultra	Slim/Tablet
Processor	386DX	386SX	Pentium	Pentium II	Pentium III	Centrino
Storage	Floppies	40 MB	340 MB	6 GB	20 GB	120 GB
Screen	G&W/Plasma	CSTN	SVGA TFT	XGA TFT	Poly TFT	UXGA TFT
Size	9.5"	9.5"	10.4"	14.1"	15"	17"
O/S	DOS 3.1	Win 3.0	Win 95	Win98/NT4	Win 2K	XP/Tablet
Optical	None	FDD	CD-ROM	DVD	CD-RW	DVD-Multi
Battery	Mains	NiCad	NiMH	Li-Ion	4 Hour	All-Day
Comms	1200 Baud	14.4K	28.8K	56K/ISDN	56K/ISDN	ADSL
Connectivity	Nothing	Proprietary	PC Card	PC Card	Int Ethernet	WiFi
Entrapment		Restriction		Liberation		Freedom

Figure 7.3   Portable PC performance timeline

Channels to success

For Toshiba, marketing effort was channeled into helping the user make sense of technology and its application plus a great deal of more generic brand building. How though do you excite people with lumps of electronics? There was always an element of sexiness about the notebook PC and interestingly most users were incredibly attached to their machines, so it was important to play to this. To support the marketing of this 'subversive' technology, a radically different advertising approach was taken, characterized by images of recognizable technology but given an interesting twist. Known within Toshiba as PSWAT (Pack Shot With A Twist), this campaign served to build brand image as well as sell the technology.

A good example is the introduction of optical drives (CD-ROMs) into the notebook form factor; this meant greater adaptability, greater utility and greater flexibility – hence the image of the lump of clay being moulded into a computer to suggest that the machine could be many things to many people (everything from a business machine to an entertainment center).

Users had to be able to relate a rapidly evolving technology to their everyday lives if we were to stand any chance of persuading the buying public that the mobile PC was everything a desktop PC could be and more. Much more.

All the advertisements of the day were geared around particular aspects of the technology (size, speed, weight, flexibility, storage capacity, connectivity) or highlighting the wide range of products available – something to suit every pocket and every mobile computing need whether simple or complex.

But what of place? Toshiba decided early on that a strong reseller channel was vital to long-term success. Unlike its competitors, however, Toshiba chose not to work through the large IT distributors but directly with the resellers themselves. Moving to a two-tier channel model did not happen until much later. This meant several things. Firstly, it could gain access to large customer bases and technical expertise that would have otherwise taken many years and a high level of investment to build. Secondly, it meant that channel diversity could minimize risk through balancing the mail-order operators against the large corporate resellers and the smaller value-added resellers. Thirdly, the reseller channel quickly provided, in quantity, comprehensive service and support capabilities. It also meant being better able to fine-tune channel programs and incentive schemes to suit the route to market.

Channel programs were focused on reward for technical expertise, quality of operations and measurable customer service excellence (the adoption of EN ISO 9000 by the industry was also in full swing at this time). Even in the early days it was recognized that one key factor to the success of the mobile platform was the ability of the portable PC to behave like a fully networked PC whilst away from base. One of the key focuses as a result was connectivity and, in the

Figure 7.4

early years of mobile computing, a great deal of effort went into recruiting value-added resellers (VARs) with the capability to make mobile PCs communicate with the back-office systems of the day – more often than not demanding expertise in 3270 and 5250 (IBM mini- and mainframe emulation) connectivity.

The link to Customer Relationship Management (CRM)

One of the largest determinants in the steady growth of mobile computing has been the corresponding growth in the philosophies and science that underpin CRM. It is therefore worth digressing briefly to examine the development of CRM in the context of increasing mobility.

In the late 1950s, the now all pervasive 80/20 (the vital few and trivial many principle) rule became widely accepted and it was realized that not all customers represent equal value in a sales and marketing sense. It wasn't until the 1980s that organizations actually began to address the challenge this presents when dealing with thousands (or even millions) of customers across many products and channels to market.

It was the boom economic conditions in the late 1990s that provided the right environment in terms of business thought leadership, technology, financing, increased competition, both local and global, and to a great degree, customer expectations that led many organizations to examine how to best 'touch' their customers.

This obviously demands investment in the technologies that allow for and facilitate integration of back-office systems such as MRP, ERP, Web, Call Center, Customer Services, Marketing and Sales, for without a holistic view of all the interactions an organization has with its suppliers, customers and stakeholders there is no possibility of knowing what effect any action has on the fragile customer relationship.

CRM systems for office-based workers have been around for the last 10 years (think of Tom Siebel's success), but the practical technology that would truly extend the power of a good solid CRM strategy to the 'road warrior' has only just become available.

Sure, we have been able to gather data out in the field for many years – even if only via paper form-based systems (I cringe when

I remember the reams of triplicate forms I used to fill in as a sales representative in my early days in sales), but when translated over to computer-based systems most organizations have had to make do with electronic variants of their paper forms. Add to this the need to plug in to a phone socket (rarely available at a motorway service area) or attempt to use a GSM phone to replicate data with the back-office and most remote users' experience of late twentieth, early twenty-first century CRM has been fraught with frustration.

We all know about, and have no doubt experienced at first hand, the rise of the call center, the endless questionnaires, surveys, focus groups, mail shots, door drops, magazine and newspaper inserts, website banner advertisements and e-shots over the same period. These have, and continue to be, great ways of getting messages out and customer or prospect information back. Where face-to-face selling is an integral and important part of the sales and marketing mix, the need for up-to-date or even real-time customer information at the point of sale plus the need for the salespeople to differentiate themselves in the face of escalating and increasingly sophisticated competition meant a corresponding rise in the use of technology at the 'coalface'.

Whilst IT plays a huge role in CRM, it is globally acknowledged that CRM has to be an all-pervasive philosophy that underpins an organization's quest to extract the greatest value from all its customers over the whole customer life cycle (however long or short that might be) if the promised returns are to be realized. It is equally true that poorly executed CRM systems, especially when evaluated from the field operative's perspective, even if attached to the greatest CRM strategy, usually sound the death bell for CRM initiatives the world over.

More than anything, any CRM system delivered into the field has to enhance the selling process and not hinder it. Salespeople are notoriously unforgiving when it comes to abandoning poor sales tools, techniques and methodologies. Most good salespeople will try anything that has the potential to help them achieve their targets but the converse is also true, except the time to abandonment is shorter.

The principles of CRM, and therefore the need for robust supporting systems, can equally well be applied to healthcare, emergency services, law enforcement and education as to the commercial space. Arguably, the need to deliver the benefits of an integrated back-office is even greater in many public services, where the lives of individuals could be at stake as opposed to the possibility of a lost sale (something even a salesperson will get over in time).

The possibilities are endless, but the basic need is the same, i.e. the ability to get the best view of the 'customer' (customer, student, casualty, patient, etc.) at the point at which it is most useful or valuable. That point will be where all the accumulated knowledge and information about the customer or prospect has been transferred, allowing the individual on the spot to make the right decisions to secure the best outcome. This capability is truly empowering, and combined with properly delegated authority, allows organizations to become highly flexible and capable of dealing with the client or customer in a personally tailored way. A corollary of this is the ability to differentiate oneself against the competition in as many different ways as there are clients or customers and therefore to retain customers better.

To achieve this, a number of ingredients have to be present and mixed in the right quantities:

- A CRM philosophy supported and evangelized from the top.
- Good integrated back-office systems.
- Widely available fast, high-speed, secure, low-cost wireless communications.
- Robust middleware.
- Easy-to-use, lightweight devices that work away from fixed power sources and are suitable for the situation.

A long time coming

The transition from entrapment to freedom has largely been a technological one, i.e. incremental improvement in processing power, storage capacity, screen quality, reliability, form factors, portability and plummeting costs, combined with the ubiquity of mobile voice communications.

The ability to move large amounts of data using the same wireless public networks has been a long time coming. Mobile phones have been around since the early 1980s and voice communication has developed apace. Unfortunately for the heroic road warrior, the ability to send and receive data across the network reliably and cheaply has up until now been something of a pipedream.

What GSM (or second-generation mobile communications) did for voice, 3G will do for data. The interim GPRS service (cumbersomely known as 2.5G) goes part way to achieving decent data rates and a degree of robustness.

Concurrently, and in some ways we have the inability of the USA to decide on a continent-wide standard to thank, a wireless networking standard called IEEE 802.11 has gathered momentum at a phenomenal rate. From the ratification of the 802.11b standard in 1999, there are now estimated to be approximately 9000 public access points to the world's communications networks and thousands of community public access projects that, when combined with IP-based telephony, present the network operators with a growing challenge. No longer are wireless communications, wireless access to the Internet and wireless access to private networks the preserve of the major network operators. There is, in the best possible way, a subversive, revolutionary alternative and certainly where the network operators deem it uneconomical to extend their services into remote areas, WiFi, even if linked by satellite, is an extremely viable option.

There is an unprecedented thirst to be plugged in. Whether that means plugged in to a network of personal contacts, the Internet, the office or customers, suppliers and anyone else who might be useful, it quickly becomes apparent that a key element in the slating of this thirst is mobile computing.

Putting aside a brief foray into the world of the desk-bound PC, Toshiba has always been a mobile computing specialist and well positioned to take advantage of the ever-changing wireless landscape.

Recognizing the benefits

A founder member of the Bluetooth SIG (Special Interest Group), Toshiba saw the benefits of cable-cutting technologies for PAN (Personal Area Networking) at an early stage, but it was the widespread adoption of the WiFi (IEEE 802.11b) standard across many geographies that led to low-cost wireless public access becoming a reality and truly ubiquitous in many places. A recent survey showed around 8000 public access WiFi hotspots in Manhattan alone.

Today, around 50 percent of all the notebooks (many of them Intel Centrino® based) and PDAs that Toshiba sells have wireless communications, either 802.11 or Bluetooth, built in as standard or easily upgradeable via low-cost, add-on hardware. In addition, Toshiba also manufactures a range of wireless enabled servers (both Linux and Microsoft based) and wireless devices like WiFi cards, Wireless Routers and Access Points.

We have the technology (apologies to the Six Million Dollar Man), but technology *per se* has become something of a 'so what'. For a manufacturer this is bad news, but not surprising you might say when one of the biggest technology user groups are children and teenagers, who are not at all concerned with *how* things happen but more with how the application of technology impacts upon their lives – just think of SMS and the rapid rise of the ringtone business (estimated to be bigger than the CD single business by the end of 2004). In this environment, Toshiba needed to find ways of further encouraging the widescale adoption of mobile ICT and so, in March 2003, Toshiba America Information Systems (based in Irvine, California) launched a WiFi hotspot program (SurfHere™) designed from the ground up as a low-cost-of-entry, low-cost-of-usage public access offering.

Uniquely, at the time of launch, this offered ongoing revenue earning potential for both hotspot operators and the location owner and, as such, was an excellent channel proposition which gave the reseller community a reason to go to their customers with something more than just another faster, prettier, lighter PC.

The UK public access WiFi landscape featured everything from free shared community access through to sophisticated offerings from players like BT Openzone, The Cloud and Swisscom Eurospot, to name but three. However, whilst some were expensive to install but offered revenue earning potential and others very low cost but with no revenue earning capability (the motivation to install being that of having another hook to keep a customer *in situ* for additional time in the hope they would purchase an incrementally greater quantity of whatever the location sold), there was a gap in the market for a low-cost installation coupled with the ability to earn revenue purely from the data traffic.

It also meant being able to extend the reseller network into the traditional telecommunications channel – a segment that had, in the main, avoided getting too involved in data, but to their cost as the IT reseller channel started muscling in on the voice business via IP telephony backed by some of the largest data networking vendors, like Cisco.

In June 2003, Toshiba Information Systems (UK) began piloting a localized version of the same solution in the UK before extending into the rest of the *Europe, Middle East and Africa* (EMEA) Region.

In support of the mobile user, services such as global on-site service and support, and all risks insurance designed to cope with the brutal lives that many mobile devices are subject to, have also had to be developed. After all, there is little point in winding up an enthusiastic user, sending them off into the wild blue yonder because they can stay connected all the time if they drop their machine or run over it and then have no way of being helped.

Full circle

In some ways we've come full circle and the marketing effort to drive wireless enhanced mobility is very similar to that which was needed in the early pioneering days of mobile PCs. The leaders and early adopters now are not, however, the large financial institutions or the field sales and service forces, but small businesses and the education sector. At the time of writing, large corporates have scaled back their investment in new technologies (the Millennium Bug scare made sure that IT spend plans are being much more heavily scrutinized and high return on investment demanded), whereas unencumbered by legacy installations and the need for high security, smaller organizations are actively looking for ways to increase their presence and agility without physically expanding. We're back to evangelizing, educating, and investing in pilot sites and projects.

The objections that need to be overcome are somewhat different to the early adoption phase of mobile computing, with security concerns now at the top of the list by a country mile. The 'war-chalking' phenomenon has exposed many poorly executed wireless networks which, in turn, has highlighted many organizations' cavalier attitude to network security generally. But that is a different story.

Adopting flexible working

An issue that few organizations have fully come to terms with is that of working practices that support the mobile worker whether truly peripatetic or ad hoc. Far-sighted organizations pay equal regard to ensuring that the practical considerations of health and safety, social support infrastructure and tailored facilities relating to the technology are not overlooked. In some ways, it would be highly advantageous if organizations (especially the HR and IS functions) assumed that all their knowledge workers were mobile – not unreasonable when current estimates suggest that 50 percent of knowledge workers are mobile to some degree or other. Working backwards from this assumption would lead to some interesting changes in working practices and business management. After all, any user regularly away from their normal place of work needs a support infrastructure quite different from a desk-bound colleague – there's little opportunity for a support engineer to 'just pop down and have it fixed in a jiffy'.

The need to address issues such as quality of life and work–life balance are as important as, and have a profound effect on, business productivity, and the great thing from a marketeer's point of view is that here is a technology that supports the growing burden of legis-lation like the EC Working Time Directive 93/104, which allows knowledge workers, given the blessing of the most senior manage-ment, to approach their working lives in radically different ways for joint benefit to both themselves and their employer. The promise of being able to work as effectively on-site as back at base is being fulfilled – at last!

Toshiba, in association with HOP Associates, a leading flexible working consultancy, published a comprehensive guide to mobility and flexible working. As part of the marketing mix this kind of activ-ity, combined with participation in seminars, round-table discus-sions and workshops on flexible working, reinforced the general messaging that was being promoted at the same time. This was all about positioning Toshiba as a champion of the mobile user from both a technology and a best working practice perspective.

Encouraging home networking is another element to achieving high volumes. Cabling in an existing house is difficult and unsightly, but easily available, low-cost wireless networking products from leading retailers means a huge improvement to IT in the home and moving away from the anti-social PC in the dining-room to the PC in the lounge, kitchen, bedroom, garden and, heaven forbid, even the WC!

From technology play to lifestyle play

So, is wireless technology something to be marketed in its own right? To those who like to roll their sleeves up and get stuck in, or for those tasked with implementing complex wireless infrastructures, yes of course. Whilst standards are still being fought over and ratified there is still confusion and here marketeers still have a role to play in ensuring that their products are positioned properly from an inter-opability and performance perspective. Like mobile phones though, where the 'wireless' element is no longer marketed, so it will be for wireless computing. For most, then, we are selling a particular work–lifestyle and the benefits of wireless technology are intimately connected with those of mobility. No one really cares (OK, the tech-nofreaks do) how a seamless and reliable 'connection' is facilitated so long as there is robust security, the range and coverage are adequate, and the system, whatever it is, is always on, easy and inexpensive to use, easy to buy, and the quality of service meets or exceeds expecta-tions. The devices themselves must have long usage life in the field, be easy to use, easily carried, and be capable of delivering services and functionality the user appreciates and values.

Marketing wireless technology as applied to information technol-ogy is changing from a technology play to a lifestyle play. The good thing is that the benefits are legion and the scope for innovative advertising promotion huge. Here are just some ideas:

- Always in touch (always on email and Instant Messaging).
- Information when you need it, where you need it (getting closer to the customer).
- Two-way. Information fed back into the system means central records updated quickly – just think of the benefits in the NHS if patient records were always up to date and instantly available wherever you happened to be.
- Productivity improvements (do it now, no need to wait until 'back in the office').
- Death of 'dead time'.
- Enhanced responsiveness.
- Independence.
- Workplace enhancement.
- Extension of online services to remote workers and populations.
- Remote monitoring capabilities (security, healthcare).
- New business opportunities (services and content delivery).
- Better work–life balance (can work just as well at home as in the office).
- Reduce stress levels.
- Better staff retention (flexible working).
- Cost savings from better utilisation of more efficient office space.
- Environmental benefits (cut car journeys).

Now you can study in the quietest place in the house.

Figure 7.5

- Possibility of fewer devices to carry (your PDA could be a phone as well as a computing device).
- Entertainment revolution in the home – low-cost way of distributing and controlling audio, video and Internet all around the house to many concurrent users.

However, the need for strong products, promoted well and delivered through the best channels (whether direct or indirect), at the right price, has never gone away. Combine the well-worn basics with communication, powerfully and effectively targeted at the potential buyer from harnessing the power of CRM and the marketeer has all the ingredients needed to sell not just wireless technology, but the difference the technology will make to almost any market segment.

Turning dreams into reality

Many of those dreams of the 1990s can now become reality, as the 'always-on' society is fast approaching. When you consider that a Bluetooth chipset is about the size of an adult thumbnail and costs around US $5, our ability to wirelessly enable and therefore inter-connect virtually any object is no pipedream.

We will, through wireless technology, soon become wholly inte-grated into the data matrix that is the Internet. We will all become 'net-entities', with the capability of being seamlessly connected (should we choose to be) to millions of other net-entities, both animate and otherwise.

Some will feel an icy chill of doom at this concept, and no doubt the most ardent civil libertarians will oppose the widespread adop-tion of ubiquitous connection, as misuse could have serious conse-quences – shades of Orwell's *1984* perhaps.

On the other side of the coin is, in information technology terms, an enabling technology that has the potential of revolutionizing the way we interact with our world (both public and private). It is enor-mously exciting and a privilege to be awake in the early morning light of such a liberating technology.

Chapter 8

Marketing wireless: a manufacturer's perspective

Nick Hunn

Managing Director, TDK Systems Europe

Most marketing professionals would claim that before you start to market a product you should have a clear understanding of what it is. Wireless is particularly challenging in that respect. It's a strangely tenuous medium. You can't see it, you can't smell it and you can't touch it. Yet marketers need to find a way to grasp hold of it if they are to persuade the public to buy wireless products.

We are now over 100 years into the history of wireless and it has spawned some major applications which have quite literally changed the world. Today, at the start of the twenty-first century, it's difficult to imagine the sheer awe which greeted the first national radio transmissions, bringing distant sounds and voices into homes around the globe. Perhaps it can be judged from the fact that the term 'wireless' grew to encompass not just the content and the hardware, but the medium of transmission as well.

More magic followed with television, which brought the moving pictures of the cinema into the living room. A grateful and credulous public took it to their hearts. In the last decade mobile telephony has also made its mark as a ubiquitous method of personal communication.

Now the electronics industry is trying to play the wireless game again, with wireless networks and cable replacements touting proprietary names such as Bluetooth, Wi-Fi, ZigBee and UWB. Whereas the first three major incarnations of wireless grew upon accepted behavioural models of cinema, gramophone and telephony, these new pretenders attempt to generate new usage models for consumers. They are also characterized by a two-fold task: first, market the concept to a fickle industry that often appears willing to jump to a new standard each day of the week, and then, once a critical momentum is achieved, market the benefit to an often sceptical consumer audience.

Some 200 years ago, Bishop Berkeley asked the question: 'If a tree falls in the forest and no one is present, does it make a sound?' Were he aware of the plethora of competing wireless standards he might ask: 'If a wireless technology is developed and no one wants it, will the marketers still make a sound?' The answer is much easier – they do. Regardless of the application or its suitability they bellow from every treetop.

If we look back at those big success stories of wireless, there is a common theme. In the case of broadcast radio and television, the services started in each country with a single monopoly player who had the time to install an infrastructure, commission the consumer equipment, develop content and then market the solution to the end-user. To this day the result is still incompatible national standards within television, where the USA and Europe have different systems. However, the application is essentially non-mobile, so the problem is limited.

A similar but slightly evolved model existed for mobile telephony and, once again, differed between continents. In Japan there was a monopoly supplier – NTT's DoCoMo subsidiary, who was able to define the service and even specify handset design. The result was a popular product that worked well and rapidly gained a large user base.

In Europe, after a number of proprietary systems, the European Commission mandated a single, digital standard – GSM. This was developed by a standards body – the European Telecoms Standards Institute (ETSI) – and then implemented by a limited number of handset and infrastructure manufacturers. The standard imposed rigorous conformance testing, and this was augmented by the mobile network operators. Once again, the user experience was fairly smooth, allowing marketing to concentrate on benefits and ensuring a rapid acceptance.

The US was the only major continent not to mandate a single standard. The consequence was an unnecessary degree of confusion for the customer, who had no desire to understand why their phone did not work across the country – they just wanted a solution. The ensuing technical rivalry diverted the industry from where it should have concentrated – on marketing a simple message to the consumer. The effect of the lack of original mandate still resonates around the US industry.

There are lessons to be learnt from these experiences. Foremost is the need to insulate the user from the technology. The second is to work together for single, global standards so that the user message is not subverted by incompatibility and interoperability fears. And the third is that, in wireless, it's not a bad thing to have a monopoly. Unfortunately, it is unlikely that the third one will ever be met again.

Over the past 20 years, there has been another change taking place within wireless. That change is sufficiently subtle to have evaded the notice of many marketers, but has immense impact for the success of a wireless marketing strategy. New wireless solutions were moving away from the dependence on infrastructure that television, radio and mobile telephony had required and were starting to put wireless in the hands of the user, with no need for infrastructure. Cordless telephones, CB radio and DECT would make the user responsible for the wireless installation and move the controlling infrastructure owners out of the picture. Wireless was getting personal.

Cordless telephones presented an interesting proposition. No new service was offered, but the user could pay for the option to cut the cable on their domestic handset. The initial products were highly proprietary – brand A would never work with brand B (in fact, different models from the same manufacturer were unlikely to work together) and the quality was poor or variable. Yet the marketing proposition was straightforward and they sold.

The ETSI standards body took a classic European view. They decided to develop a digital cordless standard which would bring wire-line quality to cordless telephony. The European Commission backed the initiative by reserving spectrum for this application, effectively freeing it from interference, and the first DECT handsets came to market. They worked well, but it became apparent that the standard allowed different manufacturers to implement it in different ways so that, once again, there was no interoperability. It may seem strange that this was a problem for a product which would typically be used by itself, but negative publicity stalled the market. The industry reacted by defining a compatibility standard – the Generic Access Protocol (GAP) – and bringing a new generation of handsets to market.

From this point, despite the higher cost, DECT handsets have steadily pushed traditional cordless telephones out of the European market. Although business was always predicted to be the key market for DECT, it has been enthusiastically adopted in the home.

DECT was the first of several clear lessons that compatibility is a key marketing requirement. Although this has been questioned as a peculiarly European consumer response, recent wireless experience with Wi-Fi shows it to be just as important in the USA.

CB radio provided another interesting wireless consumer experiment and the first of a number of unexplained wireless success stories for marketers. It was a US phenomenon which barely touched Europe, and many theories have been put forward to try and explain this. Whatever the reason, its success should have rung alarm bells amongst wireless marketeers, as its growth and usage followed an anarchic, personal subculture, rather than anything the industry had dreamt up for it. The users were taking the first steps which have led to the success of Napster and Kazaa. They demonstrated that they would use the technology as they saw fit – not as a marketing department did. This showed that, given a tool, the user may find a totally different use from the one expected.

CB took on a life of its own, even inventing a new language. With the benefit of hindsight it has much in common with the success of SMS texting – another wireless subculture that was invented by the users against the best efforts of the wireless marketing industry, whose imagination could not extend beyond notifying sports results and stock prices. In both cases the best brains in wireless marketing were simply unable to place themselves in the position of the user – typically a user with spare time on their hands but with no desire to use that time for work. The irony with SMS is that it now represents the most profitable portion of business for most network operators.

These episodes brought out some important messages that wireless marketing needed to take on board:

- It must be compatible.
- Business usage may not be relevant.
- Don't believe you know what the user really wants.

But wireless marketing was about to face an even bigger challenge as the whole development cycle of wireless changed. Up until now, wireless applications used reserved spectrum and were essentially driven by the limited number of infrastructure owners. A new generation of wireless applications were about to emerge that would compete with each other. Marketing needed to fight to pitch the technical standards against each other before the first prototypes were even constructed, let alone before they were offered to consumers.

That change started with CB radio. For the first time a wireless application had come to market which had neither been defined by an international standards body nor a monopoly infrastructure owner. It was a success and started people thinking about how else wireless could impinge on everyday life. There was just one problem – spectrum. The radio spectrum is heavily regulated and only a few regions are available for general use without a license. These regions, known as the ISM bands, were about to become a battleground. Although they are designed to be shared, vested interests began to circle like vultures awaiting the kill. Manufacturers were beginning to dream up applications but realized that, to succeed, some degree of cooperation would be necessary. It was time to look again at the concept of standards.

Wireless standards used to be developed behind closed doors by engineers. In the last 10 years that has changed. The availability of spectrum has generated a plethora of schemes to promote short-range wireless as a means of dispensing with cables. Standards groups have addressed the opportunity, new groups have been formed and an underbelly of proprietary technology continues to come to market. However, wireless imposes certain disciplines on its users. These fears, along with a need to generate a critical mass of companies to develop complex new technology, have meant that the standards makers have had to start to consider how to promote their own wireless technology above others to the manufacturers as well as the user. It is not an exercise that has come comfortably to the standards bodies. There is no doubt that the historical development model of standards bodies has been irreparably altered, with engineering thoroughness now having to compete with commercial vested interest. A comfortable, largely altruistic community has had to come to terms with some fairly unattractive commercial animals with big, sharp teeth.

The need for standards

There is a general acceptance that standards are a good thing. From a consumer viewpoint it is always advantageous if products from different manufacturers work together. Wireless has a special, almost magical, attraction in that it removes the cable that is so often either incompatible or lost. If wireless could be used to connect everything together seamlessly, then the general feeling is that it would be a good thing.

In fact, wireless needs standards far more than most other areas of technology because of the inherent limitation of spectrum. Even within technical circles, most people have a very incomplete understanding of spectrum. The PC industry has conditioned us to believe that every year things get faster and more information can be transmitted. In the wired world, the transition from copper to fiber has multiplied the capacity for transmitting data a million-fold and can be extended almost infinitely by laying more strands of glass around our planet. In contrast, wireless spectrum is bounded. It's a finite resource, which needs to be shared amongst all users in order to provide the best possible service. Where different users of the same band are likely to come into close proximity, there are potential problems of interference and, if usage is high enough, everything could grind to a halt. Spectrum does run out and we cannot manufacture more air to carry more radio waves – we have to find ways of using it more effectively.

Historically, the wireless spectrum has been controlled by governments and the military. Vast chunks of it are off limits and almost all of what is available for public use requires a license. The past few years have seen a predilection for licensing the more attractive commercial areas of spectrum as a source of revenue. The greed evidenced by the 3G debacle may yet come back to haunt those legislators who felt spectrum was the route to a quick buck. Outside these regulated areas, a few chunks of the wireless spectrum have been designated for 'free and open' public access. These are termed the ISM bands – initially put aside for Industrial, Scientific and Medical applications. There are strict controls on how they are used in terms of transmitted power and the percentage of the available spectrum which can be utilized but, unlike almost every other part of the spectrum, the purpose to which the ISM bands are put to use is not defined. That marks them apart from every other slice, such as mobile telephony, DECT, air traffic, broadcast TV and emergency services, where the type of service is rigidly defined. In contrast, the ISM bands are open for innovation. In the technical climate of the late 1990s, that meant open for exploitation. A cavalcade of proposed usage that threatened to be a new South Sea Bubble inundated the industry, taking the airwave legislators by surprise.

Although these bands were allocated many years ago, it has taken time for applications to develop. Wireless development is not an easy task. Silicon chips for wireless can take up to five years to develop and radios capable of transmitting significant quantities of data are complex and expensive. Because of this, early usage of the ISM bands was either for coarse applications such as heating (with microwave ovens a key use), or for limited throughput, such as radio-controlled toys. Outside these areas, development concentrated on solutions that could bear the cost of a high-priced radio. The prospect of new mass deployment applications paid lip service to the complexity of the task. Alliances started to come together to propose new models which would eat into the spectrum and form a new model for standards development. But behind the proposals a new fact was dawning: without an infrastructure in place it would take time to develop the technology and attain the critical mass of users for it to become accepted. It was going to be necessary to sell each competing proposal to the industry itself to ensure enough momentum to take it through to adoption.

The five steps to wireless success

A new model of wireless marketing was about to make its entrance. As it evolved, few if any of the players could predict where it would take their industries and their profitability. As the resulting products are emerging onto the market, it is becoming evident that the process has been particularly brutal and few of those involved will emerge unscathed.

In the mid 1990s a head of steam had started to build up within the wireless industry. It was apparent that advances in silicon technology could not only put the processing power necessary to run complicated protocols onto a chip at low cost, but it would soon become possible to squeeze the traditional black art of radio frequency design onto that chip as well. By the early twenty-first century it would be possible to achieve a complete wireless product cost-effectively on just a few integrated circuits. Ideas abounded – the question was which ones would gather the necessary momentum to win. While some concepts such as HomeRF fell by the wayside, others invented a new *modus operandi* to ensure their existence. The history of Bluetooth provides an excellent overview of how wireless marketing had to adapt on the fly in order to win.

Bluetooth was a late starter as a wireless technology. 802.11 was already well down the path towards completion, DECT was shipping within Europe and a hybrid, HomeRF, was being promoted within the USA as a data/voice solution for the home market. Bluetooth had some history – it was in a demonstrable state, having developed from an internal Ericsson project called MC-Link, but it needed to catch up fast if it was to stand a chance.

Bluetooth came into public existence through the actions of Intel and Ericsson. Intel had been evangelizing Bluetooth through its Mobile Data Initiative and had seen the potential of the Ericsson technology. Together, they forged a consortium of five of the most powerful players in the PC and phone industry by adding IBM, Nokia and Toshiba. Between them they took their concept to industry partners. The new marketing life cycle was about to begin.

Stage 1: Sell your idea for a standard to the people who will make it

The five founders were well aware of the task they had. They had a basic demonstration and some usage scenarios, but needed an industry to gather around them to turn the concept into a reality. They decided on a brave course of excluding all other companies from the specification process – a valid way to stop too much discussion, but had to find a way of persuading several hundred other companies to put their money and development effort behind an as yet unpublished standard. To do this, they took the bold step of announcing the initiative to the world, including the media, at a series of launches. It is difficult to underestimate how brave this was. The proponents were probably aware that real products were at least three to four years away, but the most important step was to gain more prominent industry supporters than any competing wireless technology.

To place Bluetooth onto the technical landscape, the Bluetooth SIG turned the traditional marketing approach to technology on its head. Rather than take a low-key approach within industry standards bodies, they launched Bluetooth onto the world with all the razzamatazz of a finished product. Worldwide press conferences were organized to include consumer as well as trade press to sell the usage scenarios of Bluetooth. The technical detail was limited, although it was sketched out. Instead, the emphasis was on the detailed ways in which it would touch our everyday lives. Despite the fact that there was only a partially complete standard, no compliant silicon and no software protocol stacks, aggressive time-scales were given for the general availability of Bluetooth products.

It was an audacious and unprecedented approach. An immature technology with insufficient backing to be called a standard had taken the moral high ground and managed to put established and emerging standards such as 802.11 and HomeRF on the defensive. One of the advantages Bluetooth offered was its ubiquity – unlike other wireless standards it replaced any cable, a feature which would drive the next stage of marketing, as it gave developers the opportunity to dream.

Stage 2: Recruit the foot-soldiers

However successful the pre-emptive attack, to continue the momentum and catch up Bluetooth needed foot-soldiers to turn the concept into a reality. In order to get to market in a reasonable time-scale (which would still be way beyond the initial promises), a large number of developers would be required. The ideal scenario would be to gain a critical mass of companies producing silicon chips, software and development systems to ensure mutual competition. The added advantage of producing an overheated community would be that they would provide the development funds and take the development risks. It would also allow the original promoters to get on with the detail of producing the standard. All a company needed to do to join the party was to sign an adopter's agreement – it didn't cost anything, but if you were to move forward you would need to invest in your own development.

Throughout the first six months the SIG worked hard to bring key companies on board as early adopters. Although they were to make little tangible contribution to the development of Bluetooth in this period, they provided the weight and names behind the standard that would be needed to take the next step – providing the momentum to bring new startups and venture capital on board as the driving force to accelerate Bluetooth's march to the market.

Stage 3: Invest to win the big prize

The next stage of marketing Bluetooth could not have been better timed. The technology frenzy around the Internet boom was in full swing. The five founder members were probably well aware that they did not harbor the flexibility to bring Bluetooth into existence fast enough. They needed smaller, leaner entrepreneurial companies to take the risks, burn the midnight oil, and move heaven and earth to be first to market. The question was how to attract that momentum. The answer was to offer the prospect of very big riches at the end of the rainbow.

The late 1990s saw a fascinating parasitical partnership between three sectors – bright entrepreneurs feeling stifled within larger companies, venture capitalists and market analysts. They were about to fuse together in a mutual feeding frenzy to generate a hothouse atmosphere of technical development unlike anything that had been seen before. Five years later the fallout would happen, when it became apparent that too many players were competing for the same prize, but in the early days of Bluetooth the dot.com crash was still the stuff of scary bedtime stories.

Once again the usage scenarios, initial projections and stature of the five founders of the SIG was to lend weight and credence to a dream. The story was told well and analyst after analyst began to confirm the projections that Bluetooth would be huge. By 2003 there would be over one billion Bluetooth handsets in circulation. So began a cycle of hyperbole and self-perpetuating exaggeration. Bluetooth was rapidly extended beyond its initial role of expediting phone and PC convergence into a panacea for every wireless problem. Fertile minds dreamt up Bluetooth toys, Bluetooth tyre pressure sensors and that ultimate folly – the Bluetooth-enabled Internet fridge.

Nobody questioned the dream. Startups were formed, which persuaded the analysts to increase their market projections. That, in turn, convinced more venture capitalists to invest in the hope of a fast return and more startups to emerge to satisfy the demand to throw money away, confident that each would have the unique selling angle which would lead them to an early IPO and untold wealth. At this point, some warning bells started to ring within the circus. When it became apparent that over 30 companies were developing silicon, it was obvious that many were setting themselves up to be casualties – no other wireless product area (including mobile phones and TV) supported more than four or five. But still the fervour continued unabated and the funding continued to flow.

Stage 4: Where are the products?

So far the new wireless marketing scheme had succeeded – the SIG had boosted the awareness of Bluetooth to a level unprecedented for this stage of any technology development. Over 2000 companies had signed up, tens of thousands of engineers had been harnessed to bring all aspects of Bluetooth to fruition and well over $2 billion of private and venture capital had been committed. Whereas Bluetooth could easily have been steamrollered by the earlier competing wireless technologies, not only had it made its mark, but it had destroyed HomeRF and caused serious (albeit unfounded) concerns within the 802.11 community.

Early in 2001, the first problems with this new marketing strategy started to surface. Bluetooth had made immense progress by selling a story to the general media. By Christmas 2000, the patience of the media had begun to evaporate. The question 'Where are the products?' started to be publicly asked. Unfortunately, the few nascent products were distinctly shaky in performance and interoperability. An ill-judged attempt to promote Bluetooth by distributing prototype access points throughout an exhibition hall at the major CeBit exhibition ended in disarray and started a period of intense negative coverage.

Timing did not help. The technology bubble had begun to burst and media coverage turned from euphoria to cynicism. The key promoters were late with products and under pressure to cut their marketing budgets. At the point when Bluetooth needed most support the money had started to run out. It was left to a few companies and individuals to promote the technology to the media. For 12 months the SIG was largely silent. They were relying on cash from the approval process to fund themselves. A lack of products meant a lack of revenue and no marketing budget. Bluetooth made its commercial debut in the marketplace with the quietest of whimpers.

Stage 5: What is it?

During 2002, Bluetooth started to appear in a significant number of mobile phones. By the end of the year we estimate that over

20 million handsets contained Bluetooth, yet few of their owners were aware of it. In 2003, that number will grow to a total of around 75 million, yet it is still unclear how widely used Bluetooth will be. Other chapters of this book take a more detailed look at the state of marketing today but, after the success of marketing itself into existence, Bluetooth has hit a problem of marketing itself as a solution. It suffers from the problem of being too universal a panacea. Television could market itself as pictures, mobile telephony as voice. The ability of Bluetooth to do so much has posed its biggest challenge – how can it market itself? The story is still unfolding. The number of new Bluetooth handsets suggests it will be the second highest wireless solution shipping, surpassed only by GSM. However, it has to find out what to shout about.

An important aspect to grasp about Bluetooth is the distributed nature of the products. As so many different products contain the technology, a final solution will often be a combination of products from more than one vendor. The most typical example is that of a mobile phone connecting to a PC. The user will buy these from different manufacturers and often from different shops. To further complicate the process, the solution they may want, such as remote email or Internet access, requires service provision from a third party – a network operator.

This poses a marketing nightmare. Any one of the three suppliers who wants to promote Bluetooth must put effort into an offering which sells other vendors' products. There is typically no one supplier who owns both ends of a Bluetooth link. Even worse, the companies involved often fail to understand each other's usage models. The inevitable result is that Bluetooth is marketed only as a 'tick box' feature and not an end-to-end solution. The ideal answer would be for the Bluetooth SIG to put money into selling the overall solutions proposition to the customer, but so far that has not happened. Instead, holistic marketing of Bluetooth has been limited to a few technology suppliers and some adventurous High Street retailers.

The end-to-end wireless experience

In contrast, its companion 802.11 has had a very different marketing history. 802.11b should have had a very straightforward task. Like Bluetooth, 802.11b is a cable replacement technology, but the proposition is markedly different as it only replaces a single cable – the wired Ethernet connection. To make it even easier, most vendors supply both ends of the wireless link – adaptors for the PC and access points – giving them the advantage of being able to promote a complete solution. Unfortunately, the path of true marketing rarely runs smoothly and 802.11b has done its best to throw away its inherent advantages.

The gestation of 802.11b was markedly different to Bluetooth's. It grew from a standards-based background in the IEEE over a course of six or seven years. Over the specification period only a few silicon vendors were involved and there was little public exposure of the progress of the standard. The standard was completed and approved and the first products launched into the market by established PC networking companies who offered a complete wireless experience.

As products started to emerge the first problems appeared. Products from different manufacturers were incompatible, casting doubt on the validity of the standard. User reaction was to abandon the technology and wait for this to be fixed.

The underlying cause of the problem was a fundamental difference between computing standards and telecoms standards. The computing industry has a somewhat cavalier approach to inter-operability of 'let the best man win'. PC standards rarely encompass any requirement to meet minimum standards of compatibility and the 802.11b standard was no different in this respect. In contrast, telecoms standards mandate rigorous testing and interoperability. (One can argue that these diverse approaches are symptomatic of the two markets. The PC industry's prime motivation is to ship essentially incomplete products to a user who will then spend more money on add-in boards, software and updates to make it work, so there's little incentive to solve the problem of producing a perfect device. In contrast, the telecoms hardware suppliers sell equipment whose fundamental purpose is to provide a source of ongoing revenue for network operators and that will only happen if their products work out of the box first time every time.)

The 802.11b suppliers eventually realized their problem and belatedly set up an independent test and qualification body called WECA, which specified a baseline level of interoperability for which a product could gain a 'Wi-Fi' logo that would 'guarantee' compatibility between products from different manufacturers. Around this, WECA and the individual manufacturers started a marketing campaign to promote the benefits of Wi-Fi. Adoption started in the business community and everything should have been in place for rapid deployment and success.

With everyone finally singing from the same song sheet, a cruel diversion appeared. 802.11b had built in a basic level of security to stop unauthorized intrusion. A few academics managed to find ways of cracking this and the press seized on the story that Wi-Fi was insecure. A concerted marketing response should have ensured that this was no more than a temporary aberration. Either WECA or the IEEE should have made the point that this was of purely academic interest only, as security should take place at a higher level, since every physical connection is intrinsically insecure. Instead, they denied it. Finally, it was admitted and a new scheme proposed, which was just as promptly hacked. From a point of inter-operability, individual vendors started to break ranks and promote their own, proprietary security enhancements. The coordinated face of WECA shattered into a thousand pieces. It was manna to the press. They shouted the story of compromised wireless security from the rooftops until every executive in every boardroom became aware that wireless was insecure. (As with all mud being thrown, the episode managed to blacken other wireless technologies.) To this day, business customers have still not forgiven WECA and moved forward to embrace wireless LAN – the target audience has stayed away. Instead, it has been the domestic customer that has provided the growth in Wi-Fi sales.

Both experiences provide cautionary tales. Wireless is tenuous and provides numerous pitfalls. In many ways both Bluetooth and Wi-Fi have been failed by the marketing expertise of their umbrella organizations – Bluetooth in failing to take up the banner and pro-mote an essentially disparate collection of enabled products as a valuable solution, and WECA in failing to have the honesty and humility to tell its customers the truth. Both cases highlight the dif-ficulty of trying to promote a wireless technology by relying on the individual companies selling the products. Glancing back once again to the success of mobile phones or television, they succeeded because of a unified message from what was initially a monopoly supplier. Without that single voice, commercial attempts at differen-tiation and competitor knocking will easily turn the user benefit into confusion and incompatibility.

The conclusion is that wireless marketing needs strong central voices to explain the usage models and interoperability. Most impor-tantly, wireless marketing needs to forget the technology and explain the benefit. Few people can explain why the room gets brighter when they flick the light switch, but we all understand the benefit. Wireless marketers must forget frequency hopping and WEP, spread spectrum and piconets, and focus on the user advantage.

The last five years of wireless has taught us many lessons. It has generated a completely new model of marketing, which targets developers to fast-track products – a technique which is already being used or abused by Ultra Wide Band and ZigBee, but it has still to succeed in finding a marketing model which manages to sell these non-infrastructure wireless solutions to an end-user. It's a period of rapid evolution for wireless marketing. The other authors give a fascinating insight into some of the ideas and opportunities. For the time being my crystal ball remains firmly wired.

Chapter 9

Mobilian marketing: using all available channels for marketing influence and intelligence

Wade Gillham

Marketing Director, Mobilian Corporation

The Mobilian Corporation is a wireless silicon and systems company that designs and develops analog integrated circuits, digital integrated circuits, and host and embedded software for standards-based wireless communications. The first product in the company's evolution, and the subject of the following chapter, is TrueRadio™, a two-chip chipset that enables simultaneous operation of Wi-Fi (802.11b or WLAN) and Bluetooth short-range wireless protocols.

Wireless standards background

The IEEE 802.11b Wireless Local Area Networking (WLAN) standard has experienced a whirlwind of success from late 1999 to 2003 and onward. Over the course of three years, industry experts modified their WLAN forecasts from expectations of 14–16 million units by e.o.y. 2005, to expectations of up to 90 million units by e.o.y. 2005. The IEEE 802.11b WLAN standard started the revolution, but since early 2002, it is now complemented by higher speed, more feature-rich WLAN standards, including 802.11g and 802.11a. All these standards together are collectively known as Wi-Fi, a marketing brand certifying interoperability and managed by an independent body of industry participants, the Wi-Fi Alliance. IEEE 802.11b and 802.11g currently dominate the market in volumes and both operate in the same unlicensed worldwide spectrum at 2.4 GHz.

Bluetooth is a complementary standard to Wi-Fi. It has a range of about 10 meters and a data rate approaching 1 Mbps. Wi-Fi has a range of about 100 meters and a data rate of 11 Mbps. And while Bluetooth's market is currently less popular than Wi-Fi's with the media, it still ships in the tens of millions of units per year in devices ranging from cars to cellphones. Like 2.4 GHz Wi-Fi, Bluetooth operates in the unlicensed 2.4 GHz spectrum.

To further explain the differences, and as introduced in Chapter 2, Wi-Fi is typically used as a wireless networking protocol, implying that many clients or remote nodes can be associated to a single access point,[25] and is able to transmit as much as 300 feet in all directions. Bluetooth is more of a cable replacement technology and not a classical networking standard. It operates over relatively short distances – about 30 feet maximum – in a master-to-slave topology, wherein slaves or clients do not transmit unless they are asked to do so by the master. The master is defined by the capabilities of the participating devices, and can be many things other than a classical AP. For example, a cellphone can be both a master in a phone-to-headset configuration and a slave in a laptop-to-cellphone configuration. Conversely, Wi-Fi is based on Ethernet, the basis for many of today's highly complex wired business and metropolitan networks, and operates according to Ethernet's sophisticated networking protocol, allowing the scheme by which devices access the network to govern the network traffic and facilitate efficient communication. Therefore, a platform such as a personal computer (PC) or hand-held (PDA) could benefit from both types of wireless technology, and in many cases would rely on both through combination cards.

---

[25] An access point (AP) is the network hardware where the wired network joins the wireless network. The AP typically has more functionality than the clients and can support an unlimited number of clients in Ethernet theory. In practice, the ratio of clients to AP is about 15:1.

The catch here is that the dominant Wi-Fi standards operate in the same unlicensed 2.4GHz spectrum as Bluetooth. While the two standards are complementary in feature and function, they tend to conflict with one another if they are in the same platform, which is exactly where they need to be.[26]

Product definition – customer driven

Mobilian's founders saw the paradox of Wi-Fi and Bluetooth in early 1999, and came up with an hypothesis that there was an opportunity to create a combination chipset to accommodate both standards in a small form factor, allowing them to operate simultaneously without degradation on each other. This is the premise upon which the company was truly founded and funded. The idea was good. The venture community loved it, but we had no customer validation of whether there would be a market.

It is classic marketing to define a product based on market research, previous products, in-house skill sets, etc. Our approach was to carry out the market research background via traditional channels and the VC community, but since we had no previous products and our skill set was really yet to be defined based on the talent we would hire, we validated our product idea with our customers' customers, the PC vendors. As shown in Figure 9.1, Mobilian would largely sell to Taiwanese network interface card (NIC) manufacturers, who would in turn sell NICs with our chips and features to PC vendors.

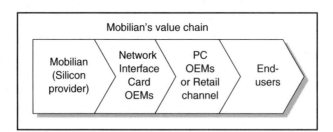

Figure 9.1   Mobilian's value chain

---

[26] More information on the potential interference between 2.4GHz Wi-Fi and Bluetooth can be found in the white paper section of Mobilian's website at http://www.mobilian.com.

By presenting our understanding of the market requirements to our customers' customers, we were able to refine our value proposition and feature set based on direct 'end-customer' feedback very early in the product development phase. We presented the TrueRadio product concept to a majority of the leading PC vendors, and continued to make every effort to show them progress throughout the development project. As a result, we incrementally changed the product's features and target pricing along with our corresponding cost targets, and our target time to market.

Also, we identified that our product offered more than interference-free Wi-Fi and Bluetooth wireless connectivity. It offered a completely incremental value derived from cost avoidance. Because it removed the majority of interference that could occur between Wi-Fi and Bluetooth, it offered insurance to the PC vendors against costly technical support calls resulting from frustrated users. According to a 1999 benchmarking study for a large PC vendor, a typical tech support call could cost as much as $80. Given that margins on wireless cards at the time were around $40–50, it is easy to see that one technical support call could erase the margin from two card sales. Since then, the prices and margins on wireless cards have come down substantially, further validating the point. Likewise, it offered insurance to the PC vendors' Enterprise customers against costly in-house technical support.

Another aspect of Mobilian's cost avoidance resulted from TrueRadio's high level of integration and corresponding single form factor card and only one antenna. This removed the additional cost of designing communication subsystems for both Wi-Fi and Bluetooth in the platform. We played to this finding extensively, producing application notes addressing relevant subjects on how to build wireless into PCs and PDAs, required antenna isolation, etc. These provided meaningful information to our target platform customers and consequently they heavily downloaded and distributed them from our website. These papers allowed Mobilian to influence our target platform customers' development efforts in designing and building platforms that would come to market at the same time as our product.

By taking the time to canvass our customers' customers with our product idea, we not only identified incremental features to make the product more attractive, but also whole new categories of value that made selling our product an easier proposition.

Also, by raising awareness of the pending product with our customers' customers, we created industry 'pull'. Since our customers'

customers knew of our product and its benefits, they asked our customers about it, or at least served as a positive reference point if our customers wanted market validation of the need for our product. As a startup, it is extremely powerful to visit a customer with a multibillion dollar client of theirs, and say: 'This client of yours would like to see our product in your solution.'

Finally, this work also assisted Mobilian in securing funding, since the market itself was a testament to the potential value of our current and next generation products.

Industry standards bodies – influencing our destiny

Once we had defined the product and received customer confirmation of its value, we set about the task of developing it. There were many obstacles along the way, and Mobilian made every effort to manage those from a business perspective, prior to impacting our engineering team with change orders. One type of potential obstacle the business team proactively managed resulted from evolving industry standards.

There are two types of standards bodies in the short-range wireless industry: technical standards bodies, such as the IEEE and the Bluetooth Special Interest Group (SIG); and their respective marketing counterparts, such as the Wi-Fi Alliance and the Bluetooth SIG, Incorporated. Mobilian participates with each type of standards body for the benefits each can gain the company.

Technical standards bodies

The technical standards bodies typically govern the behaviours and specifications of short-range wireless radios in unlicensed frequencies worldwide. In the USA, the IEEE and FCC play this role. There are several different bodies abroad with similar functions for the EU, Japan and other regions.

The standards bodies typically determine and dictate the behaviour of the radios that operate in the spectrum they are responsible for.

While on the surface this may appear straightforward, in reality it is a highly complex and complicated network of individuals working together and trading political favors to arrive at company-driven agendas. The standards bodies are comprised of working groups that focus on separate functionalities of the radios. For example, in the IEEE, there are groups focused on higher speed standards than 802.11b called 802.11g and 802.11a. There are also groups focused on enhanced security, international regulatory compliance and a host of other features. All these groups can potentially affect a product's development by changing technical specifications that impact upon the product's design.

Mobilian hired a long-time member of the standards community as VP of Business Development, and invested heavily in the standards bodies' activities through participation on relevant working groups, and if possible, through officer positions in those groups. By so doing, we were able to insulate ourselves from changes that other companies had to undergo, negatively affecting their development timelines.

Participation in the standards bodies also allowed Mobilian to maintain customer relationships and competitive intelligence, as a majority of industry participants were also involved. It became a secondary channel for business development with many networking opportunities. From a competitive intelligence point of view, Mobilian was able to not only occasionally influence groups' activities negatively toward our competitors' products, but also gain valuable insight into their strategies.

Marketing standards bodies

Mobilian also invested heavily in the marketing bodies. While this did not have the immediate technical benefits of the IEEE or Bluetooth specification bodies, it did provide a good amount of market intelligence and goodwill. Another result of being involved here was the ability to use the standards bodies' conference activities to our advantage by leveraging our involvement into speaking slots, presentations, participation in floor pavilions, etc. Of course, Mobilian employees who participated on the marketing standards bodies contributed to their activities heavily, influencing the marketing messaging of those bodies toward our objectives. It must be clearly pointed out that our objectives were largely in alignment with the 'good of the market', otherwise we would not have been as successful in leveraging the marketing bodies to our benefit.

We continue to reap good returns with our standards and marketing bodies involvement, as our VP of Business Development is now on the IEEE steering committee, and therefore holds veto power over any working group's activities. This becomes extremely important when pushing for political favors in other areas.

Market priming – fear, uncertainty and doubt

When Mobilian began marketing the TrueRadio solution, the short-range wireless market was in its infancy. There were many unknowns about how the standards would eventually shake out, interoperate and coexist with one another. The main area Mobilian concerned itself with was coexistence of 802.11b and Bluetooth. As we mentioned previously, the two standards are highly complementary, but when located in close proximity, as in a combination card or platform, they can interfere with one another. The degree of interference in a real-world usage model is something that even today remains unquantified. But at the early stage in the market's development when Mobilian began to market itself, the interference was something terrible and unknown. We played on this fear, uncertainty and doubt (FUD) to our great advantage.

Creating a messaging strategy

The foundation of Mobilian's marketing was a sound and cohesive messaging strategy. Everything we put into the public domain supported our messaging in one way or another. It was based on classic marketing. First, we established a serious and growing need – interference between Wi-Fi and Bluetooth. Second, when possible, we demonstrated the need in a real-world, relevant example. And third, we provided an outstanding solution to address the need.

This may seem elementary, but it is a fundamental concept that many, many companies fail to execute upon. They may have a messaging strategy, but adherence may not be good. Or they may have never taken the time to figure out how their product should be positioned according to a messaging strategy, and therefore their messaging is relatively unfocused. Mobilian worked very hard to focus on our message in most of our marketing activities. You will notice it throughout the different aspects of our marketing campaign, as discussed in the following paragraphs.

Product demonstrations

With any technical product, demonstration of forward progress is something engineers must count upon and build into their development schedules. With this in mind, Mobilian's first product demonstration at the COMDEX technology conference in November of 2000 was also our 'coming out of stealth mode' launch. We demonstrated our chip technology running in code on an FPGA[27] and the problem it solved to over thirty potential investors and customers. The response was impressive. Soon after, we closed a round of funding at a high valuation and signed multiple letters of intent with customers around the world, including leading-name PC vendors.

What we showed was the crucial element in these early successes. Basically, we showed the combination set-up and resulting interference without our solution, which was severe. Then, with literally the flick of a toggle switch, we engaged Mobilian's TrueRadio technology, and like magic, the interference disappeared. Then came the PowerPoint, whetting our customers' appetites and helping to prime the market for our upcoming launch.

Following this first demonstration, our engineering resources fell back into the process of bringing the TrueRadio to market on time. Along the way, as customers and investors would visit the Mobilian sites, we would demonstrate the latest progress in our development work. Today, as the product is nearing completion, there are many prototype cards in the labs that customers can touch, trial and see working. There is hardly any marketing material that lends credibility to a company like a working product does. A working product is

[27] FPGA – a field programmable gate array – is basically a large, slow, but very flexible circuit implementation of the micrologic code that is eventually embodied in a single, small, very fast silicon chip. FPGAs are typically used in development environments for troubleshooting, testing and demonstrations.

what ultimately makes a company successful. The accompanying marketing aspect can then be very instrumental as a multiplier of that success.

Getting the messaging into channels

During the months when our silicon was still in development, we based all our marketing efforts on our intellectual property surrounding coexistence, our innovative idea of a two-chip solution and the above demonstrations. Our idea was something we had confirmed was very attractive to the industry; however, we continued to prime the market with awareness of the potential conflict between 802.11b and Bluetooth, and our solution through concerted marketing efforts across conferences, product tours, media, analysts, website and white papers.

White papers

The importance of white papers to Mobilian cannot be overstated. We were in the right industry at the right time to make our intellectual property extremely valuable. Over the course of two years, Mobilian wrote and promoted at least six white papers on short-range wireless technology. These not only served to propagate the interference concerns, but also helped secure Mobilian's position in the industry as an objective, reliable source for industry insight and knowledge. This gained us many speaking opportunities and even the prestigious WinHEC Award for Advancement of the Computing Platform (2001).

White papers in themselves can be dry and dull. However, if they address areas where companies are looking to invest, i.e. where they can make money, then the analyst community, the venture community, customers, media, etc. will all be receptive to reading them. This is because there is something to gain from understanding the content. Analysts sell more reports on topics of interest to their constituents. Magazines sell more issues if they address hot topics. And on it goes. Mobilian played this strategy extremely well, and to our great benefit in market awareness, customer receptivity and marketing muscle. As we began to understand the power of our white papers, we began to proactively distribute them as soon as they were finished, and used them as hand-outs at conferences. We also created two-page summaries of the white papers for media and other interested parties with shorter time availabilities.

Leveraging the analyst community

There are two basic types of analyst firm. The first is the financial community. These analysts are paid to follow their bank's investments in particular industries and companies; therefore, one can usually expect that their research will be slightly biased in favor of their bank's investment portfolio. However, they typically write very well-informed research reports and, as a general rule, are extremely capable professionals.

The other type of analyst firm is the industry research firm, such as International Data Corporation (IDC), Allied Business Intelligence (ABI), Gartner DataQuest, In-Stat MDR, etc. These firms are much more qualitative in their analysis and, to a degree, can be both a good source of information and a good source of misinformation.

Working with these two types of analysts can provide many more benefits than simply market forecasts, as they are often in direct contact with competitors and influence the market's thinking through their publications. Mobilian targeted and worked with several key analyst firms and investment banks. We targeted the firms where we would invest our time and dollars by searching for companies publishing relevant reports to the WLAN and Bluetooth industries, and the manner and quantity of media quotes attributed to analysts at the respective firms. We identified several that were leaders in the space and bought their research to cement our relationships.

The difference in how we managed our relationships with these analysts and how others manage theirs is that we viewed the analysts as two-way communication channels. We used them in their traditional role of providing us with information and insights about our industry and competitive landscape, but we also used the analysts as extensions of our marketing strategy.

Because the space was so new, and because we were dealing in an area that was not well understood (coexistence), and finally because the analysts had many companies to follow and thus a large task of finding information, they were very interested in hearing what we were proactively communicating to them. We expended a significant amount of time and effort establishing mutual information exchange relationships with the analysts, consisting of formal presentations to them, formal and informal conversations about their research findings and even personal lives, and extensive interaction regarding our products and knowledge base.

Consequently, many times we saw our thinking about market issues such as coexistence and market volumes, as well as our own market positioning as the leaders in our area, directly reflected in the reports the analyst firms issued on the WLAN and Blue-tooth markets. In fact, many firms in both the financial analyst world and the industry analyst world published our graphics and sections of our white papers verbatim. We experienced much success positioning Mobilian as a leader in the WLAN space according to the widely acknowledged objective research analysts, and in many cases successfully solicited quotes from the analysts on our technology that we published on our website and in company collaterals.

The analysts were an extremely valuable resource for Mobilian. They provided us with market validation and credibility when many of our larger competitors used them only for their market forecasting. This was a key difference in how we leveraged the analyst community.

Media community and a good PR firm

The media community is tricky. On this front, a good Public Relations (PR) firm can be very valuable because they will have long-established relationships with the media and can assist in strategy formulation and execution. They will understand which media representatives are knowledgeable of the space and which are likely to provide good (i.e. not bad) coverage. They will also have a good understanding of the universe of players and publications in the space, saving time and effort in identifying and creating those relationships. A really good PR firm will not only provide all of those benefits, but will also provide objective feedback on strategic positioning, presentations and media interaction, as well as strategic and tactical opinions on how to best leverage the media in executing the company strategy.

Our PR firms have been both good and bad (we have had two). The first was not good, so Mobilian had to do most of the typical PR work ourselves, in addition to paying our PR firm an exorbitant monthly fee to do the same. Mobilian strategized about how best to position ourselves and our technology with the media, and in some cases we were extremely successful, getting exact relevant quotes and being called upon by key media contacts as industry experts. In other cases we were not as successful. We were quoted out of context and therefore put in a bad light. We were unsuccessful at getting media coverage. We missed many key opportunities for limelight coverage in huge publications like the *New York Times* and the *Wall Street Journal*. In some cases, our story was misconstrued into alarmism about the 'coming conflict' of 802.11b and Bluetooth, completely ignoring the second theme of our briefings about solutions and coexistence.

With that said, our key takeaway from the experience was that the media can be extremely powerful when used by an expert, but can be very dangerous if not handled carefully. Investing in a solid PR firm through a formal RFP (request for proposal) process and due diligence is a wise move. Our current PR firm, PorterNovelli, is a good one, and has provided us with value in many different areas.

Product launch

Mobilian's product launch was the culmination of all of the above work and occurred in November 2002. It consisted of long- and short-lead publication media and analyst tours, analyst dinners, participation in several conferences, multiple press releases and white papers. The launch was very successful as measured by positive coverage in targeted media, positive analyst awareness and coverage, customer appointments and demonstrations, and ultimately customer purchase orders.

Tours – preparing the market for TrueRadio

Media tours are a valuable tool because they allow a company to present its information to a relatively captive audience several weeks in advance of the marketing event for which the tour is intended. It is important, however, to carefully plan what the objectives of the tour sessions are, what the content will be and what will determine success.

During the tours the key objectives for our success were to convince the audience(s) that: (1) the market for combination 802.11b/Bluetooth devices was important and happening at the right time for our product launch; (2) coexistence was a real concern for the success of that market; and (3) we had the answer. Our content to achieve these objectives was to convey a deep understanding of our marketplace through comprehensive market knowledge, to demonstrate the problem of 802.11b and Bluetooth coexistence in a real-world application, and to show how our product could easily and cost-effectively solve this problem. Basically, this provided the classic marketing strategy of showing a problem and offering a compelling solution.

We determined when to visit our targeted media and analysts on the long- and short-lead tours according to the publication schedules of their magazines. Longer-lead publications were briefed under mutual non-disclosure up to a month in advance of the TrueRadio launch date in November 2002. Shorter-lead publications received a confidential briefing about one to two weeks in advance. These briefings were timed to correspond with the coverage the media target would be publishing in conjunction with our planned announcements at large technology conventions. As discussed in the following section, we had targeted COMDEX 2002 in November 2002 and the Bluetooth Developers Conference in December 2002 as the two key shows for our launch.

The tours were very successful. We had a 100 percent hit rate with our demonstration; in other words, the interference we sought to show was severe every time and the TrueRadio developmental solution worked every time. Also, the media we spoke with were very impressed with our knowledge of the market in general. There was no information they had which we were not prepared for in advance. We had good answers for every question they asked us regarding competitors, the market pricing trends, emerging competing standards, etc. In essence, our preparation paid off.

Conference attendance

Industry conferences are a conundrum inside the Mobilian marketing team because the multimillion dollar booths hosted by large multinationals and largely visited by a highly select group of consumers have never made obvious financial sense; therefore, Mobilian was very conservative in our conference attendance and exhibition, but very aggressive in identifying and achieving our targeted objectives. We typically spent about $10 000–15 000 on our floor presence, and about $10 000–15 000 on reserving a suite close to the floor for our product demonstrations and getting the right Mobilian employees to the show. Because of this focus, for a minimal investment, we were able to be at important shows where we could meet with most of our customers and targeted media and analysts, and where we could assert ourselves as an industry player to those same audiences, as well as our competition.

We determined which shows to target and arranged our attendance based upon the show's technical focus and our product development progress. We wanted to launch TrueRadio and ramp our participation in industry shows when the product was ready to demonstrate in a final form factor (e.g. PC card). We had already demonstrated the technology in 2000 in FPGA and this time we needed solid evidence of our progress. We thought this time frame would be around the end of 2002, and so we targeted Fall COMDEX 2002 and Bluetooth Developers Conference 2002.

At COMDEX, one of the biggest technology shows of the 1990s and early 2000s, we used our membership in the marketing standards body Wi-Fi to get an excellent booth in their pavilion. The pavilion was very cheap by comparison to a stand-alone booth (about one-fifth the cost), and we benefitted from the media attraction the standard in general was receiving. Also, there were 16 other booths and companies in the pavilion, so we benefitted from those companies' marketing dollars as well as our own.

The Bluetooth Developers Conference was much smaller, and consequently our stand-alone booth was well placed directly across from two industry leaders, and was inexpensive. Through networking with the Bluetooth marketing organization, we were also able to get on a Bluetooth SIG, Incorporated sponsored media walking tour. We were one of only two startups to do so. The other 12 companies were large, established players like Motorola and Nokia.

Our return on investment from these shows was tremendous. We had determined a set of metrics across media, sales and business development going into each show to gauge our success, and had near perfect success across all of them. Our positive media coverage coming out of the shows was around 80 percent, and we built significant momentum with our existing customers through private meetings in the suite.

Technical awards

Mobilian also sought to win two of the industry's most important technical awards, *PC Magazine*'s COMDEX Best of Show and the EDN Innovation of the Year Award. The competition included multi-billion dollar giants as well as other startups, and was judged on technical innovation, cost of the solution, relevance of the solution and other unknown/qualitative criteria. Once again we competed through a structured process of identifying the target media and analyst representatives, seeking them out when they approached our booth at COMDEX and giving them the same three-point pitch previously mentioned: problem demonstration, solution demonstration, explanation. In the *PC Magazine* Best of COMDEX show, we placed as one of two 'Finalists' for the award from among hundreds of competitors, ultimately losing to Intel's newly introduced mobile processor. At the time of writing, we are still competing to move from 'Finalist' to 'Winner' of EDN's Innovation of the Year for 2002.

The lessons

Seek the input of customers and their customers

Mobilian's relationships with our customers' customers have been invaluable on many fronts. First, we have gained market-driven insights into our product development process that have helped us to intersect the market with products that have the right feature set. Second, establishing good relationships with our customers' customers assisted us in landing new business by having them message market needs to our customers that aligned with our product's feature set. And third, by having our customers and their customers message to the market and financial industry that they needed products like the ones we were developing, we increased our ability to secure necessary financing to get to revenues.

Create, perfect and evolve coordinated, meaningful messaging

In our experience, it has been crucial to clearly identify what the right messaging is, and then consistently deliver it in almost all marketing and other relevant industry communications. We crafted messaging that was relatively simple at a high level. First, there's a real problem that could negatively impact the market. Second, we can demonstrate the problem. Third, while there are other solutions out there, we have a great solution, maybe the best one in the industry, and here's why we think so.

After formulating the messaging, we became experts at talking about our solution to anyone. We could tailor the story on the fly, depending upon the person's technical expertise, importance in an organization and ability to impact Mobilian. The messaging was prevalent in everything we did. We concluded white papers addressing coexistence with a section on our product and technology. Our presentations focused on these messages. Our fund raising centered on the necessity of what we were doing and why it was important. Our standards activities emphasized the messaging constructs in their activities. And so it went on, and still continues today.

Influence the influencers

The final key insight from the Mobilian marketing story is to identify and influence those forces which can influence you. The most readily apparent implementation of this tactic is the standards bodies. Mobilian invested heavily in influencing the politics and progress of the standards through the bodies which write them. We did this by gaining positions of influence and contributing meaningful value along the way, and once we got there. Contributing value in most areas allowed us to occasionally influence the standards in our favor when we felt it made sense.

The other groups of influencers, aside from customers, are the media and analyst communities. In large part, Mobilian established excellent reciprocal relationships with key media and analyst contacts by volunteering to provide them with high-quality objective information where we could, and by telling them valuable, meaningful information when we met with them. Because of this strategy, we are now a 'go to' company for short-range wireless information, and have largely excellent relationships across the industry publications and research houses.

Conclusion

I certainly hope this short history has provided meaningful value for you. If it has left you with more questions, or if you would like to speak with me personally, I would be more than happy to correspond with you. You may reach me at wade.gillham@mobilian.com or wade_gillham@hotmail.com. Best wishes for your success.

Chapter 10

Short-distance wireless: marketing 802.11 and Bluetooth

Tom Siep

Former General Manager of the Bluetooth SIG

The two statements:

- Bluetooth wireless technology is the same as IEEE 802.11;
- Bluetooth wireless technology is fundamentally different than IEEE 802.11;

are technically both true. A technologist will be intrigued by the contradiction and may be lured into figuring out exactly how and why they are both different and the same. Consumers – be they corporate or mass market – are less likely to invest the effort it takes to understand.

In fact, a fair number of people in the general telecommunications business have been having trouble discerning the difference and frequently misunderstand the relationship of the two technologies.

These factors create an identity problem for products employing the technologies: how can the manufacturer or the consumers tell which technology is most appropriate?

A useful term for the class of product that both 802.11 and Bluetooth technologies belong to is short-distance wireless or SDW.

Although other technologies address the same spheres as Bluetooth and 802.11b, they are arguably the most successful examples of the two classes of SDW.

In this chapter we explore what makes SDW different from other communication types and how the two major types are similar, but differ in fundamental ways that affect what markets they primarily address.

The topic of SDW is very broad. For the purposes of this discussion, when the general technology is referenced, the terms WLAN (Wireless Local Area Network) and WPAN (Wireless Personal Area Network) are used. When referencing the specific technologies within these classifications, the proper names are used. For example, in the case of 802.11, when the general behaviour of 802.11 systems is described, no letter is appended. However, when 802.11 operates in the 2.4 GHz band at 11 Mbps, the term 802.11b is used to distinguish it.

Many more differences and similarities between the technologies exist than are presented here. Attributes such as how and where the protocols are defined, qualified and evolved are interesting to developers, but not to the end-user. Only factors that influence how and why the technologies are used in wireless products are discussed.

Wireless data communication

Consumer electronics are becoming more intelligent and interactive. MP3 players, PDAs, digital cameras and mobile phones have increasing data capabilities. This capability allows the user to retain, use, process and communicate potentially large amounts of information that must be available when and where needed. For example, a Personal Information Management (PIM) database maintains personal calendars, address books and to-do lists in a PDA. The PIM database in the PDA needs to synchronize with those in other personal devices. The obvious solution for keeping these databases synchronized is to interconnect them.

Traditionally, the interconnect has been done with wires. Connecting with wires is the simplest way, providing you have the right wire. Wires have the bad habit of getting lost, broken or just in the way. Wireless is a better way, but which wireless?

In fact, many types of wireless communications are used by consumers every day. Garage door openers, TV remotes, car unlocking/alarm systems and the like are all wireless. Most of them are not obviously data oriented. More specifically, they are not readily usable as interconnects for information tools.

The first thing we must do is categorize what is available for efficient information exchange, then find the best match for getting PIM-style information moved around. Figure 10.1 shows the approximate range and data rates for the various forms that wireless data communication can take. There is great variety in terms of distances and data rates.

Wide Area Networks (WANs), such as satellite communications, have huge reach. With this greater reach, however, comes a decrease in the amount of information resource available to each user. This concept is known as *aggregate bandwidth*: the sum of all the information able to be exchanged by all the people at one time. The aggregate bandwidth of the WAN is actually quite low – if millions of people attempted to use it at a single moment, each user would see a very low throughput rate. It can also be quite expensive, making it somewhat silly to transfer a file from one PC to another using this method.

Metropolitan Area Networks (MANs) cover areas as large as cities and are primarily associated with mobile phones. Many consumers in the USA tend to think of wireless products as being the same thing as mobile phones. Most people there – including the mobile phone industry – treat the terms interchangeably. Even though

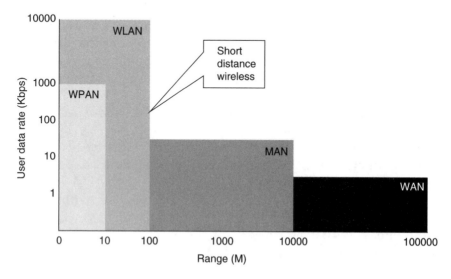

Figure 10.1   Wireless communications

European and Asian marketers generally do not use the 'wireless' term, increasingly their mobile phone networks – such as GSM and GPRS – offer data capabilities that can be a substitute for SDW. If the parties exchanging information are not in the same location, this method is pretty obvious and efficient. The systems have a lot of aggregate bandwidth and the costs are not astronomic. However, if the parties are facing each other it does not make much sense to pay the phone company to transfer a business card a few feet.

What, then, is usable as a conduit between proximal information tools? To answer this question, we need to take a look at the two categories of wireless communications which fall under the heading of SDW: Wireless Local Area Networks (WLANs) and Wireless Personal Area Networks (WPANs). Their most important characteristics are:

- Cost per transaction is near or at zero.
- Low power – does not use much electricity.
- Small footprint – does not impact the size or weight.
- Short distance – does not travel far.

The first three characteristics seem pretty obvious advantages. The last one is less so. It comes back to the aggregate bandwidth characteristic. The logic goes: the more distance the signals can travel, the larger the physical area of the network, the larger potential number of radios (cooperating or not), the smaller percentage each user can use. Simplified, this equates to: more distance = less total data throughput.

Personal versus local

Wireless solutions are implemented for two general reasons: cost and convenience. These two requirements drive the design and marketing of the surrounding technologies.

Cost is a factor when physical or logistical elements make wires undesirable or impossible. Status sensors embedded in an automobile tyre cannot reasonably be connected via wire to the central monitoring system of the vehicle. Some sort of rotor-and-brush connector could solve this problem, but is not an economic, reliable or durable solution. What is needed in this case is a solution that does not require a redesign of a fundamental subsystem in the car (the wheels), which would be a wireless interconnect.

Convenience is a less quantifiable factor. An example of this is a wireless connection to the Internet by a notebook computer that sits in an office. Connecting an LAN cable to a port on the notebook is an easy and inexpensive method of connection. It is, however, an extra step that many users would prefer to avoid – given a reasonable alternative.

802.11 WLAN characteristics

The primary mission in life for an 802.11-based product is to be part of a Wireless Local Area Network (WLAN), which at some point is generally connected to a wired network. All the different kinds of 802.11 have fundamental technologies that are pointed towards the product becoming part of the network (see Appendix A, 'Which 802.11', for a brief look at the various flavors of 802.11).

Figure 10.2 shows the seamless integration of LANs and WLANs common to all the 802.11 products. The curved arrow in the figure indicates information flow. The applications in the laptop, workstation and router need not be aware of the tasks that the PDA and

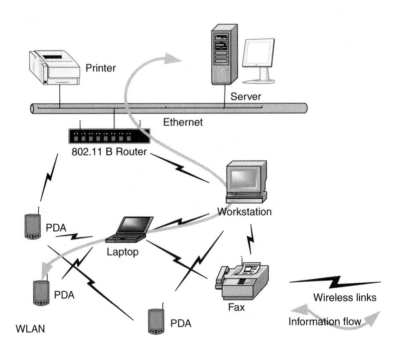

Figure 10.2 LAN/WAN example

the Server are running. They only provide the infrastructure to enable the information flow.

Until very recently, most LANs existed only inside corporations or other organizations that have a support system usually described as an 'infrastructure'. LANs and their progeny WLANs are constructed to be very infrastructure oriented. An example of that orientation can be taken from the architectural overview of 802.11, shown in Figure 10.3.

A fair portion of the structure in Figure 10.3 is devoted to 'management', which is a facility for a centralized, remote control of the behaviour of the protocol.

The initial design and marketing requirements of 802.11 are dictated not only by the consumer market but also, to a very large degree, by the business market. Interconnecting personal devices is different than connecting corporate devices to a corporate infrastructure. Typical WLAN connectivity solutions for a notebook computer user require that there be a security system that associates the user of the device with data services available on, for instance, a corporate Ethernet-based intranet.

The ability to have centralized, remote administration of WLAN devices is integral to their design. This is driven by the need for corporate IT departments to regulate the access and security of their networks. It is a formalization that is absolutely required by

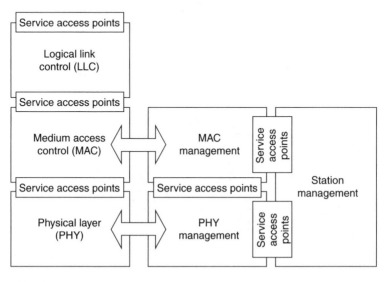

Figure 10.3 Structure of 802.11

corporations, but which non-professional IT consumers may find cumbersome.

Bluetooth WPAN characteristics

The primary mission in life for a Bluetooth product is to be part of a Personal Area Network (PAN). The PAN was coined to describe a different kind of network connection, one that does not depend on an infrastructure. The untethered version of this is called a Wireless Personal Area Network (WPAN). A WPAN can be viewed as a personal communications bubble around a person that does not reach much further than the user can see. Within this bubble, which moves as a person moves around, personal devices can connect with one another. The devices in the area can be under the control of a single individual or can be several people's devices, which may interact with each other.

Figure 10.4 illustrates how the same devices connected with the 802.11 network could be interconnected with Bluetooth technology. Note that there is a central controller of the communications.

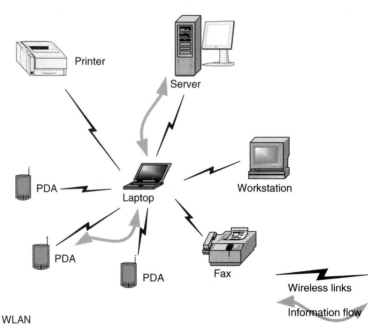

Figure 10.4   WPAN example

Information that needs to be passed from the PDA to the Server has to have the active participation of an application on the laptop. Of course, the PDA could connect directly with the Server via another instance of a Bluetooth network and avoid that overhead.

The family of Standards that the Bluetooth specification is a member of is the 802.15 WPAN. Like its cousin, it has many siblings (see Appendix A, 'Which WPAN?'). Figure 10.5 shows the structure of the Bluetooth technology as it is represented in the 802.15.1 standard.

The consumer marketplace requires a connectivity solution that takes the primary functionality of the personal device into account. For example, a communications-enabled PDA must still look and function as a PDA. Its wireless connectivity solution must not significantly impact the PDA's form factor, weight, power requirements, cost, ease of use or other traits.

Of course, not all PDAs are the same. Presently, there are two major camps: the Palm Pilot™ and the Pocket PC™. These two types are a good illustration of how a device's use affects what connectivity is most appropriate. The Pocket PC is just that: a miniature computer-centric solution that is a substitution for its larger brethren. The Palm Pilot is a more personal device.

Personal devices such as the Palm Pilot are used as a part of an individual's productivity management and entertainment tools. They may also need to interact with a corporate IT infrastructure,

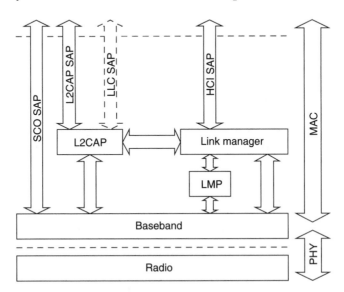

Figure 10.5 Structure of Bluetooth

but do not really become an integral part of it. Further, these devices are likely to be used in several of many different environments, such as offices, homes, in the middle of a park or industrial plants, where no connectivity is required. Many of those places will also not have power available, so power consumption is a large issue. The wireless solution for these devices must accommodate these needs.

The marketing of the corporate/infrastructure-oriented 802.11 contrasts with the intimate, personal nature of a wireless connectivity solution for the personal devices associated with a particular user, and no outside 'permission' is necessary. The user is concerned with electronic devices in his/her possession, or in his/her vicinity, rather than to any particular geographic or network location.

Short-distance wireless differences

As mentioned in the introduction, Bluetooth and 802.11 technologies have many similarities and important differences. The differences are essentially in two areas: physical and logical.

Physical characteristics are traits inherent to the construction of the wireless subsystem and prescribe how communications are accomplished at the most basic level. The most important physical characteristics are:

- Data rate.
- Organization.
- Range.
- Power.
- Number of participants.

The logical relationships between devices are more about how and when they are used. Important logical characteristics are:

- Control of the medium of the radio waves.
- Ownership of devices.
- Nature of devices.
- Lifetime of network.
- Security.

Each of these topics will be examined in the following paragraphs. Counter examples exist for most, if not all, the delineations – as is always the case. The descriptions below reflect the attributes of the technologies in relation to their most common applications. For each topic, 802.11b Bluetooth attributes are discussed, followed by an assessment of how this translates into marketplace positioning.

Data rate

As noted above, data rate is different from throughput rate. The rate the user perceives is dependent on many factors, but the primary factor is the capability of the radio.

The bit rate of the two technologies is often represented unequally in the media and even in the literature published by the manufacturers of both technologies. The only inarguable comparison in data rate is the *raw bit rate*. This is the instantaneous speed of the radio, measured in how many bits are transmitted in one second.

Bluetooth technology has a raw bit rate of one million bits per second or 1 Mbps. 802.11b has a raw bit rate of 11 Mbps, with the newer, backward compatible version of the 2.4 MHz standard (802.11g; see again Appendix A, 'Which 802.11') reaching 22 Mbps. Clearly, the IEEE standard has a considerably higher data rate.

Frequently, a speed of 'about 700 Kbps' is cited for Bluetooth technology. The number represents the maximum 'reliable' data throughput in one direction, visible at the applications interface. Obviously there have to be lots of caveats on that number, such as error-free transmissions, the ability of the transmitter to keep the pipe full and the like, but it is a good number to work with.

No such equivalent number exists for 802.11. There is not a theoretical limit on how close to the raw bit rate that two 802.11 products can get. There are some practical limitations, however. Given the way that the protocol works, a perfect one-on-one file transfer will see some 80 percent of the raw data rate. In a moderately crowded environment of four or five communicating devices, the aggregate bandwidth will likely drop to 30 or 40 percent of the total 11 Mbps, which will be divided among the users. There is a non-linear drop off in the data rate seen by the user as a function of how many users there are on the wireless net.[28]

---

[28] Incidentally, the coaxial cable version of the Ethernet LAN has a raw data rate of 10 Mbps, but will collapse and not transfer any data if the aggregate bandwidth exceeds about 30 percent. Same problem, same result.

Bluetooth technology, on the other hand, has a fairly linear drop-off in the data rate seen by the users as a function of numbers. It has the quality of having an aggregate bandwidth which is roughly constant. Add one more user to a two-user network and the effective data rate for one device is halved. Add one more and it is one-third. This works until you get to the maximum of seven units allowed in a single Bluetooth wireless network.

The differences in the raw data rates are still dramatic, especially in quiet environments. 802.11 has lots of margin for getting data from one place to another. Its downside is that it is disproportionately affected by the presence of others in the area. Products that produce or use a lot of data – typically computing devices – will cheerfully accept the impact of the presence of others. Bluetooth technology's less computing-oriented devices appreciate the predictability of the links for applications having little tolerance for non-linear degradation.

Organization

The antecedent for Wireless LAN was, well, LAN (Local Area Network). The 'Local' part of the name refers to how the network is organized. This organization is often called by the term used in mathematics to describe shapes: topology.

Figure 10.4 shows a typical topology of a Bluetooth network. It is known in topological terms as a 'star'. If this were a government, it would be benevolent dictatorship. All communications paths are controlled through a central point. No direct communications are allowed between any devices other than the central controller and its clients.

This centralized approach is simpler than most other approaches. The participants in the network – or piconet as it is called – do not have to comprehend:

• overlapping connections;
• 'charity' data storage.

Piconets allow no overlapping connections within their realm. The overlapping connections occur when two pairs of devices have direct communication paths that are independent and cross each other (there are several examples of this in Figure 10.2). Although the idea that two sets of communications can occur at the same time is attractive, it has a cost. Since there is not a practical way of containing and channeling radio waves, sets of simple radios like a Bluetooth radio interfere with each other to some extent. This is mitigated in the Bluetooth technology by the devices automatically creating a new piconet that does not interfere most of the time.

By contrast, 802.11 is characterized by democratic connections to a virtual shared bus, as shown in Figure 10.2. This topology is known as a 'tree'. Each participant is able to access any other member in the network. Any device can directly (or indirectly) communicate with any other device on its branch.

The Bluetooth protocols do not support two communicating products not in direct range of the controller of the piconet, to avoid the necessity of each device having to temporarily store information for another device. If the PDA in Figure 10.4 were not in range of the Server, no communications would be possible without specific help. The only unit that may provide help and have to provide storage is the controller of the piconet, which presumably has the resources to do so.

The 802.11 protocol, on the other hand, allows connections involving the relay of data through an arbitrary intermediary device on the network. This is a very useful function in covering geographically large areas. It does have a direct impact on the simplicity of the protocol, however. There may be times where multiple intermediaries are used and this does place a burden on individual devices to not only keep track of their own data conversations, but also those that they are supporting. One of the consequences of the complex connections is the 'charity' temporary storage of data for others. It is termed charity since the storage device receives no direct benefit. In the case where there is no interference, this storage is momentary. In the case where communications disruptions occur, the data may need to be stored for a longer period.

The 802.11 devices justify the support of their increased complexity with the additional functionality the technology provides. A side-effect of the democratic character of 802.11 is that it uses more power in listening than the equivalent Bluetooth radio; Bluetooth clients know when to listen, 802.11 devices cannot predict when they need to do so.

In the final analysis, if the communications problem to be solved requires an extended reach with direct addressing between arbitrary products, then 802.11 has the appropriate topology. If it is not needed, the simpler Bluetooth solution is often better. As is the case with all the differences between 802.11 and Bluetooth technologies, their individual weaknesses may be their strengths, depending solely on the nature of the particular kinds of communications to be done.

Range

The reach of Bluetooth radios is generally not as great as the 802.11. Although the nominal capabilities are the same on paper, Bluetooth radios tend to transmit to close-by partners in communications and therefore want and need. Typical Bluetooth radios operate with an effective range of about 10 meters.

This self-limitation of range decreases power consumption while not adversely affecting the essential function: communication to personal devices that are usually at hand. The decreased transmit power has a significant impact on battery drain at the expense of coverage. It is the topology of the Bluetooth technology that renders it more amenable to lower power operation. By definition, it is known which devices will participate in the network by virtue of their association with the central controlling device. Every node can transmit and receive the controller's signals.

Typical 802.11 radios operate with an effective range of about 100 meters. The comparatively long range of the WLAN and the distributed nature of its control mechanisms make it difficult for a single entity to control a large geographic area. This results in an issue known in communications theory as the 'hidden node problem' – where one device cannot tell if a second device is listening to a third device that is out of its range. In Figure 10.2 the Fax and the Router may be out of range of each other and both try to access the Workstation at the same time. The 802.11 protocol has mechanisms to solve this, at the cost of giving up some simplicity of design.

The range of 802.11 is very useful for maintaining connectivity over relatively long distances compared to Bluetooth technology. The overhead these 802.11 mechanisms involve is well worth the increased coverage in applications that need it. The Bluetooth topology could allow applications to set up a relay system to cover equivalent distances, but the overhead it would incur in doing so would be many times that of the 802.11.

Power

There are two aspects of power usage in both 802.11 and Bluetooth technology that should be considered. The first is transmit power – how much electricity it takes to project the signal. The other is operating power – the total amount of electricity used for communications. Of course, transmit power is part of the total communications power budget, but it is a variable, dependent solely on the amount of data being sent at a given power level. The total budget is overwhelmingly dependent on how the two different protocols work.

As mentioned in the discussion of the relative ranges, the transmit power of Bluetooth technology is usually lower than that of 802.11. This is due, for the most part, because of how it is used, but some part of it is due to the higher protocol overhead of 802.11.

The smaller power budget of the Bluetooth technology – and its smaller size – makes it necessary for the protocol to be particularly power conservative.

One of the things that makes power conservation possible in Bluetooth technology is, once again, the controlled nature of the topology. The members of the Bluetooth piconet that are not responsible for coordination may shut down their radios when they know that the unit could not possibly receive a message.

As mentioned in the discussion on network organization, the 802.11 product never knows when it may be addressed and therefore must be awake more often. This is a natural consequence of its increased flexibility.

The 802.11's greater transmit power gives it advantages in coverage and reliability at the margins of coverage. Most have flexibility in the amount of transmit power, which allows them to use only that necessary to get to the intended receiver as a coexistence and power-saving feature. This flexibility aids in maintaining a reasonable power budget.

The consequence of the increased resources demanded on an 802.11 product is an increase in operating power consumption. Power consumption affects the product design of the devices that use each communication technique. 802.11 devices tend to be run from platforms that are either plugged into the wall or have large batteries: they are 'portable'. Bluetooth technology devices tend to be simpler and are highly 'mobile'. The difference is that portable units can be moved, whereas mobile units are designed to be used while in motion. The 'style' of power consumption matches the expected usages of the two product types.

Number of participants

The nature of the tight control that Bluetooth technology exerts means it cannot tolerate an unlimited membership in the piconet. In fact, the number of members is relatively small, as mentioned above. Bluetooth technology allows, at most, eight active devices – including the controller – to participate in the piconet. This limitation is fundamental to the protocol as it currently exists. The topology of the Bluetooth technology has a reduced, low overhead addressing scheme. This simplifies the protocol at the cost of limiting the number of participants.

Membership in an 802.11 network is virtually unlimited. There is no inherent limit on how many devices can combine to form a WLAN. This is quite reasonable – and necessary – since the WLAN can occupy a very large area.

When connecting a few personal devices together, Bluetooth users are not generally constrained by the limited capacity for currently active devices. The same limitation would be unacceptable in a busy infrastructure of an 802.11 product.

Control of the medium of the radio waves

The amount of control of the radio waves needed to be exerted by each of the technologies is a direct consequence of their organizational styles, as mentioned above. The Bluetooth technology's most defining attribute is its control of the wireless medium. All information is typically passed though a central controlling entity, which essentially 'owns' the medium. An 802.11 WLAN may have some distributed control devices (defined by the protocol), but essentially there are no owners of the medium and any device can use the medium when it decides it is okay to do so.

The Bluetooth technology's tight control of the medium enables utilization of a higher percentage of the available airtime. There does not have to be any method of checking to see if the medium is clear, as is done with the basic 802.11. Since Bluetooth technology is 'personal', there are some assumptions made on how it can use the wireless medium:

1 Most data flows from a single source to a single destination.
2 For a given application, there is a controller of the data flow between two points.
3 No one else is in range, so no care need be taken to be 'polite' and avoid another's use of the medium.[29]
4 Fairness to other Bluetooth devices is not a concern, since they will use a different hopping pattern.

In the tightly controlled scheme that a Bluetooth technology uses there are no collisions within a piconet and, unless there are many colocated piconets, there will be little inter-piconet impact. All the members of the Bluetooth piconet know exactly when, and for how long, they can transmit.

By contrast, at least some of the time, 802.11 uses a contention-based scheme for allocating the scarce resource of time on the air. The devices turn on their receivers and listen for a pause in communications before transmitting. This approach allows for a great deal of flexibility in establishing communications. It is well suited to a moderately loaded environment, where the time spent waiting is not too great and the application can tolerate the listen-before-talk approach. In a heavily loaded environment, 802.11 can suffer a 'data storm' and actual throughput can fall to very low levels.

The 802.11 protocol gives up the strict control of the medium in favor of flexibility. The coverage area that a WLAN is expected to satisfy is much greater than that of a Bluetooth network. The Bluetooth method of control of the medium is not as scalable as the 802.11, since the latter has no theoretical limits on the number of participants.

Another advantage the 802.11 has with its methodology is that the existence of the network is not dependent on the presence of a single device. This is very important in infrastructure-related applications, where the continued existence of the network is critical for proper function.

The infrastructure style of 802.11 tends to make it harder to do information transfers that have time-critical attributes, for example

---

[29] With the most recent version of the Bluetooth Specification – version 1.2 – this is no longer true. The protocol now can and does assess the environment and can avoid being 'impolite'.

live video.[30] The deference to the infrastructure can lead to unacceptable delays. This same infrastructure orientation gives 802.11 a big advantage in blending in with standard networks.

The personal nature of the Bluetooth technology has just about the opposite traits: it supports time-critical applications, like real-time audio, very well but has a somewhat indirect relationship to larger networks.

Ownership of devices

As stated before, Bluetooth technology tends to interconnect 'personal' devices, i.e. devices not part of or owned by an infrastructure, but rather owned by individuals. 802.11 devices tend to be extensions of wired infrastructures which, until recently, have been the jurisdiction of corporations and their IT departments. As such, a significant portion of WLAN devices are not under the personal control of the user. The personal nature versus infrastructure nature of the two classes of devices has implications for the internal controls used by the two topologies.

An extension of a wired infrastructure needs to interact with and be controlled by that infrastructure. This remote control is affected by the use of a management information base built into the protocol of 802.11. This is a formalized mechanism, whereby information systems personnel can alter the behaviour of a network device without having to physically be present. This remote reconfiguration capability is common to many network devices.

Bluetooth devices do not generally have a formal presence in the network, although a Bluetooth access point may be connected to an infrastructure network. When it is, the only appropriate control by network administrators is in its infrastructure network functions. The traffic over the air is outside the scope of the infrastructure in the Bluetooth case.

The control that is exerted over Bluetooth devices is done explicitly by the controller of the network and is not done in the background, as is the case with WLANs. This simplifies implementations of WPANs at the cost of the lack of outside policy imposition.

---

[30] It should be noted that the higher data rate of the WLAN makes this an issue that surfaces only in moderately crowded environments.

As good citizens of the Local Area Network, the WLANs are – in one sense – more controlled than Bluetooth devices. They must implement and adhere to the remote management of their resources and operating characteristics. This remote management may, in some cases, actually reduce the need for some user interfaces (or specialized applications interfaces) on remote devices. The regularization of set-up and operating characteristics is often vital to enable the deployment of wireless technology in an infrastructure-based area.

The product impacts are pretty much identical to those cited for control of the medium.

Homogeneous networks

For many of the reasons covered in the paragraphs above, 802.11 products tend to interconnect like devices. These products tend to be computer oriented and communicate on a peer-to-peer basis with other computers that generally have similar capabilities.

The person-oriented products which Bluetooth technology interconnects are often quite different from one another. Users seldom carry more than one personal digital assistant, for example, so the only PDA-to-PDA interactions occur when business cards are exchanged.

The difference in the nature of the devices often dictates their possible role in network participation. Some Bluetooth products would be clearly inappropriate to control the WPAN. For instance, a mobile telephone headset with its small battery and lack of user interface would be a poor choice as the controller of a Bluetooth network.

As more robust devices, the 802.11 products – or their hosts – are, by definition, more capable and the distributed nature of the network topology makes the question of central control much less relevant for them.

The 802.11 devices are elements in a formal network and they must be fairly computationally capable to do so. This gives 802.11 products a tendency to be computer-centric.

The connect-anything-to-anything philosophy of the Bluetooth technology asks much less of the hosting device. This allows Bluetooth subsystems to be integrated into much less capable devices.

Lifetime of network

The amount of time a network is assumed to exist is a relatively new concept, introduced by the WPAN paradigm. The idea is that the network an individual is likely to construct will only be actively used for a short time.

Bluetooth technology itself has two specific constraints on its lifetime. First – and foremost – is that the controller's unique identifier and clock defines the hopping sequence of a network. It is the combination of those two items that defines the network identity to itself and all the members. Therefore, if the controller leaves the network, the network must cease to exist. The second aspect of the limited lifetime of a Bluetooth network is a bit more obscure. It has to do with its reliance on a 16-bit sequential counter that keeps track of the ordinal of the communications slot since the beginning of network operation. The counter 'rolls over' and goes back to zero once about every 25 hours. When that rollover occurs, the network must be re-established. The old network now no longer exists.

An 802.11 has no inherent lifetime. Its existence can continue independent of any of the members of the network. In fact, over time, all of the original devices in a WLAN network can leave the network and be replaced by other devices. If this replacement overlaps in time, the same network continues to exist.

Security

Security in wireless environments is different in degree, but not in kind, from its wired counterparts. Contrary to popular opinion, there exist no issues for wireless that do not exist to some degree in the world of wires. There are many, many aspects to security, but for the purpose of this discussion, we will only talk about security in general terms.

The obvious argument to that is that radio waves easily travel outside the user's immediate environment, and therefore the user's control. The implicit assumption is that the things in the immediate vicinity of the user are 'safe' and those outside are 'not safe'. Security experts would point out that this is a dangerous assumption. Connections to the Internet, undetected physical security breaches and similar activities can cause the most secure wired system to become

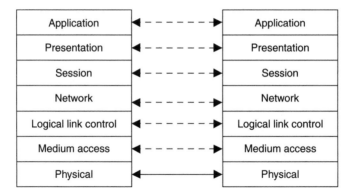

Figure 10.6 ISO OSI model

compromised. That being said, it is still clearly a concern to keep information and resources as secure as possible, and the wireless interface is a big target to would-be interlopers.

To understand how security systems work, it is useful to look at the International Standards Organization's Open Systems Interconnect model (ISO OSI). Figure 10.6 shows a modified version for the purposes of this explanation. The two stacks indicate communicating devices. The solid arrow at the bottom indicates the physical transfer of information from one to the other. The dashed arrows represent 'logical' conversations between the various layers. The rules for the ISO OSI model are that information only travels on the solid lines and is encapsulated for processing only by the peer entity.

For 802.11, the concept of Wired Equivalency Privacy (WEP) was invented to bring it 'up to the level provided by wires'. It was not meant to be a complete, robust security scheme. It resides in layer 2. Security belongs in higher layer functions, perhaps even at the Applications level. This is needed because unless higher levels identify sensitive data, such as security keys, the lower layers may inadvertently allow such information to be transmitted without proper safeguards.

Bluetooth technology defines its security higher up in the stack and is arguably better, but still could be made more robust.

Both 802.11 and Bluetooth SIG are working on improving security in their protocols. In both cases, the protocols can only provide the tools for end-users to use. Blaming the protocol for a security failure, when the user does not utilize what is there, is like blaming a lock manufacturer for a break-in when the homeowner did not lock the front door. The marketing for both technologies must educate the end-users to utilize the security schemes, so that their systems are not easily compromised. Making the security schemes easier for the end-user to take advantage of will also help.

Common issues

Apart from their fundamental traits, the 802.11 and Bluetooth technologies have some common issues with sometimes different solutions. Interoperability, coexistence and the futures of the technologies are discussed in this final section.

Interoperability

One radio is uninteresting: if you have only a receiver or only a transmitter there is not much you can do. Things become more interesting when you have a transmitter and a receiver: that gets you the ability to transfer information from one point to another, be it voice, music or data. It is much more interesting to have two transmitters and two receivers: the parties can know that each other has succeeded in their communication. It is the difference between 'communicating to' and 'communicating with'.

Having identical equipment from the same manufacturer to communicate successfully is comparatively easy. Success here is considered normal 'operation'. Challenges arise when similar or complementary devices from different manufactures are meant to communicate. Success here is termed 'interoperation'. The general problem for interoperability is that only one side of the equation is controlled by the manufacturer. It requires cooperation between potential rivals to solve the whole problem.

The mobile phone industry provides an example of the interoperability challenge. Traditionally, when the consumer purchases communication equipment from a service provider, the consumer gets a limited choice in equipment. The pre-choice is made by the service provider to limit the devices to those that have been tested and proved to work with the equipment already in place. This is one form of ensuring interoperability. With the advent of GSM-related technologies for mobile phone applications, for instance, the device being used no longer has to be specified by the telephone system company. Interoperability now becomes an issue, albeit a simpler one, because there are few service providers to interoperate with.

Virtually all manufacturers test their own products pretty thoroughly with all applicable products in their line. The vast majority also go into the marketplace, where they obtain competitors' products and test theirs alongside them.

For 802.11 products, the process is generally fairly straightforward. The essential function of the product is to access the network, just like any Ethernet network device. Qualification – proving the product works – needs only to prove that functionality, since the overlying application remains essentially unchanged. It is only one mode of communication that is being made wireless. The product functionality remains the same, but the wires have been replaced with 802.11.

For Bluetooth technology the situation is much more complex. It, too, is a wire replacement technology, but it encompasses many different kinds of cables for many different functions. The wireless link may need to replace a cable between a notebook computer and a mobile phone; a wire between a headset and a mobile phone; a connection between modem and a PDA; or an infrared beam between two PDAs. More complex yet, all these things may be going on at the same time. There is a much larger landscape to cover to ensure interoperability. These are not only different applications, they are different *kinds* of applications.

The marketing task for 802.11 is to tell what the product can do. Anything left unstated will be assumed to be absent. Purchasers of network equipment tend to be technically sophisticated, even when they happen to be ordinary homeowners. A good indicator of this is when a purchaser already has computing equipment in use and perceives the need for a network that could be wireless.

The Bluetooth technology market, on the other hand, not only includes these kinds of people, but a great many more less sophisticated consumers. These users of the technology see Bluetooth logos on boxes and may assume that they can all work together. For instance, if a consumer sees two mobile phone headsets with Bluetooth logos, the assumption may be made that they can be a pair of walkie-talkies.

The key to effective Bluetooth marketing and interoperability is not only to tell what the devices can do, but to also carefully outline those capabilities so that it is clear what the product *cannot* do. Furthermore, it is advised that if any specific interoperability issues exist with another manufacturer, then a suitable disclaimer should be made.

When worlds collide

Radio spectrum is a finite resource and there is no easy way to increase the amount available for a given technology. Obviously, if you change the technology, the amount of usefulness obtained from a given set of spectra can be increased. This was amply illustrated by the improvement from 802.11 to 802.11b. The point remains, for a given technology, the resource is finite.

This begs the question – what happens when there are too many:

- Participants in my network?
- Other networks with the same kind of radio?
- Other networks with a different kind of radio?
- Other kinds of interference?

Network capacity is handled fundamentally differently by 802.11 and Bluetooth technologies. As noted in the 'Organization' section above, 802.11 has no inherent limits, while a single Bluetooth network has, at most, eight participants. When there are too many 802.11 devices, the performance at first gently degrades then – in extreme cases – falls off precipitously.[31] Bluetooth technology, on the other hand, has a different approach. If one network reaches capacity, the protocol has allowances for creating a new independent network that can be orthogonal with the first. It is estimated that up to nine colocated networks can exist in a few meters area without significant impact. The slope of the degradation line increases somewhat for the network-to-network coordination, but remains fairly steady.

Non-cooperating networks with the same kind of radio are again handled differently by the two technologies. The 802.11b technology has three sub-bands of the ISM radio-frequency spectrum to choose from. If it is noted that one sub-band is occupied in a given area, there are the two alternatives. Other than switching the network settings, there would be no cross effect of up to three colocated 802.11b networks. When more than three networks are in an area – or no movement to another sub-band is made – then there is virtually

---

[31] It should be noted that, at IEEE 802.11 meetings, hundreds of notebook computers are wirelessly connected in the same large room. Performance is only moderately degraded, and then only during boring presentations.

no difference in the presence of a non-cooperative network: the effect in terms of throughput is the same as if the new devices were just added to the original.

Theoretically, when 802.11 and Bluetooth technology colocate there will be trouble. In actuality this is seldom the case. Coexistence between the two radio types has both some pitfalls and some ways forward. The major pitfall is when a single device has both kinds of technology and they either share antennas or have them very close together. This can cause the radios to be overdriven and little useful information can be exchanged. Many products that incorporate both technologies simply turn off the one which is not being currently used.

Still there is possible unfortunate interaction between the two technologies when used in the same area. Fortunately, both the IEEE and the Bluetooth SIG have addressed this issue and came up with a scheme where a combination of power control and what is called 'Adaptive Frequency Hopping' cope with the problem. The schemes allow the two technologies to coexist better, making the performance of each gracefully degrade.

Other forms of communication also use the band shared by 802.11b and Bluetooth technology. The largest potential interferer is cordless phones, which use the band as an analog channel instead of using it digitally, as the protocols do. This is thought to be a transitory problem, as when both 802.11b and Bluetooth technology become less expensive, it will make it more economical for cordless phone manufacturers to buy one of the technologies rather than employing a one-off implementation. Then the cordless phones become another non-cooperating network.

Non-communications equipment that emits radiation in the radio band that 802.11b and Bluetooth technology reside in can cause problems. The biggest and best-known source of this in-band noise is probably microwave ovens. Except for kitchen cooking/computing, there is generally enough distance between the microwave and the communicating product for the effects to go unnoticed.

Converging evolutions?

Many proposed features of both Bluetooth technology and 802.11 are in each other's current purview. Bluetooth radios may have higher data rates and 802.11 may become more power conservative.

If this happens, will there be any rational way of choosing between the two technologies? The inherent nature and roots of both technologies will still be there. The 802.11 will likely always be better at being part of a computer-centric network. The Bluetooth technology will likely always be better at non-computer-centric things. Unless something else comes along that can do both kinds of tasks better, both will continue in the marketplace. In the future, as is the case now, some products will embrace both technologies.

Summary

In broad strokes, the functions of 802.11 and Bluetooth technologies are very similar. The major difference is how the operational characteristics of protocols affect products – and choice of products – that implement them.

At first glance, the operation and objectives of Bluetooth technology may appear to resemble those of 802.11. Both technologies allow devices to connect to their surrounding environment and exchange data with it over an unlicensed wireless link, and will travel from country to country for use in cars, airplanes and boats. However, the kinds of products they are best suited for are different.

Products that implement 802.11 are essentially computer-centric; they are mainly using the technology to eliminate wires that connect to a wired network as a peer computing device. Their purpose is to be able to be full-fledged participants in potentially large local area networks. This technology extends the reach of portable devices to be able to fully access the Internet.

Products that implement Bluetooth technology are essentially consumer-electronic-centric, mainly using the technology to eliminate wires that interconnect a small set of specific personal devices. Although some products can access the Internet, this has not been the focus of the technology. The focus of the technology is to allow lower-capability devices – such as headsets, TV remotes and digital pens – to interact with other personal data products.

The goal of Bluetooth wireless technology is to replace the wires between objects that are close to each other and then network to the larger world when/if convenient. This wire replacement technology is intended as an embedded connection between large varieties of devices, many with limited capabilities.

The goal of 802.11 technologies is specifically to enable its devices to become part of the worldwide communications infrastructure, connected wirelessly. The design of these devices is aimed at making them a fully capable peer on the network.

The user utility of 802.11 and Bluetooth technologies is complementary. They are not mutually exclusive but instead do exist on a utility continuum – there is overlap. What kind of utility the user needs will determine the user's choice of technology.

Appendix A

Which 802.11?

One of the difficulties of marketing 802.11 is that there are so many activities going on in that IEEE Working Group. There is not just one '802.11'. They all share some of the underlying structure and functions in the way they work, but have different kinds of radios. As mentioned before, this discussion generally uses the 'b' version as the representative of this group.

Making the way the various 802.11s work the same is great for the applications programmer who wants to be able to write one program to use all these different radios. It is not so great for an end-user who sees two devices that are seemingly the same, but since they have different kinds of radios, cannot function with each other. This is an important issue for 802.11 marketing, but is outside the scope of this article.

As a summary, the following flavors of 802.11 exist or are currently in development:

- 802.11   Original Standard.
- 802.11a   5 GHz High Rate Standard.
- 802.11b   2.4 GHz High Rate Standard (11 Mbps).
- 802.11e   Quality of Service.
- 802.11f   Access Point Coordination.
- 802.11g   2.4 GHz Higher Rate (+20 Mbps).
- 802.11h   Spectrum Managed 802.11a.
- 802.11i   Enhanced Security.

Which WPAN?

Just as the 802.11 has its variants, so does the WPAN world. To over-use the term, the differences are different.

Whereas all the 802.11s share a common way of working, all three of the WPANs defined by 802.15 are very different. They each have a different way of working at the Media Access level.

In some ways this is an advantage: all the WPAN technologies are called by different names (Bluetooth®, WiMedia™, ZigBee™) and address very different needs. WiMedia emphasizes high speed with high functionality. ZigBee offers a very simple, very-low-capability data service. Bluetooth wireless technology lies between them.

Currently only Bluetooth products have a significant presence in the marketplace.

Chapter 11

A pioneer for mobile communications

Derrick Emeka

Head of Marketing, TDK Systems Europe

TDK Systems Europe Ltd began life as Grey Cell Systems over 10 years ago. As one of the early players in the mobile communications business, TDK Systems' track record includes an impressive range of 'firsts'. In the early 1990s, it was one of the first companies in Europe to offer credit card-sized network cards for notebook computers and among the first to make modems easy to use in different countries using software configuration. It pioneered the way in combining technologies such as LAN, modem, ISDN and GSM onto a single credit card-sized product.

Success with its PC Card (credit card-sized) mobile products attracted direct investment from TDK Corporation, who acquired the company in 1997 to establish their European mobile communications research and development center.

Over the last 10 years the company has grown considerably – it now employs more people and has a network of international local offices. Throughout this period of growth, TDK Systems has always stayed true to its entrepreneurial, innovative roots and it has never wavered from its core competencies.

TDK Systems is a relatively small division of TDK Corporation. You may know TDK for the manufacturing of tapes, cassettes, DVDs and other audio products. It may also stick in your minds because of the rather large corporate logos that it has positioned in both Piccadilly Circus in London and also in Times Square in New York.

Coming from a non-technological background into a world submersed with highly sophisticated innovative technologies, I naturally grimaced with uncertainty and questioned 'what I was letting myself in for', but found solace in knowing that, if I stuck to some core marketing principles, I would not be far off the mark and therefore found the challenge that faced me at TDK Systems quite a mouth-watering task.

In any new working environment, as a marketer, the key in developing a marketing strategy that works is firstly to understand what the market consists of, i.e. competitors, channels to market, a profile of your target audience, the culture of your company, etc. Conducting a marketing audit is therefore imperative, as this will provide you with a skeletal framework which you can plan, build and incorporate into your marketing strategy.

At TDK Systems, the challenge was to not only set up a marketing department, but also to change the culture of the company from being product focused to being market focused. However, there was an additional and fairly unusual challenge that faced me. As already mentioned, TDK Corporation is a well-known company and has a strong market appeal to both buyers and non-buyers of audio-cassettes. The task therefore was to market a little-known division that uses the TDK name and to associate it with something that very few people have heard of. Despite TDK having a good reputation for the audio products that it markets, it would no doubt be a challenge for users to suddenly embrace TDK as producers of something completely different. I suppose it's a bit like McDonald's making and selling washing powder but still marketing the product under the McDonald's brand.

After conducting my marketing audit, I put a five-year marketing strategy together which was designed to help position TDK Systems as a leading player within the wireless connectivity world within two years; and, within five years, to move TDK Systems from being a product provider of wireless connectivity to being a one-stop shop provider of products, applications and services (such as consultancy). This strategy would simply be a benchmark for the future, as one cannot possibly predict market changes and customer adoption for new technology. Any strategy should be flexible enough to change but should be accurate enough to use as a launching program to propel the company in the right direction.

Our marketing roadmap

To succeed within this industry, we felt that we had to achieve some key aspects, namely:

- Develop a brand identity unique to TDK Systems, which would help to increase TDK Systems' brand equity and help change customer perception from TDK Systems being associated with tapes and cassettes to making them more synonymous for the manufacture and marketing of wireless connectivity products.
- Generate awareness and interest in TDK Systems by increasing our visibility and profile.
- Become global-centric in attitude and market our products outside the UK.
- Create marketing models which would help to identify and establish a profile of early adopters and various purchase behaviours, and use this as a benchmark upon which to focus on mid to late adopters.
- Establish education programs by way of clear messaging, user guides, online training courses, on-site training, demonstrations and presentations at events and shows. This would help to show that we were prepared to stand behind the product that we were evangelizing. Additionally, we would educate the channels that sell our products in why they should sell our products and educate the users on how and why they should use our products.
- Focus more on above-the-line, below-the-line and on-the-line marketing activities, to concentrate on maximizing the return from our core early adopter customers.
- Focus more on customer relationship marketing and set measurements to help measure the efficacy of marketing campaigns.

A five-year summary

Year 1

Convert TDK Systems to a wireless company with a new identity and position it as a thought and product leader with early adoption customers.

Year 2

Drive increased revenue through education and added value marketing. This would focus on both early adopters and the next stream of customers. Specialize in business development projects to create an install base for development in year 3. Start first level of services marketing. Start focusing on the B2C market and commence e-commerce plans. Start telemarketing campaigns.

Year 3

Generate loyalty marketing initiatives. Activities such as club websites and affiliated programs will help to retain business that has been won during years 1 and 2. Move to next stage of services marketing. Develop marketing strategy across more vertical markets, helping to drive in new revenue streams.

Year 4

Initiate the start of consultancy business unit. Begin marketing professional services. Offer sales, R&D and marketing expertise as part of consultancy package. Continue to market new products and applications embracing elements of years 1, 2 and 3.

Year 5

Marketing focuses on two separate entities: (1) product and applications; (2) consultancy. Diversification means marketing can position TSE as a one-stop shop solutions provider.

Understanding the market through purchasing behaviour

In order to market wireless (Bluetooth technology), we had to ensure that we understood the reasons why customers buy technology and what they hope to gain from their purchase. Our initial focus was going to be towards the corporate and then, later, the retail customers. To this end, I devised two models that would help us segment our target audience and then, over time, deliver compelling messages and products that would stimulate not only adoption of Bluetooth products, but also demand for TDK Systems products as a first choice.

The first model was a purchasing behavioural model, which applies to both B2B practitioners as well as B2C. The aim of this model was to understand the reasons that trigger one's need to purchase technology.

The second model is called an *objective of purchase model*. If one has a reason to buy, then my belief is that the purchaser has an objective that they want their purchase to fulfill. For example, if you choose to buy a particular cup, you may do so because of its color, price, style (cosmetics), size, etc. Once you have bought it, the objective may then be to have a cup of coffee or tea, or a soft drink, or perhaps to simply use it as a decorative element and it may not even be used for a drink. In any event, there is a reason for purchase.

Technology is no different. The purchasing model looks at four key elements:

- Technology.
- Brand.
- Price.
- Solutions provider.

Each of these four main areas is then broken into a further four subsections.

Technology

Support

Support in this context has a two-fold meaning. It is determined by pre- and post-sales support, but also encompasses future-proofing a company's technology development with products that continually meet purchasers' needs and are compatible with other devices that are bought.

Reliability

Reliability refers to buying a product that is going to work with other products (what the industry terms as interoperable). It also refers to durability and longevity.

Security

Security about new technology products is a concern that affects many. Ensuring that new products are as secure as they can be, or proving that a lot of work has gone into making them secure, is something that users are likely to take comfort from when they come to purchase the product.

Best

Best technology is hard to quantify, but many end-users would like to buy, if possible, the perceived best product in the marketplace, as it is likely to have embraced the first three subheadings under technology. Products that have received good media coverage in terms of their performance and satisfaction from other purchasers go a long way in positioning themselves as the best or indeed a benchmark on which to measure others.

Brand

Affiliation

Brand affiliation is something that we define as a customer who 'lives and breathes' a particular brand. For example, if someone buys a particular brand of phone and there happens to be some negative press about one of its associated products or its methods and processes, such negative statements in the press may not deter some of its 'diehard' customers, as they may still buy products associated with this brand. As a competitive manufacturer, it may therefore prove difficult to persuade such customers to buy your brand over the one to whom they have established such loyalty. However, one of the advantages to Bluetooth being such a new technology is the potential for vendors such as TDK Systems to develop brand affiliation at an early stage.

Loyal

We define loyal customers as those who have been persuaded enough to attach a sense of commitment and belief in the brand that they are buying and therefore continue to purchase new products of this brand, if the products fit in with either their business or personal needs.

Undecided

Undecided buyers are those who are still presently doing their own audit as to what they want to buy. IT managers tend to get samples from vendors and test the products to see which ones they want to purchase based on price and performance, amongst other things. Retail customers tend to read up as much as they can about different products and brands, and then, based on their own analysis, make a calculated decision on what brand and product to purchase.

Switchers

We define switchers as those who buy different brands randomly. This can be due to two reasons:

- To test new brands out as they do not feel a sense of loyalty to previous brands.
- Because they are not happy with previous purchases.

Price

Cheap

Cheap in this instance is defined by us as a product priced at a point that is comparatively lower than competing products.

Rebates

Rebates are something that some users look for when they buy a product. From our experience, they seem to be more common in the United States than elsewhere in the world.

Competitive

We define competitive price as those products whose price competes comparatively with other similar products on the market and which perform well enough to satisfy a user's expectations.

Premium

Finally, a premium price is defined by us as a product that is priced comparatively higher than competing products on the market.

The premium price, however, does not necessarily mean that the product performs better than competing products.

Solutions provider

Applications

Applications are something that we believe add immense value to the hardware. Our feeling at TDK Systems is that, eventually as the market matures, a Bluetooth PC Card will be pretty much the same whatever brand of product you buy. However, the key differentiator will be the software inside it, which the user does not see. We define the applications here as the software that makes a customer's life easy when it comes to installing the product and unique functionalities that allow the Bluetooth product to have more value.

Partnerships/consultancy

Partnerships we believe are key to aid and stimulate adoption of Bluetooth at the early stage. These partnerships could be based on complementary device manufacturers, such as those producing handsets, PDAs and laptops. By forming a partnership with these players, TDK Systems can position itself as having products that are continually tested with mobile devices, which will help to convince the end-user that their needs for evolving mobile communications are being addressed.

Some customers will be looking for companies who can give impartial advice about wireless products. Our experience positions us to be able to deliver this and is something that we can additionally offer customers. Therefore, our message is that, when you buy a product from TDK Systems, you buy into a world of complete mobile solutions which includes applications and services. Furthermore, we can position ourselves as being supportive to the customer as their mobile communication needs evolve.

One-stop shop

Finally, our *one-stop shop* characteristic here groups customers who are looking to put all their eggs into one basket and work with only one company to satisfy all their wireless (Bluetooth) communication needs.

This model will probably not represent every individual that buys technology, but is simply used as a benchmark to position purchase behaviours and hopefully achieves an 80/20 rule whereby other purchasing characteristics will fit somewhere within the model. For example, if someone buys a particular brand of product like a Sony Mini Disc Player because of a habitual association to this type of brand or product then, as you can see from the model, *habit of purchase* is not represented. However, in this particular case, we would have positioned the buyer somewhere in between price and brand, as their decision to purchase is probably related to both price and brand.

Alternatively, if an end-user buys a particular technology because it is in 'vogue' and there is a desire to 'keep up with the Joneses', then this behaviour would be positioned somewhere between technology and brand.

A purchase behavioural model

The purpose of this segmentation is to develop clusters of similarity or dissimilarity so that the right message can be targeted to an end-user, depending on where they reside on the scale. However, until we know what stimulates end-users to buy wireless communications, it will be difficult to gauge accurately what compelling marketing messages stimulate different users to purchase.

There are 14 business sectors shown in the model in Figure 11.1; if we look at where the Electronics and Engineering sector sits within the model, it is clear that end-users buy (or would buy) wireless technology based on its perceived reliability and quality. It is also clear that the sector has a good idea of the brands that it is likely to associate with reliability, as it is positioned near the brand affiliation point.

TDK Systems therefore would need to market a message to this sector of its experience and knowledge within wireless. Even though wireless is still very new, TDK Systems was at the foundation stage of its evolution. If companies within this sector have not heard of TDK Systems, then education about our history, how compatible and secure our products are, and also our reputation in the marketplace, would be some of the messages that we would need to convey.

Purchase behavioural model

The next example (Figure 11.2), develops this model by demonstrating the types of marketing messages that can be conveyed to appeal to sectors based on their buying criteria. As already mentioned before, the Electronics and Engineering sector is clearly looking for a product that embraces reliability and security amongst other things, and therefore a premium price will be paid for a product if a buyer is confident that it embraces these qualities; perhaps this could be analogous to a user buying a *Mercedes-Benz* of technology.

TDK Systems would now need to market to this sector messages based on our reliability and experience, coupled with our strong brand recognition. The next example shows three messages targeted to three different business sectors, namely: FIRE (Finance, Investment, Real Estate), Utilities and Transport.

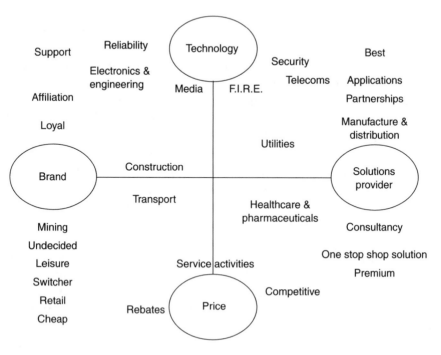

Figure 11.1   Purchasing behaviour model

Example of messages to address purchasing behaviour

For TDK Systems to position itself as a market-focused company and not be seen as a product-focused company, we felt that we needed to work with the end-user all the way through to the sales cycle; in other words, pre- and post-sales activity.

To this end, I developed an objective model (mainly for the corporates at this stage) and hoped that this method would help to develop long-term relationships with our buyers. I was also of the belief that future-proofing a company's products is all good and well, but another important element to support this is to future-proof a company or buyer's needs.

The objective model Figure 11.3 shows segmentation similar in make-up to the purchase behavioural model. If we continue to look at the Electronics and Engineering sector, you will see that they are positioned near the Business Support objective.

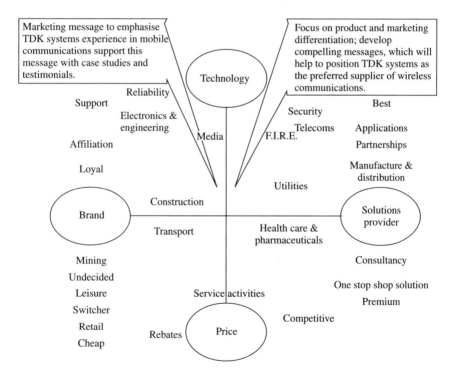

Figure 11.2 Purchasing behaviour model

Their objective is clear
'They are looking for technology that will support their business whilst they go through the process of re-engineering or restructuring their business.'

Business objective model

The objective model allowed us to try and develop a directory of case studies and testimonials segmented by business sectors, which we hope will develop 'fear and greed' within the industry. In other words, if two companies working in the same industry sector are competing with each other and one adopts and embraces wireless communication into their corporate infrastructure, any resulting growth in profit and productivity may trigger a response from their competitor, who may suddenly show more interest in wireless communications as a direct result of their competitor's improved competitive status against them.

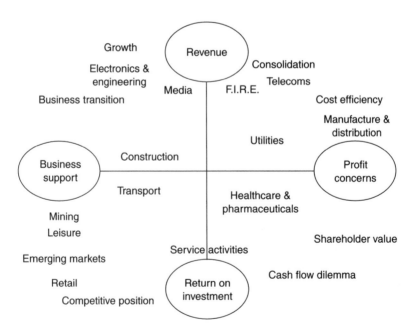

Figure 11.3   Objective of purchase model

Having developed this model, TDK Systems was well armed to try and position itself as the preferred supplier for wireless communications.

In a similar manner to the purchase behavioural model, the objective of the purchase model has four main areas for segmenting the market, namely:

- Revenue.
- Profit concerns.
- Return on investment.
- Business support.

Each of these four areas has an additional two subsections.

Revenue
Growth
We define a business's growth as being either internal or external, which has a direct result on its performance. By internal growth, we believe that a business will look to use technology as a way of increasing productivity and performance. In short, allowing the use of technology to improve and complement the existing resource that the business currently uses.

Consolidation
We define consolidation in this model as a business that has embraced technology to help it consolidate its current position in the marketplace.

Profit
Cost efficacy
We define cost efficacy as a company that is looking to achieve maximum productivity from every dollar spent.

Shareholder value
Shareholder value is where a company looks to achieve a profit for its shareholders from their investment in the company.

Return on investment
Cash flow dilemma
We define cash flow dilemma through companies who want to invest in wireless communications, but need to find ways of investing

without negatively impacting upon their current expenditure constraints.

Competitive position
We believe that most companies today try to attain a competitive position in the marketplace. Purchasing technology can help them to achieve this goal if it complements and enhances their way of working.

Business support
Business transition
Technology can aid business transition. By this, we mean transforming the culture and methodology that a company uses, by helping to secure the transition of its mindset. This can help a company to become more competitive.

Emerging markets
As companies evolve, and as industry develops, emerging markets will begin to open up new opportunities. The acquisition of new technology can help companies enter into new areas and remain competitive. For example, a furniture company could be looking at embedding Bluetooth technology into its products to add value to its existing range. This will undoubtedly open up a new audience of consumers and help to pull new business towards them. The technology can help to support the company's push to a new level.

Data intelligence

As we understood more about purchase behaviour and the subsequent objectives, we captured the data into a bespoke new database called 20/20. This allowed both the sales department and the marketing teams to gain an understanding of how best to target customers and individuals alike.

Such information would allow us to prioritize and focus on the areas of the model that we believed would bring in the quickest return. All that remained was for TDK Systems to ensure that it had the right message to complement various products and services that it was marketing to customers, based on their positioning within these models.

Bluetooth hype at CeBIT in the millennium

At CeBIT (the IT show in Hanover, Germany) in March 2001, companies showed the Bluetooth products that they were about to launch.

However, prior to this show, there were two years of hype surrounding Bluetooth and, consequently, customers' expectations were high. Due to this, we made a conscious decision *not* to be first to market. The reason for this was that our competitive intelligence told us that the products and services would fall far short of customers' expectations. If our products were launched at the same time, then we felt that their success would be camouflaged by the unhappy turbulence that would be likely to hit the media and, as a result, our products would be looked upon in a bad light.

From the start of 2001 to the launching of our first Bluetooth product later that year, we spent a lot of our time getting our branding right and ensuring that the new look and feel of TDK Systems reflected the expectations of our customers.

The launch of 'go blue'

We created a new logo and motif called 'go blue', which is the name given to our Bluetooth products. We felt that Bluetooth was not the user-friendliest name for a technology. Those in the industry were already used to this name but, to the average customer, the

Figure 11.4 The blue5

Figure 11.5   The 'go blue' logo

name 'Bluetooth' probably did not echo their feelings about wireless technology.

We also acknowledged the importance of brand recognition within the industry and, thereby, establishing a brand name to our products assumed a level of importance and trust. Customers over time would come to ask for one of our products by its brand name rather then the industry term; for example, I use a TDK Systems go blue PC Card, as opposed to a TDK Systems Bluetooth PC Card.

We launched our first products several months after our competitors. This product, which we called blue5, was designed to add Bluetooth functionality to the PalmV and PalmVx products.

What can blue5 offer customers?

The blue5 stamped TDK Systems' emergence into the wireless arena. It was launched on 31 August 2001.

By the time of the launch of the blue5 product, the TDK Systems brand was well established; however, the brand, although well known in the corporate world, was not so strong in the retail world. Our initial focus, however, was to the corporates, as it was felt that the knowledge and use of the Bluetooth products would be adopted by them and then eventually filter down to retail. However, as it emerged, the strength of adoption would be arguably stronger in retail rather than at corporate level. It was also a well-known fact that mobile phones integrated with Bluetooth would be the product driving force for Bluetooth connectivity, as you would need another Bluetooth device at the other end in order to utilize the Bluetooth functionality in the phone. As corporates continued to update their standard mobile phones, we expected that the opportunity would come where large corporates standardized on phones that had Bluetooth. This would give us the opportunity to provide Bluetooth connectivity to these phones with our blue5 product.

However, we realized that Palms were not seen as the corporate devices that mobile phones were. Although a lot of people that worked in the office had Palms, they were not part of a corporate purchase; studies suggested that 80 percent of office workers who had a Palm bought the product themselves for personal use.

We were left with two scenarios, which had to be acted upon quickly. Firstly, we had to find ways of getting users of Palms in the corporate workplace to consider getting more value out of their corporate mobile phone and their personal Palm device, by connecting the two together. This would, for example, enable them to get online whilst away from their PC.

The second scenario would be for TDK Systems to launch another Bluetooth product, which would have greater corporate appeal. The other mobile device that would allow this would be a laptop, which

Figure 11.6 Bluetooth PC Card

Figure 11.7   The BlueM product

will enable you to connect to your mobile phone and get online whilst on the move.

To this end, we launched our Bluetooth PC Card and Bluetooth USB Adaptor in October 2001. The Bluetooth PC Card added Bluetooth functionality to a laptop that had a PCMCIA slot, whilst our Bluetooth USB Adaptor added Bluetooth functionality to both laptop and desktop PCs that have a USB port.

Shortly after the release of the USB Adaptor and PC Card products, we launched two new additional Bluetooth products for PDA connectivity. We launched blueM for the Palm M500, M505, M515, M125 and M130 series of Palms. This product was positioned at users who had recently purchased Palm devices. The blue5 product was positioned at customers who wanted to upgrade their legacy Palm device.

The final PDA Bluetooth product that we launched was the blue-PAQ. This product was designed to bring Bluetooth functionality to Compaq i-PAQ PDAs.

Can Bluetooth technology coexist with WiFi?

After the launch of these products, the industry became embroiled with statements that caused confusion. These centered on other wireless standards called 802.11b and 802.11a, which are now referred to as Wi-Fi and Wi-Fi5 respectively. The statements that were made in the press about the Wi-Fi standards suggested, in

Figure 11.8 The blue-PAQ

short, that Bluetooth has no place in wireless communications; instead, Wi-Fi and Wi-Fi5 were the standards that you needed. This naturally placed the Bluetooth standard in a bit of a quandary and many authoritative speakers spoke up to put the record straight. In short, the message that came back in defense of Bluetooth was that Bluetooth and Wi-Fi are complementary technologies and not competing technologies. As such, both have a purpose and place, and neither Wi-Fi nor Bluetooth can take the place of the other.

The key factors that need to be addressed to succeed in marketing wireless

Now that Bluetooth's position in the industry was assured, thanks to the defense of those that understand the strengths and weaknesses of Bluetooth technology, all that remained was to see the adoption of the technology. From our research that we conducted at TDK Systems, it became clear that there were four key things that needed to be addressed if Bluetooth products were to be embraced.

Ease of use

If Bluetooth products were not easy to use, then customers would be put off by the technology. At TDK Systems, we felt that if you cannot get the product working within at least five minutes, then it is likely that the customer will not make a repeat purchase or, worse still, use the product that they had bought.

Compatibility

If the product does not work with other Bluetooth products, then its use is negated.

It's analogous to Alexander Graham Bell's invention of the telephone. The fact is that the best invention was the second phone, as Bell would not have been able to communicate with one phone alone.

It is essential that Bluetooth products are compatible with competing devices, as this will ensure that Bluetooth, and wireless in general, becomes the pervasive technology that is predicted by many.

Affordability

As Bluetooth products will tend to be accessories or peripherals, it is important that they are not too expensive. When users purchase expensive laptops and PDAs, the last thing that they want to do afterwards is to purchase another expensive item in order to get their device to connect to their phone. Therefore, the more affordable the product, the better. However, this is a subjective issue and it is hard to agree on what is an affordable price, as views may differ from one customer to another. At TDK Systems, we felt that if the product was arguably the most compatible and interoperable product on the market, was easy to use and was proven to be secure, then we would be able to position our products at a competitive price at the upper end, rather than at the lower end.

Security

Are Bluetooth products secure? This is a question that has traditionally plagued the uptake of new technology. Corporate and retail customers alike feel quite insecure about a new technology's level of security. Bluetooth is no different to this and the onus, therefore, has to be on the manufacturers and the Bluetooth Special Interest Group (SIG) to help eradicate fears about the technology's possible insecurity.

The fact of the matter is that Bluetooth is as secure as they come. This is partly due to the fact that Bluetooth works within a 10-meter range (although some products can work up to 100 meters) and, as such, you will be able to see if anyone is trying to interfere with your device's communication. An additional problem is that the complementary technology Wi-Fi had received a lot of negative press about its security. Because this is a wireless technology, the tendency is to bracket other wireless technologies as insecure. Bluetooth has therefore indirectly been associated within the Wi-Fi space as a technology that some believe to be insecure.

Marketing services

Over the years, TDK Systems has acquired a lot of knowledge of mobile communications. The fact that the Bluetooth industry is crying out for companies to impart their knowledge, so that users can understand the A to Z of technology, has led to a new chapter in marketing at TDK Systems and given rise to our marketing services program, which was part of our marketing roadmap.

Education is key – information is king

The emergence of b-Informed

As discussed in Chapter 3, users of technology are constantly bombarded with acronyms, or the next best thing, before they have had the chance to get used to the previous best thing. In short some, if not most, users can occasionally become bamboozled by the speed in development of technology and not achieve the full potential of their previous purchases.

We at TDK Systems took it upon ourselves to help educate users of wireless technology and tried to unravel the spaghetti that existed within the industry. Because of the importance of this, we decided to set up a new brand called *b-Informed*, which was designed to help educate both existing and potential users of Bluetooth technology.

The b-Informed brand consisted of three sub-brands or portals, outlined as follows.

Applications Insight

The Applications Insight portal consists of factual case studies to help a user b-Informed on just how wireless solutions are proving valuable to companies in varying environments. Through case studies and other examples, we feel that it goes some way to build a 'fear and greed' element in companies who are unsure about the value that Bluetooth technology can bring to a user or users within a corporate environment.

Business Source

The Business Source portal under the b-Informed umbrella brand helps a user to understand how wireless applications influence business decisions and impact on companies, in all sorts of ways.

With a focus on applications and solutions, Business Source reports on return on investment from wireless application development. Findings that were arrived at from in-depth research by consultants who worked with TDK Systems has shown how deployment of Bluetooth technology into a company's corporate infrastructure can lead to a quick return on its investment.

Candid Technology

This portal provides both business and consumers with truthful and straightforward information about changes in new and emerging technologies and standards.

b-Informed, with the latest reports and white papers, offers all the information you needed to unravel conflicting statements about technological advances. Candid Technology helps to educate users to make sense of the acronyms and allows them to make informed choices when it comes to purchasing Bluetooth and other wireless products.

We see that the onus is on vendors to educate users about new technology. For Bluetooth to become a success, it is imperative that the user understands what he or she is buying, and this means knowing its strengths as well as its weaknesses.

One of Bluetooth's issues today is that it was marketed as a panacea for all things. Because of this, customers' expectations were high and Bluetooth fell short of what users expected it to do. The technology is now beginning to become understood within the market, but there is still a long way to go, as new applications emerge that will enable the user to get more out of the hardware that he or she has purchased. This, therefore, will not necessarily require the buyer to buy new hardware, but will simply allow them to get more value from their existing hardware, thereby proving the value that one gets from Bluetooth technology.

There is an additional responsibility on vendors to provide technical or customer support to users who have purchased Bluetooth products. With any new technology, there will always be a learning curve that users will need to take until they become familiar with the technology. Until then, customers will no doubt experience teething problems from their purchase. An effective after-sales support service is therefore paramount to establish loyalty for a vendor. Manufacturers who market usable and affordable products, and complement them with an effective after-sales support service, will go a long way towards establishing a loyal customer base which, in turn, will help to develop a strong brand for the company.

To this end, TDK Systems has supplemented its education portal with an online support service, as well as a phone support service free of charge to customers. We also support users of non-TDK Systems' products, as we believe that wireless will eventually become pervasive and that everyone has the right to learn and understand how this new technology will eventually have an effect on our everyday lives.

b-Informed was the starting point of TDK Systems launching its marketing services program with a focus on education. We marketed the portals (sub-brands) of b-Informed, namely Applications Insight, Business Source and Candid Technology, as the ABC of education.

Training – making education interesting

As part of the development of our b-Informed program, we launched a training services program, which gave us the opportunity to bring a new meaning to education.

The training program consisted of two areas:

1 An online training tool.
2 A face-to-face training program, either at the customer's site or at TDK Systems. This training can be tailored to suit the customers' requirements.

This is a chargeable service, as we felt that there was an important value associated with it. There was also the feeling that, if it was marketed as a free service, it may lessen the value.

TDK Systems had, for far too long, given away its knowledge base free of charge, without getting a return from it. This was now set to change, as we saw this as an important business-generating unit for TDK Systems.

Delivery of messages to stimulate purchase

As part of TDK Systems' marketing strategy, various forms of above-the-line, below-the-line and on-the-line marketing activities were created as a way of evangelizing our products and services message. We created a pan-European advertising campaign, called the Freedom Campaign, to help us generate awareness about what TDK Systems could deliver. Added to this, we launched a global PR campaign, which helped to elevate the profile of TDK Systems within the media.

We also devised sales promotion campaigns to help attract users to TDK Systems and also to try and establish loyalty from our routes to market, which is through the distribution chain. Additionally, we delivered various messages through e-marketing campaigns such as emails and web activities.

Despite being a small division of TDK, our message reached most parts continuously, and customers within the industry believed TDK Systems to be a lot bigger in size than we actually are. Initially our message was delivered *en masse* but, as our knowledge of buyers and their requirements matured, our marketing became more targeted.

Where next for Bluetooth?

Our marketing roadmap for the next three years is set, although this may change depending of the development of the Bluetooth market. Nonetheless, we have a guideline to assess and plan our marketing future. However, the industry, as it matures, shows some obvious signs. The Bluetooth market is becoming more fragmented; products are becoming more commoditized and margins are becoming harder to realize.

These three factors were always considered to be the likely scenario for Bluetooth, but perhaps what is most disturbing today is that some companies who are part of the original Bluetooth hierarchy are investing heavily in Wi-Fi and seem to be turning their back on Bluetooth.

Bluetooth technology can only succeed if it receives the investment that it deserves, with an explanation of the technology's potency. Our marketing roadmap gives us the focus to carry this through and, despite large players seemingly turning their back on Bluetooth, it opens up a wonderful opportunity for TDK Systems to exploit the gaps left by other companies who would do well in investing a fraction of the amount that has been spent on Wi-Fi to show how Bluetooth can fill parts that Wi-Fi cannot satisfy.

We believe that Bluetooth technology will become pervasive, and we at TDK Systems intend to be a major part of its success.

Chapter 12

Marketing the advanced operating system for mobile phones

Simon Garth

General Manager, Symbian, UK

Andrie de Vries

Head of Business Intelligence, Symbian, UK

The wireless industry is undergoing fundamental change from a voice to voice-and-data proposition. This requires a new generation of device able to combine delivery of next generation data services with the traditional characteristics of a consumer-oriented mobile phone. Such phones will be centered on advanced operating systems, based around open standards, to deliver a combination of power and flexibility. Symbian OS is such an operating system that has been adopted by all the key players in the mobile phone industry to power their next generation handsets. In this chapter, we will review the role of the open operating system in phone design and consider the way in which it enables a varied proposition to each element of the mobile market, including content owners, mobile operators, phone makers and retail channels. We will also discuss some of the challenges that face the industry and explore possible solutions.

Market overview

Historical perspective

To understand the future development of mobile telephony, it is useful to briefly review the evolution of the end-user proposition.

When Alexander Bell invented the telephone, he probably did not think in his wildest dreams that there would be one billion users of his invention by the year 2000. Even less would he have foreseen that his invention would eventually go wireless. In fact, in 2002 there were 1.1 billion mobile subscribers; a mobile phone for every six people on the planet.

Technologies take a long time to mature and reach the mass market. The first analog mobile phones became available in the 1970s, and the now popular Global System for Mobile communications (GSM) technology was standardized in the 1980s, but by 1995 there were still only 100 000 mobile subscribers. Once this critical stage was reached, a surge of growth started that continues in the developing regions of the world.

Analog mobile phones, for the first time, gave users the freedom to make calls while they were away from the home or office. That was the proposition, but large handsets, limited network coverage and poor sound quality meant that initially the phones were restricted to small segments of the market (such as stockbrokers) and not the mass market. There were also significant problems with security in that it was reasonably easy to get fraudulent access to the network and make unpaid calls.

The development of digital mobile telephony solved many of these problems. It promised improved sound quality, smaller handsets and

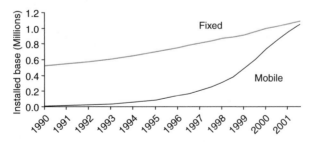

Figure 12.1 World fixed line and mobile subscribers

cheaper technology. The standards bodies also carried out huge amounts of work to encrypt the network transmission and the user identity modules. This meant that it became much more difficult to make fraudulent phone calls. The result was Time Division Multiple Access (TDMA), which provided interoperability between the older analog systems and the newer digital systems.

In the early 1980s, a group of European manufacturers and other interested parties defined a new standard for digital mobile telephony. This specification eventually turned into GSM and regulators across Europe demanded that all operators use the same standard. The impact of this standardization was profound – because it standardized both technologies and frequency allocation, manufacturers were able to maximize economies of learning and scale. The cost of equipment declined rapidly and interoperability became possible.

In North America, standardization did not happen to the same degree, with the result that GSM lived alongside Code Division Multiple Access (CDMA) and TDMA. As will be seen later, this lack of standardization was a major contributor to slow penetration rates of mobile services in North America.

Terrestrial mobile was not the only perceived solution to wireless communications. Hundreds of million of dollars were spent to launch a satellite-based wireless network. Iridium promised true global coverage – not just in those areas where a mobile network had been rolled out. But satellite phones were very bulky – the size of a laptop computer and thus only appealed to scientists or explorers in very remote areas. This, combined with the faster than expected take-up of conventional mobile phones, meant that the service never reached the critical mass required to compete. Instead of shrinking phone size and bills, the network revenue shrank and the service was decommissioned in 1999, only a year after its launch.

In parallel to the development of mobile telephony, there was a very rapid penetration of the Internet in fixed lines during the 1990s. By 2001, more than 50 percent of all people used the Internet in countries such as Canada, Sweden, Finland and Denmark.[32] The resulting Internet bubble then spilled over into the world of mobile, with many companies investing heavily in early attempts at establishing a market for Wireless Application Protocol (WAP) Internet access. In contrast to the experience in Japan, where similar services

---

[32] Source: OECD, Individuals frequently using the Internet, 2001, http://www.oecd.org/xls/M00035000/M00035855.xls.

were rolled out successfully, WAP usage had a very slow uptake in Europe. Today, with the peak of inflated expectations and the valley of disillusionment in the past, operators are seeing a slow increase in the usage of WAP and related mobile Internet technologies. Many European operators are achieving data revenue of between 10 and 20 percent – on a par with the experience in Japan. However, it is interesting to note that the European revenue is predominantly from text messaging, whereas I-mode browsing is more popular in Japan.

With the availability of packet-switched networks, such as General Packet Radio Services (GPRS) and CDMA2000, the entire infrastructure is now in place to provide a better data experience on mobile phones. This includes advanced picture messaging, email, games and music distribution.

During this rapid evolution of technologies and equipment, software had to evolve as well. Until recently, it was good enough to have a simple text interface to a monochrome screen. In contrast, the new generation of phones possess a large color screen and a graphical user interface, allowing easy, intuitive access to a calendar and contacts database. In addition, they provide the capability to take digital photographs, to look at short video clips and to play 3D games.

Evolution of the mobile phone market

The preceding sections outlined the historical development of the mobile phone market. Since the late 1990s, the industry has been heralding the dawn of the converged device, one that merges the functions of both voice and data. At that time, there was no clear

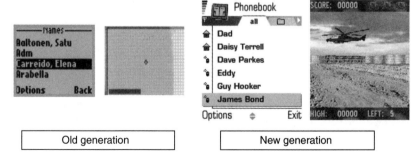

Figure 12.2

understanding of the detailed market proposition. Instead, there was a rather broad view that the worlds of computing (particularly personal computing) and mobile telephony would converge. Again, it was unclear as to whether one would cannibalize the other, or the converged devices would genuinely grow the market.

Fortunately, the combination of five years of experience, the end of the dot.com boom and some harsh commercial reality helped to resolve the situation. It is clear that neither the PC nor the mobile phone is in imminent danger of a premature demise. Indeed, further investigation suggests that, when looked at from a user rather than technology point of view, the two segments are quite separate. This may appear obvious with hindsight but, in the late 1990s, the use of PC software to drive mobile phones was regarded as a viable proposition.

Today, it is well understood that the user experience of a mobile phone is quite different to that of a PC and therefore requires a different type of software to power it. Whereas a user may have access to several PCs, perhaps one at work and another at home, they will typically only have one mobile phone that they use exclusively. The shared nature of 'personal' computers is also reflected in the sales volumes. Worldwide sales of PCs during 2002 were 132.4 million units,[33] whereas sales of mobile phones in 2002 were more than three times larger, at 423.4 million units.[34]

The relationship between phone and user makes it the ideal device to store information that is specific to the user. Today, this ranges from contact information through to individual preferences, such as ringtones and logos. In the future, it may well be a vehicle for personal identification and storage of more sensitive information, such as health records or credit card details.

The users' expectations of a phone are for a device that is 'transaction' oriented. Typically, a user will take out the phone, undertake a task (a call, a message, find a restaurant, etc.) and put the phone away. The transaction time generally spans from seconds to a few minutes, rather than minutes to hours, and must be simple and intuitive. Therefore, an operating system that takes time to 'boot up', requires keyboard typing and occasional restarts is quite unsuitable for mobile phone use.

It is this immediacy (instant access), mobility (always with you) and accessibility (can be used in almost any circumstance) of the

---

[33] Source: Gartner Dataquest, January 2003.
[34] Source: Gartner Dataquest, March 2003.

mobile phone that clearly separates it from personal computing. This underpins the market for a software solution that is designed from the ground up to meet the specific needs of mobile devices.

User evolution

The mobile phone is very firmly a mass-market consumer proposition. This is not to say that there is a lack of business or enterprise applications – far from it (and indeed some of the early market drivers for the technology will come from this segment). However, with more than 1000 million devices in the hands of users and an essentially saturated market in many countries in the Asia-Pacific region and Europe, it is clearly more of a mass-market proposition than almost any other consumer electronic device.

Marketing products and services into such a broad arena requires a number of elements:

- The proposition must be instantly compelling.
- It must be simple to access.
- It requires a vanguard group that will drive the market adoption.

In traditional mobile phones, the proposition is voice, the access is essentially the same as a standard desk phone (with the exception of the 'send' button) and the initial vanguard group was business.

Within data-enabled mobile phones, the proposition has been a combination of messaging and browsing (in differing proportions in different markets), again relatively simple to access, and the vanguard has been the youth market.

It is instructive to look further at WAP (described above) in order to learn some lessons as to how the market should be addressed. WAP is a technology initially created by one company and then developed by a consortium of organizations that represented the breadth of the mobile world. It was launched with great fanfare in 2000 but failed to meet the expected market growth. The detailed reasons for this have been well documented but, fundamentally, the service was incomplete. From a user point of view, WAP was slow, unappealing and poorly positioned. From a supply chain point of view, many of the key business decisions, such as revenue share between players, had not been adequately worked out. Early providers in the market found that they could not make a sustainable business based on the technology and many pioneering companies failed as a result.

In contrast, in Japan, NTT DoCoMo launched a service called iMode. Initially a browsing technology similar to WAP, with messaging and other services added later, iMode caught the imagination of the Japanese market and resulted in a very high level of take-up. iMode differed from WAP in a number of crucial respects:

- One company (NTT DoCoMo) took overall responsibility for ensuring that there was a viable end-to-end solution that delivered a genuinely valuable user experience.
- There existed a clearly defined revenue share model that allowed third party content providers to develop services within a predictable commercial framework.
- The services were marketed in terms of their end-user benefits ('book a restaurant') rather than in reference to the technology ('the Internet in your pocket').

There are some key lessons to be learned from these two very different experiences of market take-up.

- Firstly, it is essential that the user experience be taken into account. This is generally assisted if there is one organization that has overall responsibility for the end-to-end solution. While this may seem obvious, it is surprising how frequently this basic point is missed (we can all think of our favorite consumer disasters to illustrate the point).
- The experience must be simple to access. User research suggests that for each button press to access a service, usage drops off by as much as 50 percent. Clearly, if it takes six button presses to access a service, usage will be markedly reduced.
- The pricing model must be seen as 'reasonable' and predictable. This varies from market to market but is a key determinant in service take-up.
- The solution must be marketed to the target audience in terms of satisfying real user needs rather than in terms of the solution itself (addressing the 'so what' factor).

A key element in rolling out such services is the capability of the phone that provides the point of contact with the user. Many studies have shown that usage increases greatly with phones that simplify the user experience (such as providing color screens). The design of such phones is a major challenge, representing an investment of many millions of dollars. A substantial proportion of this cost can be eliminated through the use of an open OS such as

Symbian OS for the phone's design. In this way, phone makers can take advantage of advanced software technology to deliver a markedly improved user experience and so stimulate greater use of the phone's services.

It is critical to understand the very specific dynamics of service roll-out, according to the nature of the service. Services may be divided into three broad categories:

- Single user to single point of contact (e.g. phone connects to operator portal).
- Single user to many points of contact (e.g. general browsing solution).
- Many users to many points of contact (e.g. text messaging to other users).

These three scenarios require very different levels of infrastructure that greatly affect the speed of service roll-out. In the first example, there is a single point of contact in the operator portal. Therefore, once the portal is in place, phones may be sold in the shops and the user may instantly access the service.

The second case is similar, except that the usability of the service is determined by the number and variety of services that are accessible. Therefore, a critical mass of services is needed before the early adopters will have an acceptable user experience.

The final example is the most complex: a communication-based solution. Here, not only is it necessary to put in place the infrastructure to deliver the service and make the service available on phones, it is also necessary for the service capability to be deployed sufficiently widely that, when a user, for example, decides to send a message to another user, there is a high probability that the target user will be able to receive it. This problem is 'chicken and egg' – the service is viable only when there is a population of phones and yet there is unlikely to be a population until there is a viable proposition.

Multimedia Messaging (MMS) is a good example of the latter case. In an attempt to address this problem, providers have added the ability to send pictures to email and invested in a massive roll-out of the technology. Nevertheless, it is likely to be at least a year from initial roll-out of the service before the proposition is sufficiently widespread that it will get volume adoption.

The issue of service roll-out and the role of the phone in shortening the associated market penetration latency is discussed in more depth later on in the chapter.

Geographical segmentation

There are marked geographical variations in the evolution and marketing of advanced mobile phone services. The earliest adopters have been in Japan and the Asia-Pacific basin, with very high levels of mobile phone penetration.

In Japan, the services offered initially by NTT DoCoMo have been followed by others from J-Phone and KDDI. The dynamics of the market in Japan, in which the operator dominates the overall mobile phone supply chain, provides a simpler framework for service roll-out than in some other geographies. The Japanese market is particularly interesting for the relatively high take-up of services that are related to data and information. It is normal on commuter trains in Japan to see many people spending the time while traveling to and from work interacting with services on their phone. This provides a sound basis from which to launch further services, as long as the service itself continues to add real value to the end-user experience.

Mobile phone penetration in Europe is strong, with principally a voice and messaging proposition. The enforcement of a single standard (GSM) across Europe has led to a less fragmented market than in some other geographies and, in particular, a broad range of roaming capabilities across national boundaries. However, the relative lack of power (at least hitherto) of the operator within these geographies has been a factor that has slowed the overall deployment of data services. As we will see, this is likely to change over the coming years.

The United States has traditionally been a fragmented market, with over five different radio standards vying for the customer. As a result, coverage may be quite localized to the region in which the phone was purchased. However, adoption rates are increasing and there is a general standardization on two technologies – the European GSM standard and the CDMA standard, as driven by Qualcomm Inc. The US market has a higher degree of focus on applications for business and enterprise and, in an economy that is highly dependent on the car, solutions that are compatible with usage when driving are popular. The US market remains large and relatively untapped. When combined with one of the highest figures for per capita disposable income in the world, the market is clearly open to the uptake of services that capture the imagination of the user.

The role of software in the new value chain

The value system

Many related industries have to work together to give the end-user a delightful experience. The manufacturer has to make a compelling device and put the latest software in it. The phone has to be sold with a service contract (which could be prepaid) and the user must be billed for usage against the contract. If he or she then wants to download a Java game or a multimedia message, another set of software and content providers enter the picture.

These different strands combine to form a complex value system or value web, as illustrated in Figure 12.3.

Another reason why the value system is complex is the way in which it merges instantaneous product delivery and ongoing service provision. These services include:

- Voice and related network services, including making phone calls, voice messages, etc.
- Messaging, including Short Message Services (SMS), MMS and Instant Messaging (IM).

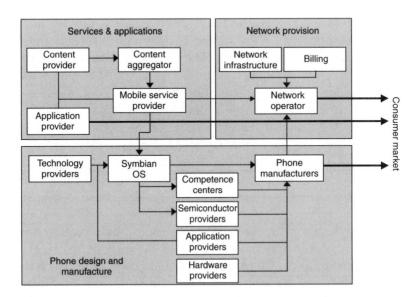

Figure 12.3   A complex value system or value web

- Online browsing in its various forms, including WAP, iMode and Vodafone Live!
- Games and Java application downloads.
- Future services, such as location, micro-payments and mobile wallet.

Phone manufacturing and design

The nature of phone manufacturing is also changing rapidly. The years between 1980 and 2000 saw very rapid innovation in new technologies. These led to end-user benefits such as miniaturization, increased battery life and very high call quality. Once mobile phones became cheap and reliable enough to penetrate the mass market, they became an expression of individuality and led to a proliferation of features to customize everything ranging from clip-on covers to personalized ringtones and wallpapers.

In a connected world, it was not good enough to provide voice communication. People were looking for alternative ways of communicating short messages – sometimes in an asynchronous way. In Europe, this gave rise to the unexpectedly rapid proliferation of SMS. The service caused a wave of improvements in the phone user interface (UI) to make text messaging easier. All of this was done through software. Perhaps the most striking innovation in this area was the development of predictive text, which afforded the user greater rapidity in keypad entry. The technology that became universally accepted was T9® text input by AOL Time Warner, which is now available in 39 languages in more than 180 phone models.

But predictive text in simple monochrome displays, while functional, limits the range of services that can be deployed. A mobile phone is perhaps the electronic device that people carry around the most. Thus, it is only natural that they will start to use it for other purposes too; to take pictures or listen to music, for example. Advanced operating system software makes these applications viable.

People have communicated in pictures for many centuries. In days gone by, people may have included a drawing of an object with a letter and, today, we still send postcards to each other from exotic locations. With the advent of digital cameras and the Internet, people are used to sending photographs to one another only hours after an event. Indeed, with cameras now incorporated into mobile phones, this can happen mere seconds after the event. The numbers speak for themselves. During 2002 there were about 20 million camera phones sold in the world – 5 percent of total phone sales – and the number is expected to rise sharply over the coming years.

Thus, the entire design of mobile phones is changing to enable the end-user to communicate with more of his or her senses. As a result, communication is moving from mouth and ear to include the eye as well.

So the phone itself plays two roles – it is a consumer electronic device in its own right and it is the medium through which a range of services and applications are delivered. A key question in the future marketing of phones will be to determine where the balance of the value proposition lies. Will the market evolve to support differentiated phones that are sold as fashion statements and deliver essentially standardized services? Or will it evolve rather like the PC market in which the phone is essentially commoditized and used as a vehicle to deliver a wide range of services? Today, nobody knows and, in reality, it is unlikely to be a binary choice. However, common to both approaches is the need for the phone itself to be flexible in order to respond to the challenges that the market throws at it.

Increasingly, the market is moving towards open phones that support software from multiple providers as a way of addressing this issue. Phone makers benefit from the ability to source major components of software without having to develop them individually (e.g. browsers, video players, etc.) and similar benefits are passed on to the operators and content providers that will interact with the phone in their role of delivering services. This ability to deliver open phones, i.e. phones to which new applications can be downloaded after manufacture, is a major selling point on the part of phone makers and, in some cases, is being used by the phone makers to extend their business model into content and applications that directly service the new generation of devices.

Network and service

The operator is central to the roll-out of mobile data services. The role of the operator varies widely with geography and, in the early market, the function of the operator was clearly defined. The operator carried the voice traffic and owned the corresponding infrastructure needed to ensure that a voice service would be supported from one phone to another. The operator's billing model was based on 'time-in-call', and the mobile phone was an object that initiated and terminated all calls. The delivery of the voice service was defined by standards bodies and, from the point of view of the operator, essentially all phones purchased for the network behaved alike in terms of the way they interacted with the operator's network. Therefore, the operator has a contained task of delivering the voice service between phones without significant consideration for the particular phone involved.

In the data world, the situation changes. Firstly, the services are no longer simple or necessarily defined by global standards bodies. The specifications that do exist frequently have room for interpretation, resulting in inadvertent variations between phones. In addition, the phone makers may explicitly add support for extensions that are not supported by other phone makers in order to be able to deploy differentiated services to their devices.

This shift from a standardized offering to a more varied one raises many challenges for the whole industry and, in particular, for the operators. Unless the operator defines the service, there is a risk of fragmentation in which the operator will need to support phones with many services that will vary from one phone to another.

To address this risk, many operators are taking a greater role in defining both the services and the phones that they will use to deliver them. This suggests a fundamental change to the operator's business model, from that of a 'pipe' towards that of a total service provider. Such a shift corresponds with a move towards greater user visibility of the operator brand and a desire to recover revenues from several locations in the value chain, including for instance content aggregation, service billing, m-commerce, advertising and publishing. Such a stretch to the operator business model provides both challenges and opportunities for the other elements of the value chain.

On the one hand, the operator becomes a route to market for services and applications. As discussed above, it is clear that an end-to-end service environment needs to be in place in order to stimulate significant take-up of services and the operator is well placed to deliver this. On the other hand, it is a threat to parts of the value chain that the operator wishes to aggregate. For instance, a content owner might wish to deliver services directly to the customer (and perhaps bill them through a subscription or existing billing arrangement, such as cable TV). This would run counter to the operator's intent and, indeed, the content owner may have a position in the market in terms of both brand and reach that would result in the operator being relegated to a low-value 'pipe' role. Therefore, those operators in a total service environment may choose to control access to other services (the so-called 'walled garden' approach) to limit the access of other content providers.

Service delivery

Operators vary widely in their approach to service delivery. Some take a hands-on role, defining and specifying (and paying for) each element of the required solution. Such approaches are particularly prevalent in some Asia-Pacific countries and for operators that use CDMA technology. Other operators take a more hands-off approach, delivering services through third parties and playing the role of a service broker rather than a service provider.

The principal challenge faced by the operators is matching the service opportunity to the market requirement that will exist when the service is available. Typically, the roll-out of new services can take upwards of two years and, in a fashion-conscious market, there is considerable opportunity for mismatch when the service materializes. Should such a mismatch occur in which the market requirement has moved faster than the product development, clearly there is a significant risk of missed opportunities and the potential for cost in the form of unsold products.

In order to address this risk and to make products that more accurately reflect the market need, operators continually seek ways of reducing this time to market, both to reduce their capital exposure and to make the business cases for new services more compelling. As we have discussed above, one of the key elements that contributes to lengthy roll-out times for new services is the need for a widespread availability of services in phones that are owned by the customer. To address this, the operators are increasingly specifying phones based on an open operating system such as Symbian OS that allows them to deploy services and applications to the phone after it is in the customer's hands.

For instance, if an operator wished to deploy an Instant Messaging (IM) solution using conventional phone technology, then the time taken for the service to grow close to its full potential is determined by the replacement rate of mobile phones. Depending on the geography, this is typically 18 months to three years and, because of the subsidy model, it represents a significant cost to the operator. If, however, users have open phones to which new services may be deployed, an entire user base can be updated instantly, allowing for a dramatic roll-out of services. This may then be coupled with a high-intensity marketing effort to stimulate uptake over a short period, rather than an elongated process that occurs with a slower roll-out. Such rapid deployment of services can only be undertaken using phones that can be updated in the users' hands – those based on an open phone operating system.

When phones used simple services, the choice of operating system in the phone was of no significant consequence to the operator (it was merely a component of the phone). In the new generation of open phones, the choice of OS is central to the operator's data services strategy and, increasingly, operators are selecting one or more operating systems to be deployed in the phones they carry in order to provide a common platform for advanced services.

Open OS phones have become progressively more widespread since 2001 from a number of mainstream phone vendors. These open phones bring with them both a developer community and a community of third party companies that have developed applications and services to target them. The operator provides the key route to market for these services, either pre-integrated into the phone before manufacture or available to be downloaded to the phone after purchase.

Content

'Content is king' is a mantra widely held in some quarters and hotly disputed in others. In the mobile world there are two broad classes of service – those in which the content is user generated (voice, messaging, photos, etc.) and those that rely on commercially generated material (browsing, music, video clips, etc.).

There is a large potential market for content delivery to mobile devices. Major companies with substantial content ownership, such as News International, Time Warner, Sony and others, have leading brands and other major media channels. Phones simply represent an additional aspect of the overall publishing mix and, indeed, initial examples of this with messaging-based services that tie into TV programming are available today.

The content owners have four challenges in addressing the mobile market:

- Route to market – this is generally controlled by the mobile carriers, and relationships need to be put in place to share brand, revenue and technology to deliver the content.
- Content protection – content owners suffer a piracy risk when content is sent to any connected device (e.g. music on the Internet) and a means of controlling distribution is essential.
- Standardization of distribution – content owners will not want to re-purpose their material for different formats of device, technology, etc. Standards need to emerge to provide a large enough target market to justify the investment.
- Content manipulation – content that is suitable for mobile use is not the same as that for the Internet or TV. Typically, content needs to be selected and possibly processed to make it compelling for small screen constrained devices such as mobile phones.

Despite these challenges, it is clear that there exists a major opportunity for the mobile phone to be used as a means of content distribution. The 'go anywhere' aspect of the proposition lends itself to touching the customer in many places and times that would normally be out of reach (for instance, to a TV company). In addition, the integration of services across multiple media channels offers new opportunities to play a greater role in the customer's overall media experience and so generate incremental revenues.

Early examples of the linkage of content and mobile phones may be seen with the recent launch of the '3' network in Europe and Asia. In contrast to conventional mobile carriers, the 3 network sees itself as a content publisher that also owns a network, rather than a network operator that has access to content. This fundamental shift is reflective of 3's view that revenue will be delivered by the value of the content and service and is unrelated to the technology that delivers it. Therefore, while some other companies choose to charge for services by the 'megabyte' of data used, 3 prefer to talk about minutes of video or numbers of messages.

With many different standards for content delivery and protection, the content providers are looking at phones based on an open operating system to ensure that the target phone is able to handle the delivered content appropriately. This is similar to the PC world, in which different video and audio players can be downloaded to handle the different content formats that are available. The open phones also allow whole applications to be downloaded that link content to other aspects of the device. For instance, it is possible to deliver TV listings to the phone and have them populate the calendar application within the phone, thereby integrating the data seamlessly with the user's normal phone experience.

We are still at the early stages of content delivery to phones. Certain basic standards of color screen, audio and video playback, browsing capability and data storage are needed before the service becomes sufficiently compelling that demanding consumers will regard it as a viable extension to their other media interaction experiences. However, with the advent of next generation phones and networks based on open standards, coupled with the ability to update their offerings dynamically, it is clear that content distribution to mobile is poised for rapid expansion.

Distribution, retail and after-sales support

Mobile telephony in the brave new world can only be a delightful experience if everything works correctly. Consumers will have different expectations of advanced phones. They will demand an experience that stimulates their eyes as well as their ears.

This may have a very profound effect on how phones are being sold. Consumers will want to be satisfied that all of the services they desire work on their phone before they leave a retail premises. Consequently, they may actually spend more time in-store when purchasing a new phone. Some of the more sophisticated retailers have recognized this and are changing store layouts to provide multiple zones. Simple services, such as the sales of pre-pay top-up, will be provided in 'zone 1', which is very close to the shop entrance. Customers who wish to make a simple transaction will do this very quickly. But customers who wish to purchase an advanced phone will be drawn deeper into the store. In this zone, they may meet a store representative who will demonstrate the phone, as well as the new services that are available. If the customer signs up to one of these services, for example picture messaging, then the store representative will ensure that the service is correctly configured.

There may also be additional software for sale in-store. Phone manufacturers are experimenting with new genres of phone, including games phones and music phones. This opens up the exciting possibility that phone retailers may sell games on memory cards in-store. This will lead to additional revenue streams, as well as the associated responsibility to provide a more comprehensive in-store range of products and services.

One of the challenges that the industry faces is the configuration and after-sales support of the handset. Until recently, most of the value-added services were wholly delivered by the network operator. These included SMS, call forwarding and barring, conference calling and voice mail. A phone could easily be configured, since every phone required, essentially, the same information – almost everyone would share the same messaging center number, for example.

This configuration task is rapidly getting much more difficult. Phones now have to be configured for email, web browsing, WAP browsing, MMS, SMS, IM, photo download sites, etc. – the list quickly becomes endless. Furthermore, the nature of this configuration information is increasingly that of a personal nature, rather than a universal nature. People will expect to download their photos to an online photo album that is unique to them.

To address these issues, network operators have a very clear requirement for over-the-air (OTA) configuration of the handset. This OTA provisioning could then be used to modify service configuration profiles. In addition, OTA provisioning opens up the possibility of upgrading software on the phone, fixing any problems to eliminate recalls, delivering new dynamic content and generally managing the state of the user's phone. Such concepts are alien to both users and providers today, but will appear in the coming years if we are to avoid the support mayhem that is the uncontrolled PC industry today.

The use of open standards helps the market to provide solutions that are not restricted to particular 'silos', but which instead will interoperate with each other. Examples of new standards include those that are under development within the framework of the Open Mobile Alliance (OMA), such as SyncML, Wireless Village and numerous forums aimed at aligning the industry in particular respects – for instance, in the way security or location information is handled. The standards themselves add little to the phones that incorporate them (the implementation is either compliant or it is not). As a result, it is attractive to select a phone operating system that embeds the standards-based implementations of particular services in order to eliminate the need to reinvent what are essentially formalized service implementations.

The counterpoint to this is the time it takes to develop new standards. Therefore, the most successful standards are often those that have been developed principally by one player (such as a handset maker or operator) and then rolled back into the standards process once a functional example is in place. This often reduces the overall development time and results in less complicated and more targeted solutions that better address the market.

Such a standards-based approach then allows both the pre- and after-market to develop support services that address a wide range of phones and minimize the disruption caused by technically complex solutions.

Challenges

It would be wrong to suggest that all of the problems associated with advanced mobile services have been solved. Many challenges remain, from the most basic elements of what the user wants (and is prepared to pay for) through to the technical and market issues of delivery and uptake.

The mobile phone business is unique. No other technology delivers a means of touching such a large number of people for such a large proportion of the day and with such a range of services and solutions. However, this very flexibility brings its own challenges. As anyone with a video recorder will know, there is a great difference between delivering a capability and encouraging users to take advantage of it (the vast majority of video recorders contain many functions that are never used). In general, this is not a problem, as there is no revenue associated with the use of video recorders. The situation is quite different in mobile phones, however, where the additional revenue generated results directly from whether or not such advanced functions are used.

In order to deliver high levels of service uptake, mobile services must deliver standards of quality and ease of use that are expected in simpler mainstream consumer equipment and are unheard of in more complex technology-oriented worlds, such as that of the PC. If new services mean a lower standard of utility for the core existing services (bigger phones, shorter battery life, etc.) take-up will be limited to a small band of early adopters. In the same way, services that rely on revolutionary changes in technology (e.g. moving from text messaging to picture messaging to video messaging) must be presented to the user as the logical progression of an idea and not as a disruptive change, even if the underlying technology has evolved beyond all recognition. Users will not read user manuals. It is the responsibility of the phone maker and service provider to design solutions that are immediately intuitive to the user in order to drive demand.

The challenges in bringing these advanced services to market may be summarized as:

- Ensuring a compelling user experience. This almost always relies on one player in the value chain (e.g. the mobile carrier) taking responsibility for the end-to-end delivery.
- Service roll-out latency – many services need a population of devices to be useful. Open OS phones provide a route to limit this latency to manageable levels.
- Creating an ecosystem – mobile data services are too large a topic for any one company. It is essential that an ecosystem is formed, in which companies and suppliers deliver solutions to make up the total offering. To do this requires standards in order to underpin a framework for such an ecosystem to develop.
- Keeping it simple – mobile is the ultimate mass-market proposition enabled by high technology. It is essential that the proposition itself is simple and compelling, and that the technical complexities are buried away from the user's view.

To achieve these goals, phones will use operating systems based on open standards, such as Symbian OS. These operating systems provide the enabling framework to allow the market to develop. It is then down to the mobile operators, service providers and phone makers to work together to deliver compelling solutions to the end customer base.

Part III

Looking to the Future

Chapter 13

Where do we go from here?

So what exactly is the future for wireless technology?

Are we all heading down a path of wireless-enabled mortality that will dominate our every waking (and possibly sleeping) moment, or will the cries of talking fridges and coffee machines become nothing more than a muffled wail of what could have been but just never took off? Espen Andersen,[35] an Associate Professor of Strategy with the Norwegian School of Management and European Research, published a fascinating paper in 2003 about his vision of a wireless future. In it, he likened the growth and application of wireless to the construction of an anthill. When observing its creation, worker ants initially appear to have no strategy, as their actions seem aimless and often completely unnecessary. However, what is later revealed as a result of their efforts is a highly organized and complex structure, which is testimony to the intelligence of the ants' behaviour. As a self-organizing system, like an anthill, Andersen portrays the growth of wireless by saying: 'The future belongs to small, connected devices that will wirelessly allow the user – and the technology – to self-organize, creating something smart out of many small and simple nodes and connections.'

This chapter explores the potential future of wireless by considering how it might impact upon a number of significant areas of industry and life, and will hopefully encourage you to draw your own conclusions as to where the real future of wireless lies.

---

[35] http://www.espen.com/.

Wireless in the home

SmartHome technology has been a staunch talking point for the last two decades, long before new wireless began to show itself to the consumer in fact. In those early days, a smart home was one with clap-activated mood lighting, remote control entertainment and security systems – a futuristic fantasyland of household gadgets and appliances that every young executive craved within their penthouse apartments, but that few could really afford. Our vision of the future back in the 1970s was, to many, a sci-fi movie-inspired one, filled with robotic household helpers and of enormous in-house computers that welcomed us home and reminded us to take a bath.

Today's SmartHome vision is not so naive, perhaps as a result of consumers becoming far more attuned to what their technology needs within the home really are. Working from home has now become a real option for us due to the increased communication channels brought to us by new technology and making the world a smaller but far more accessible place as a result.

Indeed, thanks to wireless technology, we are no longer confined to our home office to send and receive the information we need throughout the day. We can now access our email and text messages whilst we are in the kitchen making lunch and can even chair a video-conference – all through our mobile phone.

Communication has never been simpler but, as a result, has it made our lives more complicated? It is certainly impossible to escape from the influx of constant text message reminders, or the constant email inbox chanting of 'you've got mail!', which is why many researchers believe that, ultimately, communications in the home of the future need to take a far simpler route if they are to benefit from long-term adoption. On the flip side of the coin lies the message given to us by the consumers themselves that, far from growing tired of the constant invasion, they are only too willing to buy into even more ways of increasing the links from home to office and back to home again. As discussed in Chapter 3, we have bitten into the wireless technology cherry only to find that our lifestyle-model appetites have been stimulated rather than subdued by its taste. Microwaves have already been developed that have inbuilt Internet connection capability, so users can download recipes and cooking instructions as and when they need them, and work has begun on ways in which intelligent communications between store-cupboard and cooker can make deciding what to have for dinner a far easier task. Bluetooth wireless technology is set to be the prime candidate for this kind of application, due to its low costs and small chip size. Additionally, ZigBee is another prime contender, as it is specifically targeted for integration within the kind of low-data-rate applications that are typically found within a household.

Home security is also an area where wireless is predicted to play a major part. In fact, many wireless systems are already in use, to include driveway alert applications and various locational alarms. Alongside these more established wireless products, extensive work is underway to further develop a system whereby your home can be remotely monitored – and controlled – via an in-car touch-screen control system. When you leave your car, the same system functionality can then be transferred to your laptop or PDA, potentially giving you total control over your home security 24 hours a day, no matter where in the world you are. The growing need for control in all aspects of our lives is testimony to the potential market triumph of these applications, providing that cost factors do not produce too great a barrier to their widespread adoption.

Wireless sensor technology is of great interest to new home developers, both for its 'SmartHome' appeal and for its low running costs and the potential savings offered in terms of home maintenance and repairs. The sensors can be used to detect overflowing baths or, more importantly, to highlight potential problems (such as leaking pipes) before they actually happen. The systems will therefore also be of great interest to insurance companies, who may well consider a reduction in annual premiums to those homeowners whose properties contain the technology. One such example is WaterCop, a wireless early leak detection and automatic water shut-off system that has already been released in the US by manufacturers DynaQuip (see Figure 13.1). Its impressive take-up is indicative of the fact that other similar systems are set to follow in its path, each bound to play a part in making the home of the future a self-maintaining shell that requires minimum levels of input yet produces maximum output in the key lifestyle areas of entertainment, communication and security.

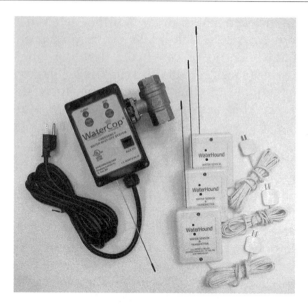

Figure 13.1 The WaterCop auto shut-off system. © DynaQuip Controls Corporation

Wireless at work

Our most obvious connection with wireless in the workplace has to be within the office. Here, we are probably already using a number of wireless Bluetooth- and WiFi-enabled applications on a daily basis, and it is this area that our thoughts probably drift towards when we think of the future of wireless at work. Certainly, we cannot afford to underestimate the ways in which our already unwired office could be improved by the further application of wireless technology and the directions in which it will evolve, but it is equally important as technology marketers to step outside of the office and into the wider world of industry, science and education to see where the true untapped workplace potential of wireless really lies.

Freedom of communication is a key area in which wireless technology can assist our working day. For example, we have already looked at how modern homes are integrating wireless technology to blur the boundaries between home and office life, making our 'working' environments either more simple or decidedly more complicated, depending upon which side of the fence you are sitting.

One area that utilizes wireless particularly effectively is that of video-conferencing where, through the application of a wireless connection, you can participate or even chair a conference from anywhere in the world. Participation in wireless conferencing has been growing in popularity over the past couple of years and many people find that, rather than isolating the participants, it actually encourages cohesion and a greater flow of ideas than when delegates are brought together in a fixed location. Features like Panopticons, where members are able to locate one another's attendance at seminars and meetings via an interactive digital map of the online conference center, are already established tools for online conference collaboration and participation monitoring, and the future may well see this kind of conference taking precedence over the traditional face-to-face group meetings of the past, with many more available interactive features being introduced along the way. Companies of all sizes are quickly latching on to the financial benefits of wireless conferencing, and it is this factor in particular that is aiding their ever-increasing global popularity. Another fascinating wireless application that attaches itself well to wireless conferencing is EtherPEG, which is, in essence, a code that works to capture a tiny part of the images transmitted to and from each of the attendee's laptops by scanning the local network. Having done this, it then creates a montage of what people are looking at, providing both amusement and potentially valuable information.

Companies like IBM believe that the office of the future will be a totally wireless environment, freeing employees from the confines of their desks and allowing them to form cohesive teams that can work flexibly within their roles, either on-site or remotely. This wireless coordination means that remote working need no longer mean being 'remote'. New wireless will allow you to still be an integrated part of a working team from wherever you choose to locate yourself and advances in 3G technology signal the ability for complex data – including digital video and detailed color photography – to be sent and received effortlessly from your mobile phone or PDA. Similarly, highly effective advances[36] in digital voice recording mean that it will soon become more commonplace to transfer your spoken words into greatly compressed digital voice files that can be transported wirelessly to wherever they are needed in a matter of seconds.

---

[36] Voice to text software has historically been problem-ridden, due to user variables in speech tone and accent.

Bluespace is the name given to a joint project between IBM and Steelcase, a US office furniture maker. It utilizes wireless technology in a number of practical ways to allow for a collaborative and highly organized workplace environment, to include such features as wireless monitoring and alerting of staff members, as well as cue software to alert colleagues of availability. Much of this technology is already available to us in one way or another. What the future will do is to clarify the functionality of workplace wireless options, separating the weak from the strong into those products and services that we really do benefit from using on a daily basis and providing them to us in the most effective and budget-friendly way possible.

As discussed in our introduction to this particular section, to truly understand the potential of wireless at work, we must, as marketers, look beyond the ever-popular office applications and to the wider workplace arenas, where there exists so much wireless application potential. We have already discussed the future use of wireless sensor systems within the home, but they present an even greater gift in their ability to help world industry use energy and resources more efficiently and to bring about increased productivity with reduced overheads. Wireless sensors can be used to measure a wide variety of industrial-related elements crucial to all aspects of effective functioning, to include temperature, humidity, pressure, vibration, voltage and current. Studies have been extensively carried out in the USA to develop a collaborative vision for the future of this rapidly evolving technology. The resulting document, *Industrial Wireless Technology for the 21st Century*, defines specific goals and challenges for industrial utilization of wireless and provides an insight into the potential power of wireless utilization at all levels of global industry.

Telemetry is another fast-growing area of wireless, particularly within the manufacturing arenas, where more efficient ways to collect, transfer and analyze data from machines and devices are continually being sought. In a recent report, the Wireless Data Research Group predicted an estimated growth in the wireless telemetry market from $1.8 billion in 2003 to $8.2 billion in 2007. Applications are already proving invaluable to car manufacturers by decreasing the amount of errors on assembly lines and allowing greater flow of communication from machinery to staff, and more work is being carried out to increase their functionality, reduce their set-up costs and make them even more desirable.

Wireless healthcare

One of the greatest challenges in adapting wireless for the healthcare industry is finding the best way to integrate its attributes into point-of-service applications that directly benefit clinicians on a practical, day-to-day basis. Wireless technology is all set to make a big impact upon healthcare in the future but, to successfully do so, it must learn from past mistakes. Unlike mass consumer marketing, healthcare marketers need to attune themselves to the 'real' and not created needs of the system if a wireless product is to truly succeed. Investigations into the reason why many wireless products and services have failed to make their mark within the healthcare industry highlight the following specific problems:

- Failure to demonstrate significant added value.
- Inconsistent technology deployment.
- The need for hospitals and healthcare centers to make a considerable investment in order for them to integrate the technology.
- Neither a real nor perceived return on investment has been substantiated.

The most important factor to be gleaned from the above is that of 'value'. Healthcare budgets are, to governments and communities alike, a bone of contention around the world, and it really goes without saying that patient care should never be placed in a compromising position due to experimental expectations that offer no guarantee of return in benefits. The creation of truly beneficial medical wireless applications is without a doubt the most challenging, yet potentially most rewarding, area of wireless technology development today. Similarly, it is up to us, the marketers, to ensure that these valuable products are presented to those that need them in the most effective way possible.

Bluetooth is a technology of particular interest to the medical profession, not least because of its suitability to adding service value to the kind of proximity-dependent procedures currently carried out. Bluetooth lends itself particularly well to many of the performance requirements specific to medical applications, and it is especially suited to those products demanding high mobility, long battery life and no infrastructure support. Another value of Bluetooth lies in the fact that it is less likely to interfere with other medical equipment, which is due, for the most part, to its ability to transmit at very low power levels. Areas of interest include monitoring of equipment and communication between the patient and various medical devices, such as a blood glucose monitoring system, where insulin intake could be regulated via Bluetooth connectivity and, in the same way, patient data wirelessly transferred to a central patient data service. Additionally, the connection could be set up to alert the patient's doctor via a Bluetooth connection with a pager or mobile telephone if dramatic variations occurred.

A number of hospitals across the United States currently employ a wireless patient scanning system, where hand-held bar scanners are linked to a central information point. The hand-held scanners are swiped across both the patient's wristband and staffs' own identification badges. The system then validates the patient's healthcare records and care requirements whilst logging both the admission process and the carer's profile. Research is being carried out into the ways in which the flow of this information could be best achieved without the need for such scanners. Furthermore, tests are now underway to trial wireless-enabled staff badges that invisibly communicate with patient's wristbands, drug dispensers and monitoring devices to provide a constant flow of data surrounding the care given, drugs administered and the patient's vital signs, including pulse and blood pressure readings.

This kind of patient monitoring also lends itself to remote care possibilities, affording patients the possibility of greater independence and the opportunity to continue to live in their own homes for a longer period of time than would otherwise be possible. For the daughters and sons of elderly parents, who are perhaps not in a position to live-in or care for their mothers and fathers, this kind of wireless application also holds tremendous value by virtue of the peace of mind it affords. Similarly, wireless monitoring products hold potential value for athletes, heart patients and all those who need their vital signs monitoring on a regular basis, but would prefer not to have to travel to the hospital every time. Again, Bluetooth is currently the number one candidate for this kind of product development for the reasons we have already discussed.

As far as the hospital buildings themselves are concerned, wireless networks offer the same benefits as those found by business users, primarily those of increased speed and efficiency. Advances in the future will no doubt see improved levels of communication between hospital administrators, clinicians and patients to the benefit of the overall smooth and efficient running of the health service.

Wireless retail

The capacity to dramatically transform current retail procedures into wireless consumer services is all too clear to wireless product and service developers alike. Basically, any retail transaction has the potential to become 'wireless' and likewise any terminal or kiosk a wirelessly enabled one. Brent Miller, the author of *Bluetooth Revealed*, talks about the possibilities for Bluetooth in retail, emphasizing that: 'a mobile phone could connect to a soda machine over a Bluetooth link to pay for a soda, or link to a kiosk at which you could buy a theatre ticket. Similarly, a mobile phone, PDA, or other device could be used to pay for goods and services using Bluetooth communication links with a cash register.' He draws particular attention to the use of access points within shopping centers, supermarkets and restaurants, as well as a variety of other retail areas where payment can occur seamlessly and invisibly, adding value to the user experience and benefitting the smooth and efficient running of such organizations.

In the same way that many supermarkets offer discount schemes and customer loyalty cards, wireless consumers could benefit from exclusive offers and additional savings by using this form of purchasing. Not only would these kind of incentives encourage widespread adoption, they would also raise the profile of the organizations who were the first to 'come on board' with the service.

Airports, train stations and bus depots are also set to become wireless retailers of the future. Trials are well underway into the ways in which Bluetooth, in particular, might be employed to allow for wireless ticket collection and check-in at airports, whilst maintaining high levels of security for passengers and staff. Here again, the wireless accessing of user profiles would allow for specific services to be offered to passengers and would instantly alert boarding staff of any special needs, such as dietary or healthcare problems, that may require attending to during their journey.

The new generation of WAP-enabled mobiles phones and PDAs are also set to have a tremendous impact upon the world of retailing. WAP suffered a great deal of bad press in its formative years due, for the most part, to its lack of services and its incredibly dull user interface, but the eagerly anticipated 3G technology has given it a much needed 'face-lift' and its new range of features and services are set to make it unrecognizable from its former tired self.

Wireless developers are keen to consider the ways in which both consumers and retailers can benefit from the new improved 3G mobile features, and are looking at ways to provide encapsulated WAP promotions that are activated by user preferences and locational prompts, such as walking by a particular store that registers potential customer interest via user profiles from a Bluetooth-enabled mobile phone. User profiles are already employed by a vast number of e-commerce applications and, again, this is the primary principle behind the customer loyalty cards that have become so popular in supermarkets around the globe; so really this concept is nothing new. What is exciting and possibly a little scary is the consumer 'grab factor' that will potentially confront us on every street corner via our mobile phones. Some will embrace it – others will despise it. Either way, it seems destined to become a prevalent and ever evolving part of our lives.

Summary

- Espen Andersen likened the growth of wireless to the construction of an anthill. His 2003 paper described the future belonging to small, connected devices that wirelessly allow both the user and the technology to self-organize.
- The vision of a SmartHome has evolved from the early days of sci-fi-inspired fantasy, to that of practicality and freedom.
- Bluetooth and ZigBee are the prime contenders for the further development of wireless appliances within the home of the future, due to their low cost and small chip size.
- Home security is also an area where wireless will certainly play a major part in the future, with devices such as driveway alerts and locational alarms already in use.
- Wireless sensor technology is of great interest to new home developers, both for its 'SmartHome' appeal and for its low running costs and the potential savings offered in terms of home maintenance and repairs.
- When we think of the future of wireless technology at work, we tend to think of office-related applications, rather than take a broader viewpoint that incorporates all aspects of work and industry. This is where the true future potential of wireless lies.

- Freedom of communication is a key area in which wireless technology can assist our working day.
- Companies of all sizes are quickly latching on to the financial benefits of wireless conferencing and it is this factor in particular that is aiding their ever-increasing global popularity.
- Companies like IBM believe that the office of the future will be a totally wireless environment, freeing employees from the confines of their desks and allowing them to form cohesive teams that can work flexibly within their roles, either on-site or remotely.
- The functionality of workplace wireless options in the future will see the separation of the weak from the strong into those products and services that really do benefit our working lives.
- The paper, *Industrial Wireless Technology for the 21st Century*, defines specific goals and challenges for industrial utilization of wireless, and provides an insight into the potential power of wireless utilization at all levels of global industry.
- Telemetry is another fast-growing area of wireless where more efficient ways to collect, transfer and analyze data from machines and devices are continually being sought.
- Wireless technology is set to make a big impact upon healthcare in the future, but to successfully do so it must learn from past mistakes concerning its *value*.
- The creation of truly beneficial medical wireless applications is without a doubt the most challenging, yet potentially most rewarding, area of wireless technology development today.
- Bluetooth lends itself particularly well to many of the performance requirements specific to medical applications, and it is especially suited to those products demanding high mobility, long battery life and no infrastructure support.
- Wireless technology also lends itself to remote care possibilities, affording patients the possibility of greater independence and the opportunity to continue to live in their own homes for a longer period of time than would otherwise be possible.
- Advances in the future will no doubt see improved levels of communication between hospital administrators, clinicians and patients, to the benefit of the overall smooth and efficient running of the health service.
- Any retail transaction has the potential to become 'wireless' and likewise any terminal or kiosk a wirelessly enabled one.
- Brent Miller draws attention to the potential of access points within shopping centers, supermarkets and restaurants, as well as a variety of other retail areas where payment can occur seamlessly and invisibly,

adding value to the user experience and benefitting the smooth and efficient running of such organizations.

- Airports, train stations and bus depots are also set to become wireless retailers of the future, where Bluetooth, in particular, might be employed to allow for wireless ticket collection and passenger check-in.
- The new generation of WAP-enabled mobile phones and PDAs is also set to have a tremendous impact upon the world of retailing. Wireless developers are keen to consider the ways in which both consumers and retailers can benefit from the new improved 3G mobile features and are looking at ways to provide encapsulated WAP promotions that are activated by user preferences and locational prompts.

Chapter 14

Conclusions drawn and lessons learned

In the minds of all great marketers lies the ability to see beyond the bare bones of a product and to capture its innate benefits in a way that will attract and ultimately reel in its target market. Even greater is the ability to bend and stretch our individual marketing philosophies across the boundaries of our existing target market to the possible avenues that lie beyond. Wireless is the ultimate marketing assault course, putting all of our skills and experience to the test. Through the pages you have read, you will have come to understand the many ways in which the market twists and turns to bring the next best thing straight to the home of the consumer; you will have experienced the trials and errors of those most highly respected within the industry and you will have ultimately formed a stronger understanding of the wireless technology that underlies the development of the products themselves.

In Part II, 'Leading Perspectives', you will have learned some valuable lessons that you can now incorporate into your own marketing perspectives and practices. For example, Wade Gillham's inspirational chapter on the value found in building strong networking relationships that act as a two-way channel to boost your products' message might well change the way you deal with industry analysts from now on. Similarly, Ronald Sperano of IBM highlights the benefits to be gained from incorporating real-time demonstrations within our promotional remit, whilst never losing sight of the bigger wireless 'LANscape' picture. He talks about the ability of IBM's products to allow the user to 'focus on the task at hand and forget the technology behind it', another vital message that is key to successful early adoption of new wireless products.

Dip into these chapters from time to time whenever you need a boost in a particular area, or perhaps an inspirational trigger. Remember the key messages they contain, as these will help to drive forward your future marketing campaigns. They are powerful reminders of just how successful wireless marketing campaigns can really be.

As for the future of wireless, hopefully Chapter 13 will have given you a starting point on which to base your own individual theories and conclusions. It is worth remembering that many new and innovative wireless applications come about as a result of simply looking at the practical utilization of existing products in a different way; this includes existing wireless products, of course, where end-user application can often become a springboard for further innovation and subsequent new product development. What starts as a simple wireless heat sensor could go on to function as a body-heat monitor, for example. And so, a new wireless product is born and a new promotional vehicle is provided for the marketer. New possibilities are created when we take the time to fully consider the benefits that lie beyond the boundaries of the drawing board and to the lifestyle models that encapsulate the true potential of wireless.

Wireless technology, in all of its forms, whether past, present or future, will undoubtedly impact profoundly upon the lives of us all. From healthcare to entertainment, its role in freeing us from the restrictions of our wired world is already proving an exhilarating and liberating roller-coaster ride for both manufacturers and consumers alike, but most especially for those marketers whose responsibility it is to effectively package and sell this 'freedom' to the end-user. Another important lesson to be learned, however, is that our excitement about the potential of a wireless technology can, in some instances, be detrimental to its public debut if we try to insist upon it 'running before it can walk'. For example, we have learned how the 'too much, too soon' approach that preceded the launch of Bluetooth wireless technology served to hinder, rather than help, its early market acceptance. Indeed, understanding the practical day-to-day usability of a wireless product and broadcasting its benefits in a way that directly relates to its demonstrable capabilities potential is the best approach to securing market credibility and acceptance at launch.

At the very least, this book will hopefully have inspired you to look at the marketing of wireless in a fresh and dynamic way that is always creative and always open to change. Unless we truly embrace change as part of our evolving marketing remit, we will limit ourselves to the boundaries of *here and now* rather than freeing our minds to the future possibilities of the products whose messages we are empowered to find.

References

Andersen, Espen (2003). Genesis of an anthill: wireless technology and self-organizing systems. *Ubiquity*, **3**, Issue 49.

Borisov, N., Goldberg, I. and Wagner, D. (2001). Intercepting mobile communications: the insecurity of 802.11. *International Conference on Mobile Computing and Networking*, New York, NY, 1 July, pp. 180–189.

Bray, J. and Sturman, C. F. (2001). *Bluetooth 1.1: Connect Without Cables*, Second Edition. Prentice-Hall PTR, December.

buy.com (2003). *PC Card*. Retrieved 2 February 2003 from the World Wide Web: http://www.us.buy.com/retail/computers/category.asp?loc=219

Conover, Joel (2001). *802.11a: Making Space for Speed*. Retrieved 8 January 2001 from the World Wide Web: http://www.networkcomputing.com/1201/1201ws1.html

Dugger, G. (2003). *Sales Questions for Selling IBM Wireless Solutions* (unpublished).

Flickenger, R. (2002). *Building Wireless Community Networks*. Sebastopol, CA: O'Reilly & Associates.

Fluhrer, S., Mantin, I. and Shamir, A. (2001). Weaknesses in the key scheduling algorithm of RC4. *Eighth Annual Workshop on Selected Areas in Cryptography*, Toronto, Canada, 17 August.

Gartner Group (19 July 2001). Retrieved 9 February 2002 from the World Wide Web: http://www.intel.com/ebusiness/pdf/prod/related_mobile/TBOwp012601.pdf

Gast, Matthew S. (2002). *802.11 Wireless Networks: The Definitive Guide*. Sebastapol, CA: O'Reilly & Associates, April.

Geier, Jim (10 October 2002). *802.11a/b Sire Survey: A Testimonial*. Retrieved 28 February 2003 from the World Wide Web: http://www.80211-planet.com/columns/article.php/1479831

Gratton, Dean A. (2002). *Bluetooth Profiles: The Definitive Guide*. New Jersey, USA: Prentice-Hall PTR, December.

Gross, Richard D. (1992). *Psychology: The Science of Mind and Behaviour*, Second Edition. Hodder & Stoughton, 1992.

Hall, Eric A. (2000). *Internet Core Protocols: The Definitive Guide*. Sebastapol, CA: O'Reilly & Associates, February.

IEEE Standard for Information Technology (1999). LAN/MAN – Specific Requirements – Part 11: Wireless LAN Medium Access Control (MAC) and Physical Layer (PHY) Specifications. IEEE, ISBN 0-7381-1658-0; IEEE Standard No.: 802.11, 1999/8802-11.

IEEE Standard for Information Technology (2002). Telecommunication and Information Exchange Between Systems – LAN/MAN – Part 15.1: Wireless Medium Access Control (MAC) and Physical Layer (PHY) Specifications for Wireless Personal Area Networks™ (WPANs™). IEEE, ISBN 0-7381-3069-9; IEEE Standard No.: 802. 15.1-2002.

Industrial Wireless Technology for the 21st Century (2002). Based on the views of the industrial wireless community, in collaboration with the US Department of Energy and the Office of Energy Efficiency and Renewable Energy.

Intel (4 February 2001). *How Wireless Local Area Networks Enhance Productivity*. Retrieved 9 February 2003 from the World Wide Web: http://www.intel.com/ebusiness/bizissue/roi/ar020401.htm

Intel (2002a). *Kellogg School of Management: Successful Wireless LAN Deployment*. Retrieved 9 February 2003 from the World Wide Web: http://www.intel.com/ebusiness/products/mobile/p4pm/wp020904_sum.htm

Intel (2002b). *Wireless LANs: Linking Productivity Gains to Return on Investment*. Intel Corporation, October.

Intel (2003). *VPN and WEP*. Intel, January.

Lansford, J. and Gillham, W. (2002). Alphabet soup: tradeoffs between 802.11b, 802.11a, and 802.11g. *WinHEC 2002: Microsoft Windows Hardware Engineering Conference*, April, pp. 1–19.

Mannion, Patrick (6 August 2001). *Cipher Attack Delivers Heavy Blow to WLAN Security*. Retrieved 25 November 2001 from the World Wide Web: http://www.eetimes.com/story/OEG20010803S0082

Messmer, Ellen, Fontana, John and Cox, John (23 September 2002). *Microsoft, Cisco Prepare for PEAP Show*. Retrieved 27 February 2003 from the World Wide Web: http://www.nwfusion.com/news/2002/0923peap.html

Miller, B. A. and Chatschik, B. (2001). *Bluetooth Revealed: The Insider's Guide to an Open Specification for Global Wireless Communications*, Second Edition. Prentice-Hall PTR, December.

NOP World (2001). *Wireless LAN Benefits Study*. NOP World.

O'Hara, B. and Petrick, A. (1999). *The IEEE 802.11 Handbook: A Designer's Companion*, First Edition. IEEE, December.

Proxim (2002). *802.11a: The Clear Choice for Wireless LANs*. Sunnyvale, CA: Proxim.

Saltzatein, William E. (2002). *Bluetooth: The Future of Wireless Medical Technology*? Medical Device & Diagnostic Industry.

Salvator, David (31 October 2002). *Building a Media Network Part I*. Retrieved 28 February 2003 from the World Wide Web: http://www.extremetech.com/print_article/0,3998,a=36375,00.asp

Siegel, P., Salomon, K. and Lane, B. (2001). *The Future of Wireless in Education*. University of Illinois.

Siep, T. (2000). *An IEEE Guide: How to Find What You Need in the Bluetooth Spec*, First Edition. IEEE, November.

VeriTest (2002). *IBM: 802.11b Distance and Performance Testing*. Retrieved September 2002 from the World Wide Web: http://www.veritest.com/clients/reports/ibm/default.asp

WLANA (2001). *Wireless LAN Customer Consideration*. Retrieved 9 February 2003 from the World Wide Web: http://www.wlana.org/learn/educate5.htm

Index